P9-DFT-786

AMERICA'S TOUGHEST SHERIFF

AMERICA'S
TOUGHEST
SHERIFF

How to Win the War Against Crime

By
Sheriff Joe Arpaio
and
Len Sherman

THE SUMMIT PUBLISHING GROUP

THE SUMMIT PUBLISHING GROUP
One Arlington Centre, 1112 East Copeland Road, Fifth
Floor
Arlington, Texas 76011

Library of Congress Cataloging-in-Publication Data

Arpaio, Joe, 1932-
America's toughest sheriff : how to win the war against
crime / by Joe Arpaio and Len Sherman.
    p. cm.
ISBN 1-56530-202-8 (hardcover : alk. paper)
  1. Arpaio, Joe, 1932- . 2. Sheriffs—Arizona—Case
studies. 3. Prisons—Arizona—Case studies. 4. Crime
prevention—Arizona—Case studies. I. Sherman, Len,
1956- . II. Title.
HV7979.A78 1996
363.2'82'0973—dc20   96-3207
                                            CIP

Jacket and book design by David Sims
Photography by Leslie Sokolow

FOR AVA
My wife, my best friend, my partner

TABLE OF CONTENTS

Introduction . . . .*ix*

Prologue . . . .*xv*

1   In the Eye of the Hurricane 3

PART I—THE TENTS

2   Another Visit to
the Big (And Open-Air) House 27

3   There's More to the Tents
Than Just Tents 41

4   Working on the Chain Gang 53

5   Joe Slept Here 63

6   And That's Not All .71

PART II—The Posse

7   Actions Speak Louder... 81

8   Volunteers Unite 91

9   On Patrol 105

10   How to Start Your Own Posse 121

11   Possibilities and Opportunities 145

PART III—The Drug Wars

12   The Problem Only Gets Worse 155

13   Lessons Learned 161

14   Winning the Drug War 209

PART IV—Final Thoughts, Future Considerations

15   The People and the Press 229

16   The Future 255

INTRODUCTION

The following pages will well acquaint you with Sheriff Joe Arpaio, his history and his ideas. As the coauthor of this work, and in the spirit of full disclosure, I thought you should know what I think and believe, and how I became involved in what I hope will be regarded as a noteworthy, provocative book.

I moved to Phoenix from New York for several reasons. Yes, the weather was a definite factor, as were several of the less pleasant realities of residing in New York City. Then there was the lure of the West, and the possibility of fulfilling that most fundamental and perhaps quixotic of American dreams: living as the rugged individual—albeit with air-conditioning.

But something else brought me to Arizona, something equally compelling. It was my growing awareness that Arizona was in the forefront of changes—political, sociological, environmental—that could sweep the country.

I met Sheriff Arpaio soon after arriving in town. I was busy talking to everybody, from opinion makers to the merely opinionated, in order to get a sense of the area when I called the sheriff, affectionately called "Sheriff Joe" by his Arizona constituents. Thanks to the media, I had heard about him and his posse and tents, and I wanted to see for myself what the commotion was all about. I didn't have a specific agenda in mind—such as writing this book—I just wanted to talk.

Within ten minutes of entering his office and shaking his hand, I knew I was in the presence of a phenomenon. Joe Arpaio was not just another politician spouting slogans, trying to suck up to the media and the public in order to get reelected. This was clearly a man who believed in what he was saying and in what he was doing. Perhaps more to the point, this was a man whose deeds matched his words, who took his experience and knowledge and convictions and put them to use in service of the people who elected him. And that's a rare man.

The sheriff was heading out to the Tent City Jail and invited me along—"if you have the guts," he said. By the end of that brief excursion, I was convinced that Maricopa County had implemented several ideas and programs worthy of notice by the rest of America, and that Sheriff Joe was the harbinger of a new force not only in American law enforcement but also in American political philosophy.

Hailing from New York, I have had enough personal encounters with crime to possess strong opinions about the problem. And though all my losses have been relatively minor—three stolen bicycles, two stolen car radios, and so on—particularly in comparison to what happens each day on the mean streets of every U.S. city, I was still outraged by having to contend with the endless threats to my person and property. And while I certainly recognize that many factors contribute to crime, that recognition does not in any way prompt me to excuse crime or those who perpetrate it. Nor is it the business of law enforcement to correct the societal conditions that can lead to crime. Law enforcement's overriding duty is to stop crime.

We live in a society that increasingly equates isolation with security. We pretend not to see the homeless man as we scurry into our guarded building or our gated community. We erect barricades to block off streets and keep out gangbangers, and we hire private cops to patrol our avenues and keep away drug dealers.

That, of course, assumes we can afford gates, barricades, and private cops. If we can't, then we are on our own.

Thus, while crime affects all of society, one quickly discovers that it affects some people more than others. Put bluntly, the rich don't ride the subways and so do not grasp that crime is the over-riding concern of most Americans.

Hence, the privileged and protected and powerful, more often than not, approach the question of crime in the same manner they approach most communal issues—from a safe distance. They cele-brate themselves with extravagant parties they call fund-raisers and write off as charity, and congratulate themselves for their compas-sion and leadership. They condemn society for its shortcomings and instruct their fellow citizens on the sacrifices that must be made in the name of justice, while refusing to consider themselves bound by the rules and conventions of the community in matters of morality.

Surely we see this throughout the country, but we see it in heightened clarity in New York, that central mecca for money and media to meet and join and bask in their mutual glory.

And so I came to Arizona.

You won't be reading a lot of overheated political rhetoric in the course of this book. It's not because the sheriff doesn't agree with the views just stated. He probably does. But speculative ruminating is not Sheriff Joe's style. Joe Arpaio is a cop, pure and simple. He was a cop for thirty-two years with the feds, and now he's the head cop of Maricopa County. Even though he's an elected official, he's not a politician in the conventional sense. He has his task, and it's always been the same: To fight crime. That's it, case closed.

So a terrific idea like the posse is widely acclaimed as a great crime-fighting tool, and stunningly cost-effective to boot. And since those obviously laudable attributes are exactly what the sheriff was seeking, he is satisfied with the result.

And while he recognizes that within the posse concept brews an important political message, that is secondary to the posse's practical intent. The posse embodies the height of the American spirit of self-sufficiency, a spirit we usually celebrate more in word than deed. This used to be a nation of volunteers: volunteers rallying to fight the British, to defend one another on the frontier, to build communities and make sure those communities were safe for everyone. People all over the country say they're tired of big government, which means we'd better do the job ourselves and not wait for bureaucrats to fix every problem. That's what the posse is all about: We the people, taking back our streets and taking back our lives.

This book is about much more than crime fighting. It's about Americans regaining the egalitarian spirit that made this land of individuals a great nation. Do we still believe in ourselves? Do we still believe in the very idea of what it means to be an American? Do we still believe in those revolutionary values that define an American? Do we still believe enough to fulfill the promise of America?

Government is not the enemy. Politics is not the enemy. Even political parties are not the enemy. They are all mere instruments of our collective will, and when that will falters, those institutions and those ideas falter. So if the government can no longer be depended upon to perform fairly and efficiently, and politicians and political parties are creaky and corrupted, then we must reinvigorate those organizations and those concepts with integrity and purpose, and jettison whatever and whoever cannot be redeemed.

The genius of America is our ability to change tangible reality without altering the intangible underpinnings of our society. We have grown from a loose confederation of communities into the mightiest empire in history, while ceaselessly expanding and restructuring the demographics of our population, incorporating new people and new traditions and new ideas into the fold without abandoning our individuality or our national character.

How is this possible? How can America not only survive such continual changes but also thrive on them?

At its heart, a nation is a myth agreed to by its people. All the other consequential factors, social, political, and economic, are tied together by the underlying belief and value system to which all citizens voluntarily and consciously subscribe.

But we are more than that. Unlike other countries, America is a faith, as tangible as a church. Unlike other countries, America is also tribal, permitting the supplicant to join or separate from the nation with relative ease. Once accepted into the tribe, one is instantly, totally American, no probation required. Try that in China or Germany, or a hundred other lands.

It is no accident that we refer to those who led our Revolution as our "Founding Fathers," an intimate and personal identification. They are fathers to all of us, whether our families were here in 1776 or arrived last week, because we are all equally American. We have no titles to hand down, no familial privileges or special rights. All Americans originate from the same mythic parentage, from the beginning, from our Founding Fathers.

This myth, this faith, this tribe gives much and demands much in return. If triumphs will be gained, then we must earn them. If tomorrow is to be successful and happy, then we must work toward that day. We, the people.

And so we come to Arizona.

Americans fear crime as much as we fear for the American future. One anxiety feeds the other, and with good reason, for the cancer of crime imperils all promise and hope. So we have a sheriff, a veteran of the crime wars, a man who has spent half his life working as a cop, who is prepared to show the way. Joe Arpaio has risked his life countless times and his reputation even more frequently in the service of this nation. Now he's prepared to do even more—he's prepared to tell us the truth about crime and punishment in this country, what must change, and what we have to do.

The words "hero" and "courage" and "character" are used loosely these days. I'm not here to claim any such titles for Sheriff Joe. I leave that to the reader.

But I shall definitively tell you that the sheriff has honorably and heroically fought the good fight throughout his career. Many cops have done the same. The difference is that Joe Arpaio has gone virtually everywhere and done virtually everything in pursuit of his duty.

And now he has come to Arizona. And this is where he has made his ultimate stand. Law. Order. Justice.

Right versus wrong.

Them or us.

Where do you stand?

LEN SHERMAN

Amerika is losing the war against crime, and we've been losing it for years, on every level, from graffiti and purse-snatching to drugs and murder. We're losing, and the way I see it, we have to change, or it's only going to get worse.

But you already knew that. You knew that when you stepped out your door and clutched your bag tightly to your chest, held your breath when you walked by a bunch of kids hanging out on the corner, or looked around cautiously before removing money from a deserted ATM machine. And you knew that after arriving home, double-locking the door, turning on the TV and seeing the news dominated by old women being raped and kids shooting strangers.

A recent *Business Week/Harris Poll* discovered that more than 70 percent of Americans are pessimistic and disheartened about this nation's future. Did I say "discovered"? Surely you didn't need a poll to tell you that. You feel it. You know it.

But I also want to tell you something you don't know—and that's how Americans can turn around the situation and take back our country. I've spent thirty-two years fighting crime around the globe on behalf of the American people. Now I'm the sheriff of a county the size of New Jersey, and I know what must be done. I'm doing it right here in my own stretch of Arizona, and it's working.

I want to emphasize that point. I'm not some journalist or politician spouting off about what *everybody else* has to do to clean up this terrible mess. A lot of people with sophisticated opinions about crime live in guarded neighborhoods, send their kids to private schools, never have to take a bus or have any contact with the problems they're lecturing about.

I have lived and almost died by my words. I spent most of my career in the Drug Enforcement Administration, a lot of it undercover, and I got very close and personal with some of the nastiest characters around. I've gone from the highest levels of federal law enforcement, where I was the only person ever to have been both the agent-in-charge in Turkey and then regional director for all of Latin America, to election as sheriff of Maricopa County, where I am responsible for maintaining law and order in an area that is actually bigger than eighteen states. (And I might be the only high-ranking law enforcement official who has made that very large leap from the feds to the locals.)

And as the sheriff, I've been elected by the people to do a job, and come hell or high water, or the media or the ACLU, I'm working as hard as I know how to make my home a place where people are safe and, just as important, *feel* safe.

And the people of the Phoenix area seem to appreciate it, which accounts for my approval rating in recent polls hovering around 90 percent, cutting across all ethnic and racial lines. These days a president hits 55 percent and he thinks he's ready to be carved into Mount Rushmore.

My popularity, and some of the things I've been saying and doing about crime, have caused me to be sought out by the media. And when I say sought, I mean *pursued*, and sometimes with a vengeance. But I'm not stupid enough to think that *The New York Times* is here one day and *20/20* the next because of my sparkling personality or endearing wit. The reason the newspapers, TV news magazines, and talk shows are trooping down to The Grand

Canyon State and knocking on my door is because crime is the number-one issue in this country. It's the number-one fear, the number-one problem, and anybody who stands up and actually does something about it is going to make news.

And that's exactly what has happened to me. I've been in the papers, and I've been on TV, and I've gone from being a lawman—which is what I've been my whole life, and which is all that I ever wanted to be—to being a symbol of how Americans can stand up to crime, defend their streets, and protect their quality of life. With this whirlwind swirling around me, I figure that if I'm going to be in the spotlight, I might as well lay out exactly what I see and what I believe, what I hope and what I fear, directly from me to you, no reporters, talk show hosts, or commentators in between.

So get ready, because I'll tell you up front, I'm not going to paint a pretty picture. The way I see it, we are either going to get smart and get tough and deal with this menace, or we are risking the very destruction of the country we love. I'm going to tell you how we permitted this threat to fester, grow, and almost overwhelm us. Then I'm going to tell you what I believe we must do, based on my experience combating drugs and crime all over the world—from Turkey to Mexico to Phoenix. Our task is as simple—and as tough—as taking back each street, each community, from the plagues of violence and fear. In my heart, I know we're up to the job.

Now for some cold facts, so we're all on the same page about the fundamental reality of the issue. Every so often, new figures are announced by one group or another, and sometimes the figures are up, and sometimes they're down. (The year 1995 saw categories of criminal activity showing dramatic reductions in many major cities, allowing politicians and police chiefs to claim semivictory and, more important, credit.) At times, the numbers can be both numbing and confusing in the same manner that on one day studies prove that coffee's bad for you, and on the next different studies claim it's okay. Ditto for exercise, chocolate, vitamins, and apparently everything else.

But some statistics are harder to ignore, particularly those that take a longer view, and here's a couple to chew on. According to the Department of Justice, as quoted in the July 1995 issue of *Atlantic Monthly*, the United States in the 1960s had 3.3 police officers for every violent crime reported per year. Some three decades later, those percentages had turned completely around, and the United States had one police officer for every 3.47 violent crimes reported. Imagine, this nation now has, as stated in *Atlantic Monthly*, "less than one tenth the effective police power of thirty years ago. Looking at it another way, each police officer today must deal with 11.45 times as many violent crimes as his predecessor of years gone by."

Let's deal with those numbers in more human terms. New Haven, Connecticut, experienced six murders, four rapes, and sixteen robberies in the year 1960. In 1990, New Haven, with a population now 14 percent smaller, sustained 31 murders, 168 rapes, and 1,784 robberies.

New Haven is not unique. New York City saw 244 murders in 1951. Last year, *the same as every year for more than a decade*, almost two thousand murders were committed in NYC.

And what of society's penalties against these outrages? Three out of four convicted criminals avoid jail. Less than 10 percent of all serious crimes result in incarceration. When a criminal is finally locked up, time off for parole and good behavior can mean that the convict actually serves a mere one-sixth of his sentence.

And try this on for size: Eighty percent of felons who commit three violent crimes will commit a fourth.

Based on all its data, several years ago the Department of Justice surmised that 83 percent of all Americans—83 percent of *us*—would be victims of violent crime at least once in our lives. For approximately one-fourth of us, Justice expected that we would suffer three or more violent, criminal encounters.

And that's not the last appalling word, because as bad as it is, the situation is only going to get worse. The reason is as simple as it is chilling, and the reason is the collapse of the American family. Children are having children, parents have forsaken their parental responsibilities, families have fallen apart— indeed, the very idea of the traditional nuclear family has been discarded in too many quarters, from inner-city youth too young to comprehend the awe-some burdens of bringing a person into the world to Hollywood stars too privileged to be bothered with common convention.

Too many of our young people have been abandoned to the streets, abandoned without any hope or purpose or morality. Whether those streets are mean, as in south central Los Angeles, or indifferent, as in Beverly Hills, the effect on our youth, on our children, is frequently the same: Left to their own devices, too many young people have substituted drugs and guns and gangs for love and discipline and education.

Compound that missing moral center with any teenager's inherent sense of invulnerability and immortality, and society is spawning a world of desperately dangerous children.

The result: Teenagers commit one out of every three violent crimes.

The result: The hackneyed phrase, "The children are our future," returns to mercilessly haunt us as we confront our brutal legacy. The teenage population, which has been stagnant for several years, is about to undergo an explosion as the children of children reach physical maturity.

In 1965, Daniel Patrick Moynihan alerted us that the growing numbers of black children born to single mothers heralded an era of individual and societal violence and chaos. When he spoke up thirty years ago, that percentage stood at 26 percent. Moynihan, of course, was denounced as a racist, and the issue was immediately abandoned by fearful politicians and academics. Moynihan, of course, was proved right over time, and his ideas gained mainstream acceptance long ago. Now juxtapose a few bits of information:

1. Thirty percent of all children in the United States live in single-parent homes, a notable increase from 12 percent in 1970. Sixty-five percent of black children born this year live with only one parent. But obviously children are not alone in being deprived of two parents. The percentage of single-parent families stands at 35 percent for Hispanic children, and 25 percent for white children.

2. More than 70 percent of the juveniles who commit violent crime come from single-parent families.

The conclusion is irresistible: Illegitimacy rises, violent crime rises, societal decay speeds up and spreads, and the cycle feeds itself with the ferocity of a cancer devouring its host.

So we are left with yet another grim Justice Department report that predicts that the juvenile arrest rate, which already had risen to almost one hundred fifty thousand in 1992, could double by the year 2010. Such a doubling will result in a terrifying increase in violence and pain and misery.

The underlying cause of youth crime has to do with many issues, from social to political to economic. The police only become involved after the other mechanisms of society—family, school, religion—have failed. Youth crime is neither caused by law enforcement, nor can it be cured by law enforcement. Nonetheless, the police are the last line of defense, and that is where I stand. My department, along with all other police departments, must be prepared to deal with this advancing onslaught.

Teenage criminals to career criminals, drug addicts to drug kingpins, gang members to mob families, muggers, murderers, and all the rest... We must all be prepared not only for the battle we are now fighting but also the battle we shall soon be fighting, because this is a fight for all of our futures.

Of course, we have been fighting, on one front or another, and we surely have the bills to prove it. Our criminal justice system costs us sixty-one billion dollars a year. Nationally, taxpayers spend an average of between twenty and thirty thousand dollars on each prisoner.

Justice is not getting cheaper. Breaking it down to just one example, the California Department of Corrections predicts it will have to build another twenty prisons, costing five hundred million dollars each, to accommodate the expected inflow of new inmates. (Incidentally, California already runs twenty-eight state prisons.)

Dissatisfied with the level of protection all this money has bought, Americans spend another sixty-five billion dollars on private security firms and crime-prevention measures. (The steering wheel locking device "The Club" accounts for one hundred million dollars alone.)

All that money, and we're still not safe. I have never believed that throwing money at a problem automatically solves it. Our national problem is crime, and our national spendthrift approach to finding an answer, any answer, no matter the cost, no matter the futility, validates my skepticism.

We cannot sit back and wait for the "experts" to arrive at neat sociological or statistical or philosophical solutions. The real solutions are going to be more difficult and, to be blunt, dirtier than that. The real solutions will not include pleasing political speeches shouted from sanitized studios for the television cameras. They instead involve daily, unending patrolling and investigating, planning and preparing, wrestling and battling between good guys and bad guys on the streets and in the trenches. Police work is not pretty. It is always hard and sometimes dangerous. But such an all-out effort is the essence of preventing crime.

Police work is not conducted in a vacuum. Rather, it is conducted as part and parcel of the community. Thus, real solutions will require the efforts of not only law enforcement officers, but the entire community.

The reality is stark—either the good guys will prevail and restore some sense of decency and honor and respect to our society, or the bad guys will come out on top and destroy everything we hold dear.

And it doesn't matter if you're reading this in Arizona or New York or Florida or California or Kansas, we are all facing the same hazard, the same threat. Just as you can go anywhere in this country and find a McDonald's or a Gap, you can find graffiti and gangs and drugs and a general breakdown in the American quality of life just as easily. Crime is not only about being murdered, it's also about feeling that the street—your street—is no longer a friendly place, feeling that you are under constant assault from harassing, intimidating forces. This degradation in the American quality of life is as ultimately destructive as any violent crime, because it causes us to lose faith in our community and our future.

As crime has changed over the years, so has law enforcement, sometimes for the best and sometimes not. When I was a police officer in Washington, most cops walked the beat, just as I did. That was how we got to know the neighborhood and how we administered the law. Over time, however, the patrol car took over, assisted by tactical units and SWAT teams and a catalog of technological toys.

Same for the war against drugs. When I joined the Bureau of Narcotics, we had little more than two hundred agents doing an arguably great job. Today, more than forty federal agencies have often overlapping jurisdiction over drugs, untold billions are annually expended, and we appear to be achieving less than the old Bureau of Narcotics accomplished, all by its lonesome.

On the other hand, on a personal level, being sheriff is the best job I've ever had. Working for the feds was great, but now I don't have to answer to any bureaucracy or chain of command. Now I answer directly to the people, who elected me.

You know, there's an irony in my new role. I spent most of my career undercover, which is about as anonymous as any person can get, and now I've become "Sheriff Joe," maybe the most public of public officials in Arizona; in the news, one way or another, for better or worse, almost every day, from here to Paris to Tokyo to God knows where.

Why all the interest? Maybe because we're trying a few things here that are working, and could work elsewhere. A few things I want to talk to you about. In fact, a lot I want to talk to you about.

Win or lose. Right or wrong. Good guys versus bad guys. Sometimes life is that straightforward.

As I said, we have a lot to talk about. So let's go.

*"Now I'm the sheriff of
a county the size of New Jersey,
and I know what must be done."*

CHAPTER ONE

In the Eye of the Hurricane

Phil was talking to George.

"George Matta," Phil said. "Can you hear me?"

This was a reasonable question on Phil's part, because George was twenty-five hundred miles away, and in jail to boot. Fortunately, the satellite link was strong, and George was beaming in perfectly.

"Yes, sir," replied George.

"What's it like living in there, George?" Phil asked.

George squinted in the midday sun and spoke in his slow, calm voice. "Miserable, sir. This place was not created nor was it ever designed for comfort. Besides the weather, we have to walk all the way inside for water. This jail is very strict. The officers rely on discipline. I admit, a lot of the inmates here, they do need discipline. They complain a lot about the discipline, about the courtesy, when the officers give them courtesy. But that's just the way this jail's run, and it is effective. To me, it's been a learning experience, sir."

This was not what Phil expected to hear. "You say it's been a learning experience," he responded. "We should say, George, that you're about to get out of there. How much more time do you have?"

A beaming Sheriff Joe in Tent City

"Three weeks, sir."

"Three weeks," Phil repeated, in a tone that sounded to me like Phil was trying to suggest that George was attempting to curry favor with his jailers. In my mind, that didn't make a lot of sense. An inmate should be interested in currying favor when he first goes to jail, not when he's leaving. Not that this was a crucial detail in the discussion—I just thought I would point it out to you.

"Yes, sir," George said.

"Right," Phil said. "You're in there for attempted murder."

I had the feeling that Phil, increasingly surprised and unhappy with George's comments, was starting to deal with him as a hostile witness.

"Yes, sir," George calmly answered.

"This was an altercation with the wife, I think, was it not?"

"Yes, sir."

"I assume that marriage is over."

"No, sir," George said. "She is still waiting for me."

"She is?"

"Yes, sir."

"And are you a rehabilitated man?" asked Phil. "No more physical stuff?"

"Absolutely, sir."

"'Sir,' Phil repeated, with a small smile. "You do sound like a recruit standing in front of that tent, but go ahead."

Just to be accurate, George was seated in front of a lot of tents.

"I will not say I will never return to this place," George said. "I will say this: I will not commit crimes as I've done before."

"How long have you been at that prison facility, George?"

"Approximately a year," George said.

This was all interesting stuff, particularly since it was airing nationwide on *Donahue*, Phil Donahue's long-running talk show. I suppose the program's producers had asked if they could put an inmate on the show to get the real inside scoop, and that was fine by me. Finding a volunteer was a snap. After all, so many reporters had already tramped through the jail that a whole lot of inmates were quite comfortable speaking with the press.

I was also on the show, along with a couple of other law enforcement officials, a crime victim, and a prisoner's advocate. A panel which fairly well spanned the spectrum of opinion on crime and punishment. And that's why this is as good a place to start as we begin our wide-ranging review of this most pressing issue.

Donahue opened the proceedings with yours truly.

"Phil Gramm is just one presidential candidate who gets a standing ovation when he says, 'I'm tired of prisons being Holiday Inns," Donahue said. "Sheriff Joe Arpaio of Maricopa County, Arizona, proud Maricopa County of which Phoenix is the county seat. You're the sheriff. Boy, you take no prisoners. Do you?"

"Oh, I take a lot of them. I need more."

"Yeah," Phil said, and then introduced George Matta, whom I could see on the big television placed next to me and facing the audience. For the first segment, it was just George and me; the others would join us later.

The *Donahue* film crew was shooting from inside the compound because, as the host noted, George was an inmate in the Tent City Jail.

"Sheriff," Donahue said, "how many people are in this prison facility?"

"Phil, it's a jail. I don't have the prisons, I have the jails."

"Oh, okay," Donahue said. "Prison is a state facility, jail is county?"

"That's correct."

Prisons are operated by the state and federal governments. Jails are run by the county. It was a distinction that many did not understand, and I made it something of a minor personal mission to educate the uninformed.

"I have a thousand in the tents, one thousand. I'm going for two thousand in three months. One thousand in the tents, free of charge. I scrounge these tents from the government. And it cost only eighty thousand dollars to build that facility."

"And it's one hundred twenty degrees in these tents in the desert of Arizona in the heat of the summer," Phil said, his voice rising as he sounded a bit excited by his own words. "That's cruel and unusual punishment, Sheriff."

"Well, our servicemen and women went to Saudi Arabia. They lived in tents in the desert, and they didn't even commit a crime. So I don't call that cruel and unusual punishment."

This struck a chord with the studio audience, which applauded heartily.

"Let's take another look at this," Donahue said as his camera crew back in Arizona showed the audience scenes from the tents. "Here is the jail that is accommodating, as the sheriff has explained to us, up to a *thousand* people." Now Phil displayed real astonishment at what he was seeing. "We'll get an inside look here in just a moment. There you are, reviewing the troops, so to speak. No, this is not *M*A*S*H**. This is a county jail. Boy, you got a lot of folks mad at you. Most of them are in that jail."

"That's okay."

"Why'd you do this, Sheriff? And do I understand you to believe that you want to put more people in prison?"

"Yeah, I'd like to be number one. I'm only number four in the nation."

"For counties, you mean."

"For people in county jails."

"You're the fourth largest population?" Phil asked, starting to repeat himself.

"Yes."

"No kidding," Donahue said. "And why do you want to do that, Sheriff?"

Phil's question was a little vague, and I tried to answer it fully. "The more people you have in jail, the fewer people you have on the streets committing crimes."

As far as the tents were concerned, I remarked that I had lived in tents when I had served in the army during the Korean War. Thus, a solution presented itself: "Why not put tents up to allow more people to come to jail, even though I had a jail overcrowding problem. So I scrounged around—I use that word scrounge, because I had to beg, borrow, and bargain around the nation to find tents from the Defense Department free of charge."

"Those are Korean War tents?" Donahue asked.

"Some have holes in them, but it never rains in Phoenix anyway."

"But one of the problems is that they never breathe," a clearly disturbed Donahue said. "That's that old-fashioned waterproofing. I mean, there's no air in there!"

This assertion left me quite unmoved. "There's air in there. I haven't lost anyone. There've been no problems in the tents with the inmates."

"Do you serve hot lunches?"

"I went to bologna sandwiches last year and saved four hundred thousand dollars, and I took away coffee and saved another one hundred thousand dollars."

"No coffee," Phil said, absolutely incredulous.

"That's right."

"Is there any TV available in this jail?"

"I just plugged in cable, and I show Newt Gingrich, the Weather Channel, the Disney Channel, and C-SPAN. (I neglected to mention ESPN, and the Phoenix municipal government channel.) That's all they watch. You won't be seen there. National TV is out."

"Ohh," Phil moaned with good-natured, mock regret. "They are some of our highest viewing areas, our prisons. Bologna sandwiches. And you saved how much?"

"Four hundred thousand dollars. Some people criticize me because it's green. I'm not a butcher, I don't know why it's green. I ate the bologna, I survived."

I'm not sure if Phil was up on the bologna being green, and, like a true professional, he just kept going. "Can I read *Playboy* magazine if I'm a prisoner?"

"No. I took all those out. R-rated movies, too. I went down to *Donald Duck, Lassie Come Home,* and *Old Yeller.* They didn't like that, no more movies in the jail system."

"Because you believe that prison should be a giant pain in the butt for those who are incarcerated?"

"I believe it should be punishment, period." That garnered another round of applause. "And you should also never live better in jail than you do on the outside."

The people seemed to like that idea, too.

That was how the show went for the first few minutes, and even if you didn't understand all the references to green bologna or tents or no coffee rules, you will before I'm through.

The preferred fashion for talk shows is to have every guest represent a different point of view, with each allocated a segment to speak his piece. And so it was today.

Phil introduced Chief Michael Becher from the Clark County Sheriff's Office in Indiana to discuss his department's introduction of the chain gang.

"We're a lot like the sheriff is," the chief said. "Trying to get these programs up and going, you have to scrape for dollars and cents to do those things."

Donahue wanted to know how it was working.

"Right now it's working great," Becher said. "Our local radio station did a poll, and we have ninety-eight percent approval in the community for these chain gangs."

Evidently, Phil found this amusing because he chuckled. "Ninety-eight percent."

"Now that's pretty high," Becher said.

"In other words," said Donahue, "of all the people calling into the radio station, ninety-eight percent agree with this."

"Absolutely."

"Does this guy follow Rush Limbaugh?" Phil asked.

"I don't have any idea," replied Becher.

Phil had already taken heed of my own chain gang.

"Sheriff," Phil said, "you're not the first one to do this, but you do have chain gangs."

His reminder that I wasn't the first hit a sore spot. "I'm the first jail system in the country. In fact, I would have been the first last year—I just didn't have the bodies who guard the inmates. Now I use armed posse men and women to guard the chain gang."

"What's the distance between me and the next prisoner?" Donahue asked.

About five feet, I explained.

"And about how many are on one chain?"

"I usually put five hooked together. Five on one chain."

"And the kind of work they do?" Phil inquired. "Clean up debris?"

"Clean up the streets of Phoenix. I give them orange uniforms and Men At Work signs."

"And to those who would say this is arcane, it's medieval, you're cruel, we do have protections," Phil said. He was starting to get excited again. "Prisoners are people. I mean, it's true, they should be incarcerated, pay their price, do the crime, pay the time. But Sheriff, we're going back to the eighteenth century, the seventeenth century, here."

I didn't find Donahue's accusation nearly as provocative as he did, (nor, from my observation, did the audience), but I thought Phil would be better off hearing it from somebody else. "Well, George was just on the chain gang."

"Is that right, George?" Donahue asked.

"Yes, sir," George answered via satellite.

"How was that?"

"Miserable, sir." His candor caused several members of the audience to laugh. "You try being chained to fifteen other inmates who have little respect for themselves or other human beings for thirty days out in the hot sun and try to work as a team. If you can accomplish the objective of not losing your temper or getting in a physical fight, you have reached an objective, and that is self-discipline, self-control."

Donahue showed videotape of inmates working outside on the chain gang in both Maricopa County and Clark County. Neither looked too harsh to me, and, once again judging the audience's reaction, or lack of reaction, neither did anybody other than Phil.

The Do-Gooder And Dostoyevsky

That's exactly what Donahue called Jonathan Smith, the director of the D.C. Prisoners' Legal Services Project.

"Here comes the do-gooder," Phil said. "Boy, you're a lonely voice on this program. Well, let me tell ya: We folks here in America don't care much for what you're doing. We think you're a bleeding heart. We think you worry too much about the criminal and don't pay enough attention to the victims. You're here to say that these are bad ideas."

"I think they're terrible ideas," said Smith. "I think the support in this country is based on a real misconception on what prisons are all about and what happens in prisons. There is all this propaganda about prisons being comfortable places, about cable television, exercise rooms, prisoners having all these luxuries. Well, it simply isn't true."

Smith said that he worked with prisoners every day, that prisons were dangerous, horrible places, and went so far as to claim that the treatment many inmates experience on a daily basis constitutes nothing less than "torture." He definitely didn't approve of tents and chain gangs, calling them part of "the dehumanization and humiliation of prisoners."

Finally, Phil had somebody who agreed with him, and he went with the flow, declaring that such treatment only increased the danger for the prison guards.

"Well," Smith said, "it's not fair to the guards, it's not fair to the community, it's not fair to the prisoners. I think it was Dostoyevsky who said, you want to take a look at the decency of a society, you take a look inside its prisons. And the United States would fail that test. We dehumanize our prisoners." He kept going, maintaining that prisons were too tough, too harsh, that incarcerating criminals with nothing to do only bred more crime, while incarcerating them with the wrong things to do also bred more crime. Smith concluded by condemning our national policy toward incarceration as twenty years of failure.

While some of what he said had value—certainly some prisons were terribly run, and certainly education and work were valuable penal tools, but the man had gone way too far in the wrong direction.

I had to say something. "Wait a minute. I was with the Federal Drug Enforcement Administration for almost thirty years. I worked in Turkey, Mexico, Iran, Iraq—you ought to see those prisons. Here in the United States, you live better in the federal prisons—you know it—than you do on the outside. They have bocci—I'm Italian, I can tell you—they have bocci, they have pizza, eggs over light, they have their own televisions. What you're saying is wrong. You're misleading the audience. It's almost like a country club."

"I don't run a prison system, either," added Chief Becher. "We're a county jail. And we have regulations that the jail must be between sixty-eight and seventy-two degrees at all times. We have other regulations that say they must be served a dietary menu. They must have exercise. We're not beating them. I believe in humane treatment to a certain extent, but these are criminals. They have violated other people's rights. Aren't we concerned about those rights?"

That last rhetorical question was another guaranteed crowd pleaser.

The Victim And the Legislator

Chris Long-Wagner woke up in the middle of the night in her Ohio bedroom to find a naked man looming over her. The man grabbed her by the back of her hair and held his hand over her mouth. He was huge and powerful, and did not need any other weapon to physically dominate Long-Wagner during the hour he spent in her bedroom, assaulting and raping her.

Later, when her ordeal was over, Long-Wagner learned several key facts. The man had raped two women in 1980, and had received a fifteen- to seventy-five-year sentence. He must have been something of a model prisoner, attending Narcotics Anonymous *and* Alcoholics Anonymous in prison, as well as earning his GED and a two-year Associate Degree. The con had been released early, after serving just seven years. Eight months after his parole, he had broken into Long-Wagner's home.

During his time in jail, apart from reforming, the man had spent countless hours weight lifting, bulking up, getting stronger every day.

The attack caused Chris to become politically involved, and she had lobbied to remove weight lifting equipment from Ohio's jails. Representative E. J. Thomas sponsored the bill in the state legislature, and he had accompanied her to the program. His bill, which not only removed the equipment but also banned martial arts training, passed the legislature easily. He explained his reasoning to the audience in a sentence: At our expense, while all the rest of us are working, he's spending several hours a day getting big and strong, so when he comes back out, that means that his next victim is going to be intimidated and overpowered by this great bulk."

Representative Thomas also had a nice word to say about my tents. He had served in the military and in Desert Storm, and affirmed that he and his fellow soldiers had all survived living in tents in good condition. He thought it was obvious that released cons wouldn't be so quick to commit another crime and return to jail if most jails weren't "fairly comfortable."

"There's no deterrence," Thomas said, "and that's why the sheriff has such a good program."

Jonathan Smith, the prisoners' advocate, made it clear that what happened to Long-Wagner was unforgivable and awful. Nonetheless...

"I think that what we're doing is focusing our attention on the wrong thing," Smith said. "Taking away the weights won't solve any problems."

"We're talking about the humiliation of the prisoners," Thomas said. "What about the humiliation of the victims?"

And there were more hoorays, even from a cynical, big city audience.

The next guest worked for the New Jersey Department of Corrections, overseeing several hundred inmates who worked on prison farms, growing food for their own consumption as well as for sale to state institutions, saving New Jersey a cool one million dollars a year. Ed Crotty said the goal of his program was not so much to turn the inmates into farmers as it was to teach them something about work, to give them dignity and some purpose.

Crotty's program made a lot of sense to me, although Donahue presented it as though it was contrary to my agenda, which was a totally fallacious conclusion. After all, why would constructive work be incompatible with tents and discipline and saving the taxpayers' money?

The Big Finish

Phil attacked me. It kind of came out of nowhere: One minute he was talking to somebody else about something else, and the next—wham!

I figured that he had just had enough. He had wanted to show that sweetness and light, compassion and commiseration, were the way to go in the penal world, that tents and bologna sandwiches and no MTV and no *Playboy* constituted cruel and unusual punishment. It was pretty obvious that he hadn't convinced the audience of any of it.

Phil started by mentioning the Department of Justice investigation into the Maricopa County jails, though he didn't mention that Justice routinely investigated scores of jails every year, that some prisoners made jailhouse careers out of accusing their jailers of innumerable slights and wrongs, that our courts were drowning in nuisance cases, that Maricopa's jails had already been cleared of any wrongdoing in several Arizona probes, and that I had been the first to detect the few problems we did have, and I had been the one to arrest two jailers who had broken the rules, and I had been the one who had them prosecuted.

Phil also didn't mention that my budget had been cut by a whopping $10 million, and I was two hundred detention officers short, which definitely didn't help my staff do its job. But I brought it up, which only seemed to make Donahue more determined. He instantly jumped off that track and took off on another. And it was a doozy of a ride.

"When you start canceling hot lunches, and feeding your prisoners bologna sandwiches," Phil said, "and you're getting a standing ovation from an angry, frightened community, that's just put another lock on their door. When you take away TV and *Playboy*; when you juvenilize your prison population, you convey the notion somehow that the prisoners really aren't human beings, and we don't have to bring to them any kind of due process, and screw the Bill of Rights.

"And more and more cops start to play more and more cowboy. And the anger builds, the divisions build, the walls between the prisoners and the guards build, and pretty soon somebody says something to somebody else and ka-boom! And you've got some real hardworking public servants in Maricopa County held hostage."

I wasn't one to interrupt, but this was really getting to be more than a little melodramatic, not to mention ridiculous. I opened my mouth to speak, but Donahue was on a roll, and he was not to be denied.

"And I want to tell you something," Phil said, his tone increasingly imploring, "if that happens, and I pray that it doesn't, Sheriff, because I'm here to tell you that I don't have all the answers. But one of the first things you're going to do is restore hot lunches to get those guards out, you're going to restore *Playboy* magazine, you're going to restore CNN and television. This is all a rootin', tootin', shootin', short-lived effort to prove that you're tough, and I think Jonathan has a point when he says it's not going to work."

That was quite a soliloquy, and since it didn't add up to much, a long answer was not required.

"Who said I'm going to restore it? You're telling me I'm going to restore it. I'm not going to restore it. First of all, we haven't had any problem. We haven't had any riots. We've had three or four problems with a hundred and fifty thousand people coming through my system—a hundred and fifty thousand a year. We run the most efficient jail system in the country. Our meals are down to thirty cents a meal per inmate. We send our inmates out to pick fruits and vegetables. I even have forty-eight thousand corn dogs free of charge from New York that I feed the inmates. I haven't had the problems."

George Matta had an opinion to contribute. "First of all, I'd like to say that not all inmates are the same. Every inmate is an individual. As far as weight lifting goes and exercising, the inmates here do not have weights. We improvise by push-ups, sit-ups, dips, you know. We overcome the necessity for doing exercises. Number two, as far as educating yourself, doing something worthy and resourceful with your time, I learned how to do bookkeeping and accounting through the jail's library. I also picked up a new skill as a barber here. I learned how to cut hair very well. Everyone comes to me for their supercuts. Like I said, every inmate here is an individual. If he applies himself to the time and takes himself seriously."

Donahue asked George whether he had ever witnessed guards roughing up the inmates.

"Personally, I've never seen any physical abuse by the officers," George said. "What I have seen is the inmates being subdued. You get a lot of inmates in here with little or no self-respect. They don't appreciate the officers or their jobs. They complain about getting no respect from the officers. The officers here work twelve-hour shifts. I know what these officers go through in a twelve-hour shift."

Phil announced once again that George was getting out in three weeks. "We should make that point," Donahue said, as if Matta's impending release somehow impeached his testimony.

That pretty much wrapped it up. Oh, there was a little more give-and-take. An audience member asked me how much time would it take before we knew whether my system worked.

I told him flat out it was going to take time. "I've just had the two years. We'll see if it's going to work. But even if it doesn't work, why should they live better in jail then they do on the outside?"

The audience showed its agreement by applauding.

George had a last word. "I just want to say that the sheriff's system has worked for *me*."

The crowd clapped for George's evident rehabilitation, but Phil was not so easily moved.

"Yes," Donahue said, "spoken like a man who's getting out in three weeks."

George stuck up for himself. "Well, sir, I've put in my time."

Phil switched his attention to a last word from Jonathan Smith, then concluded by saying: "The prison population has doubled in the past ten years. This system hasn't worked."

His comment prompted a woman in the audience to rise and respond. "I think, sir, you've lost sight of the reasons prisoners are in prison. I think the reason they're there is because of the crimes they commit. I think their solutions are saving money, and they're better than anything else I've heard."

This produced still more applauding affirmation from the people, which must have caused Phil to give it one last shot for his overtly unappreciated beliefs. And yet again I was his target.

"They're gonna rise up," warned Phil. "I mean, I read about you, Sheriff: Charles Dickens wrote about you in those schools."

That was a strange accusation, factually and philosophically—almost desperate, you might say—and not worth a reply.

And then a few more opinions about other topics were offered, and the program faded away and was over.

Not too much later I was on the plane winging back to Phoenix. I didn't like being away from the county or the office for too long. Inevitably, something new was happening, some action that demanded my reaction.

I shifted in my small seat. In case anybody wonders, *Donahue*, which must mint money, is so cheap it flies its guests coach.

I was thinking about the show. It always amazed me how little most journalists, commentators, academics, and talk show hosts actually knew about crime and punishment. Oh, many of them were familiar enough with the statistics and the studies, but that was not what I meant by "knowing." I'm referring to the reality of crime and punishment, the human cost and consequences of all the sociological theories and political deals. Victims understand crime. Cops understand crime. Talk show hosts—well, I'll leave that one up to you.

I understand crime. I've understood for thirty-six years now, thirty-six years fighting crime, thirty-six years accounting for exactly half my life. I've understood it as street crime and international conspiracy and government corruption, in Washington,

D.C., and Chicago, Las Vegas and San Antonio, Turkey and Mexico, Lebanon and Panama.

There had been so many places, so many plots, so much crime, not enough punishment. So much to consider. So much to remember.

And I remembered one cold, black night in particular, some thirty years ago, outside a remote village somewhere in the mountains of Turkey...

I'd been driving for I don't know how many hours, grappling with the wheezing, aged truck I had rented a couple of hundred miles ago. Up to now, the trek had been pretty much routine. I had driven to Ankara from my home in Istanbul in my government-issue 1957 Chevy, and picked up Commander Galip Labernas, my counterpart in the Turkish national police. He was an old pro, but his enthusiasm for crime busting had long ago evaporated and disappeared.

From Ankara, we had headed into rural Turkey, away from the bright lights—or just about any lights—and big cities. Of course, the further we journeyed from the main urban areas, the more difficult the roads became, until they were finally too much for my car, which was six years old and had been worn down traversing the rutted, dirt roads of Turkey. But that was all the old Bureau of Narcotics, forerunner to the Drug Enforcement Administration, could afford. It probably cost what the modern DEA spends on those snazzy department baseball caps.

The Chevy was the least of my inconveniences; I was one of only six agents working outside the United States, and I was solely responsible for not just Turkey but for the entire Middle East. I had been assigned to the region, put on a plane and dropped off in Istanbul, without any language courses or background information or staff to smooth the trip. It was just me, my snub-nosed .38, and a very small bankroll, up against the international opium trade.

The task was daunting in scope and importance. Turkey's endless fields supplied the opium for the laboratories of the Corsican syndicate in Marseilles, which converted the raw material into morphine base and then heroin, which was shipped to America, primarily via Canada down to New York City. This was no casual enterprise, but perhaps the most organized, continually successful criminal conspiracy in modern times: A conspiracy I would fight from Europe to the Middle East to Central America to South America; a battle I would wage, on one front or another, for the next eight years.

I would finally break the conspiracy and arrest Armand Ricord, the mastermind of the entire organization, whose power and position were so entrenched that I had to secretly spirit him out of Paraguay and to the United States against the opposition of our own ambassador. A Hollywood movie would later dramatize, immortalize, and misrepresent a small part of this criminal enterprise, known to the world as *The French Connection*.

But that was all in the future. Tonight I was just a narcotics agent doing my job, following up on a lead and preparing to make a buy in the middle of nowhere in the middle of the night.

I'd met the go-between who'd set up this transaction shortly after arriving in Turkey. He was a Lebanese "businessman," who was looking to score big in the informer game. After striking out on several deals, he had begun to click, and I'd made a series of decent busts because of his efforts. This one was supposed to be big, maybe a half-ton of opium.

I usually had some kind of Turkish cop with me whenever I went out undercover, which only made sense as I had neither police powers nor backup of my own. For the most part, the Turkish police were hardly models of law enforcement efficiency, being generally underpaid, undertrained, underequipped, and undermotivated. On the other hand, they were all I had. I had discovered that it was smart to work only with cops from either Istanbul or Ankara, because the rural authorities were thoroughly bought and paid for by the local drug dealers, and would give you away faster than you could spit.

So there we were, driving all day and all night, exchanging my Chevy for a rented, rusty heap in one village, moving on, not stopping to rest in one of the small hotels the road offered, twenty-five cents a bed, and all the bugs you can step over. I shared my whiskey and GI rations with Commander Labernas, as was expected, and kept spinning and shuddering along the narrow, rough mountain roads, used more by horses and donkeys than by trucks.

Somewhere along the journey, we picked up about twenty soldiers from the paramilitary police and hid them in the back of the truck. We kept going forward until after two days and nights, we neared the town of Goceri.

It was 1:30 A.M. I was driving without the headlights. In the mountains, an approaching vehicle can be spotted half a day off. Headlights only made it that much easier to give the bad guys an edge.

It was as dark as night can be, and I proceeded slowly. We had almost reached the outskirts of the town when I spotted the signal, a flashlight blinking twice up ahead. I stopped the truck, got out with my own flashlight and answered back. Identification established, I walked closer.

I'd spent four years working undercover in Chicago before this assignment, spinning out elaborate stories of my criminal background and intentions, proving myself to mobsters and killers, knowing that the smallest slip could mean a quick death. Turkey was very different, however, much less sophisticated and suspicious, though no less dangerous. The buy was set up by the go-between, and all the suppliers ever knew or cared about, particularly in the countryside, was that I was some foreigner—one day I was an Italian diplomat, the next a Dutch sailor—who had money and wanted to buy opium. I would show up, flash the cash, and go from there. Simple—especially in theory.

Anyway, my Lebanese informer was waiting, along with one of the farmers/smugglers who had brought the opium. It was legal to grow opium in Turkey at the time. Refined, it provided the morphine base used for medicinal purposes all over the world. And the price paid for opium by drug smugglers was two or three times higher than the price the farmer could get from legitimate buyers. However, because the government regulated the crop, each farmer could divert only a few kilos from his lawful harvest and get away with it, and so it required a bunch of farmers to add up to a take as sizable as half a ton.

On behalf of the supplier, the informer asked to see my money. I pulled out a thick roll of bills and waved it in front of their faces. Benjamin Franklin's face was on top, so the men could see I was loaded with one hundred dollar bills. Of course, the rest of the bills underneath the hundred were ones. A single hundred was all my Bureau of Narcotics' budget could afford. Fortunately, I wasn't dealing with the most sophisticated of criminals, and the farmer didn't ask to count the money. He was satisfied.

"Where's the stuff?" I asked.

The Lebanese gave me directions down a side road, where I would find the opium, and conduct the transaction. I returned to my truck. The informer and the farmer went on ahead.

This was the hairy part. If the farmers or anybody else was planning to hold me up, or kill me for my cash, it would be at the end of this road.

I cautiously headed down the bumpy lane. I had my headlights on, full force. Any possible advantage to be gained by sneaking up on the farmers was no longer possible because the farmers certainly knew I was there. At this stage, it was more important to make sure I didn't careen off the road and plunge the truck off the mountain.

The lights of the truck bounced off the bags of opium piled on the ground in the middle of the road, but in the first flash off those burlap bags I recognized that this was no ordinary haul.

I stopped the truck, but didn't turn off the headlights. I wanted to keep a little illumination on the scene. I glanced over at my Turkish policeman and nodded, a silent reminder to be ready.

I checked the .38 stuck in my waistband and stepped down.

I had never seen so much opium in any one place. It was collected in a huge mass of small and large bags, at least six feet wide and several feet high, with other sacks hanging off the sides of the pack animals, which had transported them to this rendezvous. And it was not only the sheer quantity, which was overwhelming, but also the smell, the air suffused by that unmistakable musty odor.

All this opium brought with it one complication. The more opium, the more farmers were required to contribute to the total, and every one of those farmers attended the transaction to see that he wasn't cheated out of his rightful slice of the money. Standing before me were about twenty-five to thirty farmers, tough, bearded, mountain men, quiet and grim, armed with rifles and knives.

I glanced over at my Lebanese pal, who was grinning. He had known this was something special, and had wanted to surprise me. Of course, if this had been a real deal, instead of a buy-and-bust, I would never have had enough money. Black market opium was going for thirty dollars a kilo. Considering there could have been a ton of it here, I would have needed a suitcase stuffed with hundreds, not just one measly bill plastered on top of a fake roll resting in my pocket.

The farmers were eyeing me, waiting for their money. The silence hung in the air. The moment had arrived. I sucked in some oxygen and shouted out the signal.

"*Gel!*"

That was Turkish for "come!," and that yell was supposed to bring both my temporary Turkish partner and the troops crashing out of our truck and to the stage, front and center.

But nothing happened. The farmers stared at me, confused. I shouted again, even louder, "*Gel!*"

Nothing. Not a damn peep. I was 408 miles from Istanbul, and that was where my backup might as well have been.

"*GEL!*"

And I stood there, all alone, aside from the farmers, who thankfully still waited, confounded by this clearly crazy foreigner, evidently still anticipating their money.

I knew the farmers wouldn't stay frozen forever, so I did what came naturally: I attacked, which in this case meant pulling my gun and shouting, "Interpol!" ("Police!" wouldn't have worked because I obviously wasn't Turkish. And "United States Bureau of Narcotics!" would have been a meaningless jumble of words, so "Interpol!" was the accepted, recognized shorthand for some kind of foreign cop.)

So there we were, me and my six-shot revolver with the two-inch barrel, taking thirty-odd Turkish opium farmers into custody,

which, I mention quite incidentally at this point, I had no authority
to do. I needed my Turkish compatriots to make the bust official.

For some reason, the farmers didn't move. Perhaps they
thought my performance was just too funny to interrupt. I don't
know. All I do know is that they didn't shoot me, and that was good
enough for me.

Then, all of a sudden, the cavalry woke up and started leaping
out of the back of my truck. (It's possible they were waiting to find
out if the farmers would quickly kill me, thereby closing the case
and rendering their participation unnecessary.) The soldiers didn't
believe in quietly flanking the enemy and taking prisoners, because
they emerged from the truck screaming and firing their weapons in
the air. This utterly stupid barrage only served to spook the farmers, most of whom instantly turned and fled with their animals into
the night.

One farmer just a few feet away raised a rifle and pointed it at
me, and there was nothing I could do. He had me dead. But either
his rifle jammed or he simply didn't fire, because nothing happened. And then other bodies got in the way, the action shifted, and
it was over.

The farmers were vanishing, which, upon reflection, was
preferable to them deciding to shoot it out with the soldiers, with
me in the middle. At that instant, however, with my adrenaline
pumping, I was furious that people were escaping. I saw a donkey
getting away with probably a hundred kilos strapped to his back,
and I fired at him. Maybe because he was fading into the darkness,
or maybe because a revolver with a two-inch barrel is accurate at a
distance the length of the average living room, or maybe because
I'm a lousy shot, the donkey got away without a scratch.

So did, by the way, most of the farmers/smugglers, who melted
away in the night. Pursuit was impossible. These were their mountains and valleys, and they knew every rock and path and hole.

Still, we rounded up a handful of the farmers, and somehow
managed not to get anyone killed. I didn't reprimand my Turkish
allies. I had figured out there was really no point; one accepted the
way things were or one asked for a new assignment somewhere else.

Anyway, I had something more interesting to do. This was my first opportunity to take a good, long look at the catch. This was one ton, minimum. Unbelievable. I had never heard of anybody snatching so much opium before.

To a cop, all this confiscated opium was a beautiful sight.

It wasn't too smart to spend a lot of time standing around congratulating ourselves. We were deep in hostile territory, and the farmers could conceivably organize themselves into an ambush. I helped the troops load the opium and the prisoners into the truck, and away we went.

Same as on the trip out, I drove pretty much straight through, and two days later I was back in Istanbul. The prisoners were led away, and the opium was weighed. The haul was an extraordinary one ton plus, the largest seizure ever made in Turkey. The case received worldwide publicity. Even so, I could not help thinking about that donkey and the hundred kilos that got away.

I went home, took a shower, and went back out to make the next buy and the next bust. It was early morning when I left the house...

The plane was nearing Phoenix. No time for talk shows or Turkish memories.

The real world was approaching, fast.

PART I

The Tents

CHAPTER TWO

Another Visit to the Big (And Open-Air) House

T he press conference was ready to begin. The media was assembled inside the dining room, one of the few permanent, or "hard," structures in Tent City Jail: Three local television stations, two radio stations, a reporter from the Associated Press, a writer from a Norwegian magazine, and a crew from French TV. A typical assortment of journalists, congregating for another event at the tents.

Today's occasion was a visit from Senator Phil Gramm, Republican from Texas. Gramm was running for president, campaigning through the state. He had stopped at the tents in part for the photo op, and in part to make some pronouncements about getting tough on crime.

The tents were quickly becoming a favorite gathering spot for politicians, in and out of Arizona. The former governor of Louisiana, running for office again, was flying in to offer his own statement, and have his picture snapped for the folks back home.

It made sense that politicos and the press *The tents* would appreciate the photogenic quality of the *attract more* tents. The Statue of Liberty embodies freedom. *than prisoners* The Tomb of the Unknown Soldier represents the sacrifice and suffering of our fighting men and women. Well, in a similarly symbolic vein, the Tent City Jail can stand for a new approach to crime and punishment. And that's why the requests keep coming in to view, tour, photograph, videotape, film, and, in a single, stark word, *use* the tents, for better or worse.

Arizona's own Senator John McCain made the introductions. He graciously included me, declaring that I was "the best-known and most popular politician in America, and most popular sheriff in America, and a man who has revolutionized the office."

McCain said he had recently received phone calls from the *Philadelphia Inquirer* and a national magazine soliciting comments about me.

Next it was Senator Gramm's turn at the podium. He said he had journeyed to our tents to show his support for our jail, and not only in erecting the tents but also in the many other programs my office had initiated.

"Increasingly," Gramm said, "people all across America know about Joe, and approve of what he's doing. It's time for federal prisons to stop resembling Holiday Inns."

The senator wanted to turn every prison in this country into "mini-industrial parks," with prisoners working during the day and going to school at night.

With that, we took a spin around the grounds, stepping inside the tents, chatting with the inmates, standing beside the flagpole as the media watched and recorded.

Happily, the smell wasn't bad today. The Tent City Jail is located in southwest Phoenix, where the city ends and the desert begins. Just over the hill to one side is the city dump. On another side is the county pound, where they destroy and cremate the many unwanted animals.

On many days, when the breeze is blowing right, the smell can be more than unpleasant, and the crosswind from both facilities is just about overwhelming. However, the air was quiet that day, and though my distinguished guests didn't know it, they were lucky.

The event progressed as planned, and eventually Senator Gramm, Senator McCain, their aides and the attending press climbed back into their vehicles and drove off. Another press conference was successfully completed, but the work of the tents continued, work that is unending and indispensable, sometimes controversial, and frequently dangerous.

And that work is what I shall discuss now.

At the time I became sheriff more than three years ago, the jail system in Maricopa County was desperately overcrowded. The various jails were constructed to hold approximately three thousand prisoners, while more than five thousand were actually incarcerated. Such crammed conditions must breed stress and anger and, inevitably, violence, whether we are talking about rats or humans occupying those too-small quarters. And so it was in Maricopa County jails. Prisoners were fighting one another as well as guards, and both prisoners and guards were constantly being injured.

This situation was hardly unique to Maricopa. Let's briefly examine statistics for the year 1992, as compiled by the Department of Justice. In that year, state and federal prison populations totaled 883,656 inmates. Local jails held another 444,584 men and women. (Not surprisingly, men heavily outnumber women. Of those 883,656 state and federal prisoners, 789,700 were male.)

Think of those figures this way: Out of every 100,000 in this country, fully 518 were in prison or jail, the highest ratio in the Western world. Viewing these numbers through still another perspective, in comparing the years 1980 and 1993, (which saw a rise from the previous year of another 7 percent in the prison population), 2.9 times as many people were incarcerated in 1993 as had been just thirteen years earlier. Said in different form, 2.9 times equals an increase of nearly 150 percent!

Though prison spending has increased on both the state and federal level, it does not come close to matching the rising prison population.

A similarly sad state of affairs certainly ruled in Maricopa County when I took office. We needed more jail cells, but there was no money to build them. In fact, the Board of Supervisors, the body that rules the budget for the county and my department, was busy cutting funds for the Sheriff's Office to the tune of an astonishing $10 million. That was $10 million removed from my entire budget of $92 million, which meant that that $10 million accounted for more than 10 percent of my department's total budget!

The ongoing budget battle was and is all about local politics. The Board of Supervisors, undoubtedly in the temperament of political bodies everywhere, wanted to aggrandize its power through domination over other governmental bureaus. Add that instinct to the board's evident resentment of the positive press and poll ratings I was receiving, and its collective appetite was whetted enough to attempt to seize effective sovereignty over the Sheriff's Office. When that failed, the next move was to try to achieve the same result by cutting my budget. Of course, the only result for which the board could claim credit was damaging its reputation, damaging my department's ability to serve the people, and, ultimately, damaging the public safety. After a standoff lasting about a year, the board gave up and belatedly began restoring the missing funds to the Sheriff's Office.

In any event, I had already hit upon the idea of using tents when I ran for office in 1992. Neither budget problems nor jail overcrowding had prompted the idea. Instead, my motivations were absolutely simple and direct: I wanted to put more people in jail and I wanted to do it while spending as little of the taxpayers' money as possible.

At the same time, the military was in the process of downsizing and discarding obsolete equipment. I contacted the army and asked if they had any extra tents. The army was only too happy to give us whatever they had available, at no cost. Before we could accept the tents, the Sheriff's Office had to obtain a special Pentagon rule change that allows local government departments to obtain federal equipment for little or no cost.

The truth was, the tents—mainly twenty-bed tents, with a few forty-bed units included—weren't worth much on the open market. Many of the canvas coverings were first used during the Korean War, while a few were as old as the First World War. Some had holes or were definitely fraying at the seams. But they had survived the Persian Gulf War, they were still serviceable, and that was more than good enough for me.

The tents were the key ingredient to my plan. All we had to do was pour the concrete foundations for the tents, build fences, install electricity and plumbing for bathroom, kitchen, and medical facilities, as well as the evaporative water coolers and electric heating provided for the tents. Water foundations and portable toilets placed around the grounds augmented the indoor facilities.

Though these expenditures were far from great, I wasn't dunning the county for any assistance. Instead, I was using fines imposed on the inmates to pay for various infractions.

Before anything else was built or assembled, the concrete was mixed and set for the flagpole, which soon rose from inside the compound, hoisting both the American flag and the Maricopa County Sheriff's Office standard as they flew far above the tents.

On August 2, 1993, at high noon, Tent City One was formally inaugurated and opened. With a bit of a melodramatic flair, I scheduled the press conference for high noon. I was hoping that the temperature would hit 120 degrees "to make the reporters sweat," but the summer day only reached 113 degrees.

My message was succinct. "Did anybody see that movie, *Field Of Dreams*? They said, 'Build it and they will come.' Well, I built it, and they will come!"

And very quickly they did. The tents soon held one thousand prisoners, every one a sentenced convict. The handful of critics who spoke out scoffed, saying that the tents wouldn't work, that they were dangerous for inmates and detention officers, that they were backward and ridiculous. But, as usual, the critics didn't know what they were talking about. In fact, they were dead wrong.

(Example: The *Village Voice* in New York City actually called the tents "concentration camp-like," which would have been funny if it weren't demented. It makes me think that the article's writer not only needs to go to the library and check out a book on World War II and the Nazis—preferably a book with photographs—but also get out of Greenwich Village every now and then.)

To begin, the idea that housing prisoners in the desert in tents constituted some sort of cruel and unusual punishment was patently ludicrous. Here's the short answer: If our troops in Desert Storm could live in the Saudi desert in tents for months, heroic young men and women who were faithfully serving their country, then why aren't the tents good enough for sentenced inmates? (And let's not forget that living in tents and eating lousy food was the least of our soldiers' concerns.)

And so what if the tents were less than pleasant—I think the very least we can ask of our criminals is to sacrifice a little for the taxpayers.

As to the potential danger to both detention officers and inmates: The budgetary gash the county Board of Supervisors had inflicted upon my department had seriously affected the number of detention officers I could hire. We were exactly 167 guards short and didn't have the money to fill out our roster. Across the nation, the ratio of guards to inmates in the prisons and jails averages one guard for every four inmates. One to four.

With a constantly growing inmate population, I simply couldn't afford that ratio. In our hard facilities, (i.e., permanent structures), the ratio is one to eight. In the tents, two detention officers are in the yard at any one time, guarding one thousand inmates. That's two for one thousand. Only the most experienced detention officers are recruited for this duty, which partially explains why problems and confrontations in the tents have been much less frequent than in the hard facilities.

The other reason the tents provoke less violence is clearly due to the nature of the compound itself. Unlike inmates in a hard facility, the prisoners in the tents get to roam the grounds, to stretch their limbs in a manner impossible in a cramped, permanent structure, and that surely makes a difference—probably a very significant difference, indeed.

Tent City One was such an unalloyed success that we quickly made plans to open an adjoining compound. I dubbed this new facility "ConTents," and announced its commencement at a ceremony on its grounds on May 10, 1995. This addition contained twenty-three tents which held twenty bunks each and three forty-bunk tents.

On that occasion, I noted that Maricopa County Jail held 5,803 men and women, the largest number in the county's history, a number that was certain to continue growing. Keeping up with this influx of prisoners was a logistical and monetary nightmare. The solutions hit upon by other jurisdictions totaled precisely two—build new jails or release prisoners early.

In Minneapolis, for instance, a new jail had recently been constructed. It is a hard facility costing the taxpayers a cool $200 million to hold between nine hundred and fifteen hundred inmates. You read that right—$200 million! I know that, because the sheriff from Minneapolis was here for a visit to check out our tents, and you know he was impressed.

The taxpayers of Maricopa County shouldn't have to spend $200 million or $100 million or, at the generally accepted low end, $40 million to house malefactors. Each tent city I have erected has cost between $80,000 and $100,000. Even if I hadn't been able to use the money paid by the inmates for different fines incurred during their sojourns with us for construction—even if the taxpayers had been forced to put up the money—and of course the money collected for the fines was used and the taxpayers paid nothing—contrast and consider: $200 million versus $80,000. Or at their low end against our high end, $40 million versus $100,000. Any way you cut it, which would you choose if the choice were yours?

Well, you know which I choose. Now the tents are not a blanket solution. Tents in Minneapolis wouldn't work too well in the dead of winter. And serial killers and other outright unrepentant, incorrigible, vicious, murderous animals shouldn't be kept in tents of any kind. (In fact, when someone causes enough trouble and additional punishment is due, we take that person out of the tents and place him in solitary confinement, or "lockdown," in a hard facility.)

So while the tents won't always work, they certainly can work often and in many locales across this country. And from all the interest displayed by cities and counties calling my office and visiting the tents, I am sure you will be seeing Tent City jails springing up in many jurisdictions and many states, to the grateful cheers of the public.

But that discusses only the first solution to overcrowding, the tried-and-true "throw more money at the problem" solution. The other remedy law enforcement officials have discovered is less expensive in terms of dollars, but infinitely more expensive in terms of the real, final cost to society.

An example will suffice: The sheriff of Los Angeles County was recently faced with not only an exploding prison population but also had *his* budget reduced by $7 million by his Board of Supervisors. His response to these dual strains on his department's resources was to order the early release of three thousand prisoners. Three thousand convicts handed a free pass because there wasn't room for them in the jails.

The sheriff of L.A. County is hardly alone in adopting that course of action, or rather, to my way of thinking, that course of *inaction*. All across the United States, officials responsible at every level of the criminal justice system are doing exactly the same thing: They are forsaking their sworn duty to serve the public and justice by taking the quick, easy way out and letting the inmates go free. Such ethical abdication makes a mockery of our entire legal system. A rational, democratic society depends upon *authority* as much as *power* (the former referring to the *right* to command while the latter speaks to the *ability*, the strength and force), and society's authority and power are diminished and ridiculed when the guardians of law and order—society's first obligation to its citizens—do not keep their word.

In this instance, when society judges an individual guilty of a crime, metes out an appropriate sentence, thereby showing its commitment to not permitting such behavior, and then lets that criminal off because punishing him is "inconvenient" or "difficult," then all of society suffers. Society and its rules and prerogatives are held in contempt by precisely the people who will jump at any such weakness to abuse society's leniency or weakness or vulnerability. And that kind of contempt and weakness only leads to more lawbreaking and injustice and suffering, and as more people are incarcerated and then given early release, the cycle only gets more and more disturbing and dangerous.

So there has never been even the smallest possibility that I would ever release people from jail early. Never! Police officers are risking their lives every day making arrests, and I shall always have room in my jails, whether in the hard facilities or in the tents, for their prisoners. We must make room for those who deserve incarceration. There is no other choice.

By the time you read this, our newest innovation will hopefully be nearing completion and preparing to open for business. As I have mentioned, only sentenced inmates have been permitted in the tents so far, because the law states that those awaiting trial may not be housed in temporary structures, and, legally, tents are considered temporary structures, though I will never take them down.

A pressing need is for more structures to hold those awaiting trial, so we are constructing two barrack-type dwellings, housing four hundred inmates. Because the construction demands of this facility are substantially more involved, the complex will cost approximately one million dollars, a lot of money but still a pittance compared to a conventional jail.

When this third unit is up and running, we'll have two thousand inmates in the entire Tent City Jail. Just in time, too, for there are now more than six thousand inmates in the Maricopa County system. And if people keep committing crimes, and police officers keep arresting them, I'll put up as many tents as we need and keep putting them up, until we run out of criminals or tents, whichever comes first.

I was showing a French television crew—*another* French television crew, from another French station—around the tents the other day. They were doing a documentary about America, about the "real" America, whatever that means, and I was being profiled. They had already followed me around for three days, and while I am always happy to talk to the media, three days was getting to be a bit much. But the boys from France were intent on doing a thorough job, so here we were, at the tents, for their last day of filming, thank God.

It was the middle of the afternoon. About fifteen inmates were inside the dining hall, watching television. *Montel Williams* was on, and the men sat in chairs and watched several people argue about custody of a baby. I didn't stay long enough to get the whole story, but it seemed to me they all deserved to be in somebody's jail somewhere. The prisoners were more animated and talked back to the screen in the way people do, as though the screen might answer.

We were too late for lunch and too early for dinner, which was going to consist of some cold meat sandwich, as usual. No loss there.

The television crew took a stroll around the compound, filming this and that. The inmates were used to seeing the media and were ready and willing to give the roaming journalists what they wanted. They practically lined up to talk, to voice their complaints, to announce their innocence, to say the things prisoners always say everywhere. The French producer was pretty much enthralled with his encounter, and he ended up burning a lot of tape listening to their sad tales of injustice at the hands of an uncaring society.

Now I'm not going to drown you in inmate talk (the way a poor French audience is evidently going to be suffocated), but I thought I'd provide some highlights so you get the gist—that many inmates simply do not understand that breaking the law is wrong. I know it's hard to believe that *that* basic concept can elude anyone, but listen and learn.

One fellow complained about being deprived of the pleasures he was accustomed to, asserting, "We should have the same rights as people on the outside." Now that's an interesting concept, though it pretty much eliminates the whole point of jail.

His friend modified that a little, saying "Yeah, we should have the same rights we do in our homes."

Of course, if he had stayed at home enjoying his rights, the fellow wouldn't have wound up in jail.

On the heels of that, another inmate chipped in with the comment that, "Yeah, we didn't ask to be here."

Actually, asking had nothing to do with it.

Perhaps the summit of laughable arrogance was one man's complaint—and I quote word for word—"We are treated like criminals!"

Wow. Consider the mind of somebody who thinks like that. Consider how they regard basic matters, like truth and reality and right and wrong—in particular, *your* rights and *their* wrongs.

Another popular line of criminal logic dealt with convicts complaining that they absolutely, positively didn't belong in jail. One inmate pushed his face before the camera to allege that he was only incarcerated due to a "miscalculation." This avowal was seconded by a host of other convicts, though of course on behalf of themselves, not the first guy. One prisoner said he had been arrested as a result of "a case of mistaken identity." Another shouted that "somebody was out to get him!" and had framed the poor soul. Another guy declared that not only had somebody been out to get *him*, but that particular somebody had been his own cousin. More than a few blamed the cops, the courts, their friends, their enemies, in no particular order and in varying combinations.

In this cauldron of drug dealers and users, muggers and thieves, rapists and killers, was a lawyer, who, not surprisingly, had the most creative reason why he didn't belong in the hoosegow. According to the lawyer, he was either in jail because of a) real estate fraud, or b) a civil contempt citation. He was talking so fast that it was hard to tell which was the underlying cause of his troubles. In any event, he had been representing a client, or maybe himself, in the middle of a real estate deal when something happened to the documents, and they went before the judge, who got mad at the lawyer for no good reason, and the next thing he knew, he was on his way to an unwarranted, undeserved, unjustifiable, unquestionably unconstitutional stint in the county pen.

Of course, it would already have been straightened out if the judge hadn't immediately gone on vacation for an extended weekend, which, by the way, the lawyer suspected was planned just so the judge didn't have to hear the lawyer's explanation. Given all that, couldn't I personally intervene on his part and go to the judge and straighten the whole thing out?

Despite the obvious soundness of his position, I declined to interfere with the court's decision.

I could go on forever, *ad nauseam*, but you get the idea. I'm not guilty, I'm a victim, I don't belong here, I am being held against my will and unjustly, and society owes me big, and, given half a chance, I will collect one day.

In all fairness, not everyone is quite so blindly, stupidly self-serving. Several inmates admitted that, yes, they had sold drugs or bought them or robbed or assaulted or committed other crimes that had landed them in jail. And once that leap of honesty is made, it is usually easy to reevaluate their lives and decide that they don't want to make the same mistakes and find themselves back in jail.

"I've been in this system fourteen months," a man said, "and it's time for me to get back to the outside world. And when I do, I'm never coming back here."

A second young man said he was caught and convicted of passing bad checks. He was in his early twenties, rather quiet, obviously bright and very well-spoken. He said he had been sentenced to six months and would finish up his time in another few weeks. His crime had abruptly interrupted his college education, and his mother had gone to Arizona State University and arranged for her son to enroll upon his release. It was a break this young man said he wasn't going to blow, that he was going straight, and never returning to this awful place.

Listening to that young man, I sincerely hoped that he lived up to his newly affirmed standards and his own best expectations.

The theme, "Jail is an awful place, and I'm never coming back," was heard over and over. Those words were music to my ears. I *wanted* the inmates to hate my jail. I *wanted* them to hate everything about it, from the heat to the food to the work to the drudgery. I *wanted* them to remember for the rest of their days that this was a terrible experience they never wanted to experience again. I *wanted* them to walk the straight and narrow, in the best circumstances, because they've seen the light and had a change of heart, and in the worst case because they wanted to stay out of jail.

I *wanted* them to never want to come back. If that feeling took hold in only one out of ten inmates, then that was one in ten inmates the public and the police would never have trouble from again. And that sounded like a worthwhile goal.

CHAPTER THREE

There's More to the Tents Than Just Tents

While the tents are the most substantial and visible part of our jail program, they do not stand alone. Other measures also embody my philosophy of making the entire Maricopa County jail system less pleasant, more efficient and less burdensome on the taxpayers.

The bottom line can be summed up in a line I constantly repeat: *Our inmates should never live better in jail than they do on the outside.* It's that simple. Jail should be a place nobody ever wants to return to. That doesn't mean that inmates should be treated cruelly or inhumanely. Such behavior is not only ethically and legally unacceptable, it also is not productive from an institutional viewpoint. Indeed, arbitrary or barbaric management merely serves to render any jail more violent, unruly, and dangerous for both inmates and guards. Jail should be uncomfortable, not unsafe. Thus, the key concepts underlying my *modus operandi* are discipline, hard work, and a total absence of frills.

The media attention is okay by me

Once again, keep in mind that these measures apply to all Maricopa County jails, tent and hard facility, canvas and concrete.

41

We start with the prohibitions I instituted: No smoking. No *Playboys*, *Penthouses*, or any nude magazines. No coffee. No violent television shows. No "NC-17," "R," or "PG" movies.

(I cut out movies altogether after I showed *Old Yeller* and the inmates wildly cheered when the poor dog died.)

The prisoners don't like it. Every time I visit the tents, I hear the same thing: Why can't we have coffee? Why can't we have cigarettes? And my answer is always the same: Because you're in jail! (The irony, of course, is that by helping them quit smoking or, to a lesser extent, stop consuming coffee, we're actively promoting their health and well-being, whether they want to or not, whether they like it or not.)

It may be hard to believe, but many inmates cannot seem to grasp that some of the rights and privileges they enjoy on the outside are forfeited the moment they are incarcerated. For too many inmates, jail is simply a way station, even a respite, between other criminal destinations. One day they might be scoring in a crack house, another day breaking into someone's home, another in custody, another back on the streets, on and on, round and round they go, smoothly moving from one stop in their desultory life journey to another. You might be surprised to discover how basic are the needs of many criminals: Food, shelter, television, cigarettes, drugs, sex. As long as they can satisfy those desires, they are momentarily content. So when they move from the street, where they might have been mugging or robbing or dealing or even murdering to get what they want, to the penitentiary, and find that they can live just about as well or even better, without having to put out any effort (even criminal effort), what do you think is the result? What do you think *they* think? Do you think they fear jail? Do you think they pause before hitting a little old lady over the head to steal her bag and say to themselves, "Gee, maybe I shouldn't do this because if I'm caught I'll have to go back to that terrible place? That place where I can't smoke, have coffee, eat steak, do drugs, and have sex."

Of course not.

Instead, they say, "Hey, being locked up wasn't so bad. I did pretty much anything I wanted, I had my conjugal visits, and my

friends brought me drugs, and I could buy cigarettes in the com-
missary, and the food was better than I was used to, and I got to sit
around all day watching TV and lifting weights." Even if they are
caught and convicted, they know they have a good chance of getting a deal from the overworked assistant district attorney, and getting probation from the overloaded court. And even if they are sent
away, they know they probably won't get too much time, and even
if they do, they know they'll probably serve only one-third of their
sentence, getting out for "good behavior," whatever that fraudulent
term means, or even get kicked loose, free and clean, only because
the warden's jails are busting at the seams, and the warden decides
the easiest way to deal with the problem is to just open the doors
and let out a bunch of convicts.

So what's there to worry about? What's there to fear? You know
the old saying, "Don't do the crime if you can't do the time"? That
used to mean something, something to consider long and hard.
Now it's a joke. "Do the time?" Fat chance!

So I'm doing what I can to alter the penal equation. I'm not in
charge of the courts or the county attorney's office. I am in charge
of my deputies and my jails, and I have been changing the way my
institutions handle their responsibilities.

Other than the tents, the most attention I've received from the
public and the press concerns the green bologna. That green
bologna, comprised of part fact, part fiction, is only the most
famous piece of the entire food story, a story with which you should
be more familiar.

And don't fret; I'll explain about the green bologna in short
order.

As I've previously discussed, the Board of Supervisors slashed
my department's budget soon after I took office. My ongoing efforts
to uncover ways of tightening up control of the jails, toughening up
the system, and sparing taxpayer funds, now took on extra urgency.

The not-so-secret secret to increasing efficiency is thinking
creatively; contemplating angles others haven't contemplated,
mediating on solutions untried and untested. That's precisely what
we did with our food service.

Before I was elected, the Maricopa County Sheriff's Office (MCSO) food service operated pretty similarly to every other sheriff department's food service. The service purchased food based strictly on the low bidder system—the manufacturer or supplier whose prices were the lowest for a particular item won our business. That's certainly a fair and straightforward system, but not necessarily the best. In other words, working solely through low bids does not necessarily maximize the assets available both in and out of our department.

So we changed the way we did business. In the process, we tried some things nobody had done before. We mixed it up, combining some old ideas with some new ones, and discovered a slew of options that fulfilled a variety of requirements.

Frank Russo, our Food Service manager, came up with one terrific innovation. One way to preserve food, and thus save money by not having to throw out whatever is not immediately used, is—stated as simply as possible—to cook food at 165 degrees, bag it in cryovac bags, and then place the bags in refrigerators or freezers set at a temperature of 40 degrees or lower. In short, this is a method of pasteurization.

So far, so good. The rub begins when we consider that the apparatus used to accomplish this is called the Cook Chill System, and costs in the neighborhood of half a million dollars. That's half a million my department absolutely did not have.

So Frank improvised. He gathered together four hundred steam kettles, each kettle capable of holding one hundred gallons, and called a company that modified the kettles. The company attached pumps and whatnot, and suddenly we were the proud owners of an almost homemade Cook Chill System, capable of preparing and preserving everything from beef stew to vegetables to spaghetti sauce, all for the bargain basement price of $80,000.

Another innovation: Many local farmers have responded to our money-saving efforts by donating parts of other fields for our use. Thus, we have five department trucks that take inmates out to pick these fields for whatever is waiting for us, be it tomatoes or potatoes, carrots or cauliflower. The farmers are then given receipts so they can write off what is taken as tax-deductible contributions.

At this point, we are receiving so many contributions from farmers that our five trucks are not sufficient, and we are renting several more to meet the demand.

All this effort has paid a most important side benefit. In late 1993, George Graves of Distribution and Food Services was assigned to find "free" food. As I have just described, George was wildly successful. But his labors did not end there.

In the course of making contacts with farmers, George became aware of the Arizona Gleaning Coalition, a consortium of growers, private corporations, state agencies, and food banks.

At first, MCSO was only a recipient of surplus food from this network. Quickly, however, George realized that MCSO had resources that the coalition needed. He realized that MCSO could enter into a very fruitful partnership with the coalition, and that something very exciting could emerge from this union. And so we started to use our trucks to transport food around the state, picking up from farmers and other providers and bringing it to food banks. The impact of this intensified distribution is clear: Since March 1994, the Arizona Gleaning Coalition estimates that food distribution has doubled to food banks throughout the state, food that otherwise would have gone to waste. We're talking about more than $800,000 in food product.

In addition, George has arranged for the assignment of working inmates to all of the valley food banks, providing the charities with a reliable labor supply.

George Graves has been named to the Coalition's Operations Committee, and continues to work to further its laudable goals, both at the office and at home. For his inspiring example, George received a special commendation from the Sheriff's Office in 1995.

Our relationship to the farming community continues to grow, sometimes in unexpected directions. For example, we have been giving our garbage to pig farmers, garbage being a pig delicacy. In return, every now and then the pig farmers supply us with a couple of animals, which we have slaughtered and then cooked.

Then there's our computer system. Actually, it's just a pair of PCs backed up by a fax machine. The fax is tied into a network of food vendors and manufacturers, and we are constantly searching for special buys. For example, we might call Oscar Meyer and find out whether they have any products that could be labeled "seconds" for sale. Seconds are not spoiled or distressed products, but foodstuffs that have some cosmetic defect that renders them unsuitable for the retail market. It's no different than going to a clothing outlet store and paying just a few dollars for an expensive garment that is marked down, because a few stitches are out of line, or a button is missing. That's what we do every day, seeking out those discounts and deals.

And Oscar Meyer is very happy to respond, because the company is glad to help out law enforcement and also because the company is glad to have a market for what is none-too-marketable. Oscar Meyer has sold us sliced turkey, salami, olive loaf, pimento loaf, and, yes, bologna. We'll take whatever the company has to offer, and we've paid as little as twenty-eight cents per pound. Along with Oscar Meyer, we deal with a host of other major concerns, including Kellogg's, Armour, and Swift.

And don't neglect the savings from even an isolated measure like cutting out coffee, because cutting out coffee saved $100,000 a year. In similar fashion, the switch to cold meals saved another $400,000.

We've received so much media attention for our efforts to hold down costs that some vendors have contacted us with substantial donations. For instance, not long ago a New York manufacturer heard about what we were doing out here in Maricopa County, and contributed 450 cases of corn dogs, each case containing a hefty seventy-two corn dogs. The manufacturer donated the dogs for less than the cost of shipping them west, which meant that we had to lay out a measly eleven cents per case. And these were no seconds, but the same corn dogs you can buy in your favorite supermarket.

Donations keep flowing in. In fact, so many of our local farmers want to help out by providing us with acreage and crops that we are looking into starting our own production kitchen, where we could prepare some of our excess food to sell to other governmental bureaus and departments, from prisons to hospitals, at a cheaper rate than they could find elsewhere. In this way, we can generate some income and save even more money, while reducing expenditures at other government institutions as well.

Through all these measures (and also employing some skillful bartering, trading, and negotiating), we have cut the average cost of a meal by more than half, from sixty-five cents to approximately thirty cents, the least expensive meal in any sizable jail or prison system in the country. I'm talking about serving 25,000 meals each and every day (adding together adult and juvenile inmates). I'm talking about teaching 300 inmates to work in our kitchen, learning to handle food and cook and bake. I'm talking about providing two hot meals and one cold meal a day, all meals and menus approved by a county dietitian to ensure proper nutrition.

Our system works so well that we get calls from prison and jail systems from Maine to New York to California asking for advice and assistance in incorporating our programs into their plans and designs.

Not bad. Not bad at all.

So after all this talk about pasteurizing and farming and haggling, you're probably wondering exactly what the inmates eat. The *New York Post*, in typical tabloid style, provided a day's menu, under the unblushing headline, "Yummy, yummy! Green bologna for the tummy."

"Breakfast: Cereal; tasteless and runny scrambled powdered eggs; leftover fruit gleaned from local farms by inmate labor; bread, and buttermilk.

"Lunch: Two white bread sandwiches, one green bologna, the other peanut butter; fruit; carrots; Kool-Aid.

"Dinner: A runny Sloppy Joe-like mixture with one slice of white bread, and a half-cooked potato; a wilted salad; Kool-Aid."

So judge for yourself. The menu might not be your idea of culinary delight, but then the odds are that if you're reading my book, you're probably not an inmate in my jail. I'm saving money while providing an officially approved, nutritional dietary plan for 6,000-plus prisoners. So where's the problem? What's the controversy?

I don't see any but sound management practices and a rational penal philosophy.

Oh, and about that bologna: It turns green when the meat isn't mixed exactly right, and the air gets in and oxidation occurs and colors appear and eureka!—you have green bologna, or maybe blue or purple or red. For some strange reason, everybody wants to talk about the bologna, from *The New York Times* to Tom Snyder, which just about scans the spectrum. (Tom, in particular, seemed to really get a kick out of the bologna. At the top of his show, before I was introduced, he stated that I was "said to be the toughest sheriff in America. This guy feeds the prisoners bologna sandwiches." Dramatic pause. "*Cold* bologna sandwiches." Pause. "*Green*, cold bologna sandwiches." And then Snyder and his off-camera audience broke up laughing.)

The media attention is okay by me as long as the reporters and the public understand the central point, which is, in a sentence: I will do what it takes to make my system work and work the best it can, effectively, efficiently, and within our budget. And if green bologna has somehow come to symbolize our efforts, well then, that's what symbols are for.

So we continue to work on making our jails tougher and better. Inmates were smuggling in drugs and other contraband in their long hair, so everyone gets a haircut, the job done by other inmates, which turns out to both save money on professional barbers, and provide on-the-job vocational training. Network shows are out, and television viewing is restricted mostly to C-SPAN, ESPN, the Disney Channel, the Weather Channel and the local government access channel. I also pumped in Newt Gingrich's ten-part videotape series on revitalizing our American civilization. It seemed self-evident that the inmates could use as many lessons on good citizenship as they could get.

I'm still not exactly sure why, but my decision to show Newt Gingrich's tapes caused quite a media dustup. I had actually purchased the tapes, with inmates' funds, naturally, long before anybody in the press heard about it. So I was kind of surprised when a few journalists got wind of my video viewing plans, and this not-entirely-new, not-exactly-news story suddenly zoomed around the world.

Much of the media wasn't certain how to react. Some decided to express approval, a few went the other way, and many smartly opted to stick with being amused. I'll leave it to Rush Limbaugh, surely the most influential political commentator in America today, to explain what I did, and what I meant, as he told the story to his television audience, in the studio and throughout America:

"In addition to taking away coffee and other perks, he's decided to add the ten-part Newt Gingrich course on renewing American civilization. Is that not great?" The studio applauded as Rush beamed.

"Now here are a couple of fascinating quotes from Mr. Arpaio," Limbaugh said, "because of course... this is an engraved invitation to the ACLU to come give him trouble. In fact he says, 'I understand some people might call this cruel and unusual punishment, but so what?'"

Rush spoke over the applause. "All right! Now, my friends, get this one. He was asked, 'Well, wait a minute. So you've got Mr. Newt's ten-part video course that you're going to show on your ex-cable TV system. Don't you need to balance Mr. Newt with some Democratic tapes?' And he said, 'For one thing, I don't think there are any Democratic tapes. And some people might say these guys already got enough of their ideas anyway.'"

Laughter and applause resounded through the studio.

"But lest you think Sheriff Arpaio is political," said Rush, and he paused to give a big stage wink, "here's a little video clip of Mr. Arpaio so you can actually hear and see him yourself."

And Limbaugh showed a tape of me stating that I'd take anybody's video series, as long as it was good, including President Clinton's, if of course he had produced a sufficiently interesting program.

Rush ended his piece by staring at the camera and intoning, "You don't have to worry about that."

But enough about the tapes—back to the inmates: In the never-ending attempt to procure favorable treatment, convicts were abusing the right to visit the nurse or doctor, so we instituted three dollar co-payments for inmate-initiated medical services. (If an inmate does not have three dollars, he will not be denied medical attention.) Inmates are subject to random drug testing, and the tactical squad periodically searches the jails for drugs, weapons, and other illegal or prohibited goods. Violation of the rules is punished by inmates being confined to lockdown, i.e., twenty-three hours out of every twenty-four in solitary. In addition, inmates who have been sentenced must work or go to lockdown.

The truth is, I don't think these measures are that tough, they're just common sense. However, unlike many of my political counterparts, I'm willing to actually implement these ideas and accept whatever consequences might come.

And let us not forget, if an inmate follows the rules and tries to make something of his life, he can study and get his high school equivalency or participate in a work assignment or gain some vocational training or get help with his substance-abuse problem. You see, even in jail, even in a very tough jail, an individual can learn and ponder and change and emerge a better human being.

Sadly, most do not make that choice. I know I've said it before, but it's worth saying again. Most—and I mean almost 70 percent—choose to learn nothing, choose to keep breaking the law, choose to keep returning to jail. If all those inmates who comprise that 70 percent are too stupid or corrupted or just plain vicious to go straight for their own good or the good of their families, then maybe my jails will convince a few, or maybe more than a few, to obey the law and get an honest job just to stay out of the tents and away from the green bologna.

A visiting reporter from a Minneapolis television station found and interviewed an inmate who also hailed from Minnesota, and the convict's feeling about his experience in the Maricopa County jails warmed my heart: "It's going to deter me from coming back to Arizona, that's for sure. I'm going back home, and I ain't coming back!"

I regularly visit my jails, talking to the prisoners and the officers. I listen to their complaints and their problems. The hard truth is that most of the prisoners are con men through and through. They walk up to you and look you in the eye and say they never did anything, that this is one big mistake or conspiratorial frame. All they want to do is get out and be the upstanding, outstanding citizens they really are. And, finally, inevitably, invariably, can you help them out with—select one or more—the guards, the courts, the parole board, the mayor, the governor, the Pope, you name it.

Forget the social workers. Forget the shrinks. Forget the ACLU. That's the way it really is. Those are the kind of people you're usually really dealing with. Given all that, there's only so much you can do, only so much you can really hope to accomplish in the way of rehabilitation.

So, save the ones you can save. Help the ones you can help. Control the rest.

You don't like that word? Then how about manage or check or intimidate? Take your pick. Just get the job done, within the bounds of ethics and law.

Save the ones you can save. Help the ones you can help. Control the rest.

That might sound harsh to you. I don't know. If it sounds harsh, that's all right, because jail is a harsh place. Jail is not a reward or an achievement, it is punishment.

Amazingly, much of society seems to have forgotten that unvarnished reality.

If you've ever visited my jails, tent or hard facility variety, you know I haven't forgotten. I promise the people I never will.

CHAPTER FOUR

Working on the Chain Gang

I was ready to inaugurate my chain gang concept a long time ago, but, thanks to the aforementioned Board of Supervisors budget cuts, I couldn't afford to. I was already short detention officers in the jails, and didn't have any to spare for outside duties. Then I remembered the posse, and we were back in business. But I'll get to that in a minute.

What most of us know about the posse comes from the movies. From *I Was A Prisoner In A Chain Gang* to *Cool Hand Luke*, chain gangs were rightly exposed for their shocking brutality, rampant racism, and systemic injustice. It wasn't long before public outrage caused the chain gangs to be eliminated throughout the country.

But as the years have passed, and society has changed in so many areas, including virtually all aspects of the criminal justice system, we are able to view chain gangs from a less emotional and more rational perspective. In doing so, I discovered that it wasn't the *idea* of the chain gang that was flawed, but rather the *administration* of the chain gangs.

Chain gangs offer a chance to work outside

When I realized that, I was ready to work the chain gang the way it should be worked, so it made sense for both the system and the inmates. The

Maricopa County Sheriff's Office Last Chance Program was introduced in May 1995.

Chain gangs were not only brutal, racist, and unjust, they were also essentially tools to humiliate the prisoners, to break them down physically and mentally. All inmates enter my jails absolutely equal to one another. They have the same privileges and the same responsibilities. They have the same opportunities to gain even more privileges, including the chance to work outside the jail.

At the same time, they have the opportunity to lose those privileges and responsibilities. They can violate the rules or disobey the officers or smuggle in contraband or cause trouble in a thousand different ways. When they do, when they endanger themselves, other inmates or the guards, they have to suffer the consequences. If the infraction warrants it, they can be placed in lockdown for twenty-three hours each day for as long as the offense demands. The inmate gets one hour a day to exercise. Phone calls are only allowed on the weekends, which means that the con gets two hours a week to try to reach the phone to make a call.

Not a happy situation.

The old saying applies, even in the pen: Don't do the crime if you can't do the time.

When an inmate has his privileges revoked, that includes forfeiting the privilege of being a trustee, which translates into no longer being permitted to have a job. Since all sentenced inmates are required to have a job, losing that privilege does not bode well.

In addition, to many prisoners, a job can mean a lot. It might provide a measure of authority, particularly a measure of self-respect. It can also break up the monotony. Given the right circumstances, the inmate can leave the jail during the day, and that means everything.

So the trustee position is important and valuable, and about 85 percent of our prisoners achieve it. But if the inmate screws up—and so many of them do—then the trustee position is gone, and he can be transferred to what is referred to as permanent no-work status. The path out of this dilemma, the path back to regaining privileges, can be the chain gang. If an inmate successfully completes the thirty-day program, which entails more than just working on the chain gang, then his privileges are restored, and he can reenter the general jail population. If they fail to successfully complete the thirty-day tour, then that's it. No more chances.

That's why we call the chain gang our Last Chance Program.

No one is forced to work on the chain gang. Inmates must volunteer. They must petition the appropriate detention officers for the opportunity to join the chain gang.

So you can begin to see that instead of using the chain gang as it has traditionally been used, as a means of humiliating the prisoners, our chain gang functions in precisely the opposite fashion, as a way of encouraging the inmates to work hard to rejoin their fellow prisoners in rights and privileges. In other words, instead of acting to *bring down* the prisoners, our approach to the chain gang seeks to *raise them up*.

The inmates know the rules. They usually know them before they apply. If they don't, they are certainly informed of them soon enough.

The rules are easy to remember, because there are only a handful, and they are written down. After the inmate asks to be placed on the chain gang, (and the guards receive five or six handwritten notes every day), and if that request has been accepted, then the inmate must sign a pledge. The pledge specifies that he is voluntarily participating in the Last Chance Program. He promises to comply with all instructions. He states that he is aware that profanity and insolent comments will not be tolerated. He agrees to sport a military-style haircut and forego facial hair.

The pledge states, "I will be a model inmate." And the prisoner signs his name.

Since the chain gang goes out into the community, my detention officers are very careful whom they allow to participate. Child molesters are not accepted, nor is anyone involved in long-term domestic violence situations. Nonetheless, the approved volunteers have been convicted of crimes ranging from manslaughter to vehicle-related offenses.

The drill is as follows: Fifteen men are selected for the chain gang. Each inmate is issued an orange baseball cap stamped "INMATE" and an orange jumpsuit, a web belt, a canteen, and a pair of combat boots. Prisoners are forbidden to alter their uniforms in any manner.

The detention officer in charge of the detail arrives at the jail at 5 A.M. The prisoners are up and ready somewhere between 5:15 and 5:30 A.M.

The inmates stand outside their cells while the officer inspects their quarters. If anyone's area is not clean, or the bed is unmade, the inmate is not permitted out. Since the inmates are well aware of what is expected of them, that is a rare occurrence.

The inmates themselves undergo inspection. Heads up, hands at your sides, feet pointed at forty-five degrees—and the detention officer checks them over.

Two, sometimes three, posse members arrive at 6 A.M. Along with their sidearms, they are issued shotguns. Their task is to provide the security for the detail, while the detention officer oversees the work. If posse members were not always willing to volunteer and help out, if my office did not have this resource available, the chain gang would not be feasible.

The detention officer orders a right-face, and marches the inmates out of the pod where their cells are located. The program operates with something of a boot camp flavor, with quasi-military discipline employed. The inmates address the officers as *sir* or *ma'am*. While on the job, an officer might punish an inmate who curses—which is against the rules—with an order to drop and perform ten push-ups.

The detention officer directs the inmates to lock themselves together. The inmates are linked in three groups of five men per chain. Each chain is fifteen feet long, so the prisoners are separated by five feet of metal. The padlocks, which are basically the hardware store variety, are attached to one ankle around a combat boot.

Once chained together, the inmates are paraded out of the facility. This is one of the most difficult times during the day, because the other inmates in the yard sometimes yell out uncomplimentary comments at their fellow prisoners. Interestingly, as months have passed, and the inmates have become more familiar with the chain gang's administration and goals, the ridicule and insults have decreased.

While marching, the detention officer often establishes some rhythm by calling out a responsive chant, same as in the army. This helps the prisoners get used to walking in step with one another, which is pretty crucial when five men are chained together.

The inmates and officers board a bus and head out to that day's site. The workday commences around 7 A.M.

The chain gang's fundamental duty is to clean up—clean the streets of Phoenix, clean the county parks and state parks, clean graffiti off public buildings and structures—and clear away—clear dead branches from trees, clear brush from fields and washes. The cleaning up beautifies the county, while the clearing away reduces the risk of brushfires.

The inmates work on publicly owned property, with an occasional detour to assist a church or some similar institution sweep up its yard. The aim is to do work that benefits the entire community.

The inmates employ common yard tools, including rakes, water hoses, shovels, as well as small sickles and weed-eaters. Once, an inmate even handled a chainsaw.

The officer in charge decides when the prisoners need a break. In the summer, the heat demands that the breaks are more frequent and the day ends earlier, maybe around 11:30 A.M. At cooler times of the year, the detail is extended a couple more hours. (Detention officers work ten-hour shifts. Thus, when they start at 5 A.M., they have to get back by the afternoon in order to have sufficient time to get their prisoners and paperwork squared away.)

The prisoners get a half hour for lunch, and eat the same bologna sandwich they would receive back in jail. A port-o-john is carried in the bus and set up outside for the prisoners' use.

The inmates are hardly hidden away. Instead, they are right out there for the world to see. In case anyone misses the point, signs are posted: "Sheriff's chain gang at work." When the chain gang was new, people driving by often honked their horns to show their support, or flashed a thumbs-up sign.

To answer a popular question, no one has ever attempted to escape. Nor have there been any problems with prisoners fighting among themselves, or confrontations between the prisoners and the public.

The chain gang works six days a week and completes a lot of jobs that otherwise would never get done. The reason is simple: The county doesn't have enough workers for all the necessary tasks, and, besides, it lacks the money to pay them. We've figured out that if Maricopa paid its workers just minimum wage (which it surely doesn't), the efforts of our chain gang would cost almost five hundred thousand dollars in 1995 alone, our first year of operation!

The end of the detail sees the inmates heading back to the jail on the bus, then marching back to their pod. The inmates unlock the padlocks and remove their chains. They return to their cells and wash up. They trade in that day's clothes for fresh socks and underwear and jumpsuits, and get ready to do it all over again tomorrow.

What does it all add up to? Well, there's the benefit that accrues to the community, which I've discussed, and then there's the benefit to the inmates. Amazing as it might sound, for some inmates, the chain gang represents the very first time in their lives that they have actually followed through with a commitment from beginning to end. This shows them something they haven't seen before, something within themselves, something worthwhile. This shows them that if they can accomplish this, maybe they can accomplish a lot more.

In short, they gain some self-respect. They learn about the merit of discipline. Hopefully, they get a glimpse of possibilities beyond simply bouncing aimlessly and dangerously through life.

Perhaps that's asking a lot from chaining a bunch of guys together so they can pick up trash. Perhaps, but it works, at least some of the time. It's not a snap program. A few prisoners get themselves bounced out of the program each month. Sometimes, particularly in the beginning, as many as thirteen out of the fifteen would be expelled for violations of their pledges.

On the other hand, many of the prisoners appreciate the chain gang. You heard what George Matta had to say on *Donahue* in the first chapter, and that's not atypical. Some of the inmates ask to remain on the chain gang when their thirty days are up, preferring to work outdoors, actually gaining the satisfaction of seeing the results of their labors. On July 6, 1995, a reporter from the *Mesa Tribune* posed as an inmate, and spent the day working on the chain gang. The prisoners did not know who he was, and neither guards nor inmates conducted themselves in any way out of the ordinary.

Journalist David Leibowitz wrote that he was more than a little scared before joining the chain gang, uncertain and anxious about what awaited him from his fellow prisoners, the guards, and the detail. Many journalists and commentators have analyzed and criticized the chain gang, passing judgment from afar. Leibowitz was about to experience the real deal. Let's briefly view the Last Chance Program through his eyes.

Four inmates are on sick call so the chain gang is down to eleven volunteers, plus Leibowitz.

The detail begins. The reporter's first concern focuses on the lock attached around his ankle, but he finds that it is "tight enough to feel, but doesn't pinch."

One hurdle down. Next, the inmates are driven to Ninety-first Avenue and Camelback Road in west Phoenix where they spend three hours picking up debris. The temperature climbed past the hundred-degree mark.

Leibowitz's description of the reaction of the public to the inmates, and vice versa, is very interesting:

"Cars honk, the gang waves. Shame, if present, is hidden. In fact, oddly, there seems to be only pride: Each inmate has volunteered for this—to get out of lockdown and to relative freedom from Sheriff Joe's 120-degree tents—and the chains razz and race each other. The roadside looks noticeably better as we go."

By midmorning, they stop for lunch. Each man gets a bag filled with two pickle-loaf sandwiches, a wedge of cantaloupe, and a doughnut.

"Everyone eats fast," relates Leibowitz, "ready for more work."

The day progresses, including a visit from yours truly, escorting a television crew from the Australian version of *60 Minutes*. The TV correspondent asks them what they think of the chain gang: "'I'd rather be busy than locked up,' is the day's most uttered sentence."

After the Australians and I depart, the eleven inmates and the reporter go back to work. Eventually, they board the bus and return to jail. Marched back inside, Leibowitz suddenly discovers himself alone with the general prisoner population, without any guards. The reporter feels that old "twinge of fear" again, but the feeling is "needless: The chain gang has cult status. We get quizzed about the heat and our detail."

The article closes with the removal of the chains and padlocks, and Leibowitz walking out of jail. I believe that the last few lines are worth repeating in full:

"Unchained, my foot feels light. As I leave, I notice the sound of my step. No chain rattling, just the slap of boot on tile. It's a sharp, clear sound, one that stays with you. For me, I think, that sound—of freedom—would be enough to keep me out of jail.

"That's not the real question, of course. The work is bearable, not nearly inhumane. The shame is minimal. Will that sound, I wonder, be enough for the other eleven?"

No other sheriff, and no other county jail system in the country, runs a chain gang program. Nor does our chain gang operate like any other. Alabama has its inmates breaking rocks; we don't waste our prisoners' efforts, and we don't squander this estimable resource. In our program, the prisoners are not humiliated but encouraged through hard work, discipline, and appropriate rewards. Getting out of lockdown and regaining their privileges certainly counts as valuable remuneration to the inmates. However, the true value is earning some self-respect, because that can last a lifetime, and keep them from making the mistakes that got them tossed into jail in the first place. To encourage these ideas and foster self-respect, I formally graduate those who complete the program and even award them diplomas.

For some inmates, the Last Chance Program works. For others, it doesn't. But even if only a handful of inmates see the light and change their ways, isn't that still enough to make the entire effort worthwhile?

And don't forget—the streets look a hell of a lot cleaner.

Same as with several of our programs, we get phone calls from correctional institutions across the country asking about our chain gang. We tell them anything they want to know, because the Last Chance Program works and should be exploited to its fullest, near and far.

CHAPTER FIVE

Joe Slept Here

It was at least ninety degrees, about average for a springtime afternoon in the Arizona desert. The press conference was wrapping up; statement given, questions asked, background pictures taken. I had announced this, they had asked that, media satiated, over and out. Nothing out of the ordinary.

But the day wasn't done, and the ordinary was about to be forgotten, because I had a special event planned for that night. I was going to sleep in the tents alongside the prisoners. My rationale was pretty obvious and worth whatever risk was involved. I had been listening to complaints from prisoners, lawyers, the media, and special interest groups about how awful it was in the tents, and I was sick and tired of it. Since when was incarceration supposed to be a vacation, or even pleasant? The fact was, the tents were tough, but they were far from brutal. I was spending the night to prove exactly that.

The bottom line was, if I could take it, then so could the inmates.

The time had arrived to enter the dragon I had done it once before, a few months back, with a police lieutenant from Little Rock. The fellow was running for sheriff back in Arkansas, and had traveled to Arizona looking for my support. In the course of our visit, I had taken him on a tour of the jail, and rather spontaneously invited him to join me for a night in the tents. Maybe, because I had invited him in front of the press, the lieutenant had quickly accepted.

Unfortunately, by his own sleepless account, he had not enjoyed the experience at all.

This time, I was bringing along a reporter and photographer from the local paper, *The Arizona Republic*, and also a correspondent from a Phoenix TV station. They were seeking the kind of colorful story that sounded like an adventure, and I was prepared to oblige.

The time had arrived to enter the dragon, so to speak. We started in the Estrella Jail, which borders the tents, and were fingerprinted and photographed, same as any convict. Next, we exchanged our clothes for prison garb—orange slipover shirt and blue pants. As quoted in the *Republic*, I regarded myself in the mirror and said, "I look like a smurf."

Then we stepped into the compound. Make no mistake, I knew this wasn't going to be any walk in the park.

After all, the tents weren't only for drunk drivers and purse snatchers. We were entertaining drug dealers and sex offenders and murderers, too, with no more than two or three detention officers guarding them at any one time. I hadn't ordered extra guards just because I was in the tents. The reality is that no number of guards, especially in a compound filled with tents, can fully protect an individual against a determined attack from somebody who moves fast. You have to know how to protect yourself, it's as simple as that. And after a career spent among nefarious evildoers, I felt pretty confident I knew how.

First rule: I didn't intend to turn my back on anyone.

A little excitement goes a long way in prison, where unending routine is the name of the game, and the appearance of the sheriff and a media contingent rapidly attracts a crowd.

The word went out, and, once again, I rely on the *Republic* to give an unbiased, accurate account:

"The moment Arpaio entered the yard, the shouting began.

"'Hey, it's Uncle Joe!'

"'Wow! It's Joe hisself. God almighty!'

"'Hey, Joe, come here, I wanna talk to you.'

"As Arpaio walked, prisoners rushed to his side, talking excitedly, demanding answers, complaining, laughing, cursing.

"Arpaio didn't turn a hair."

In short order, I was surrounded and bombarded with hostile questions. How come I wouldn't let them smoke cigarettes? How come I wouldn't let them read *Playboy* or *Penthouse* magazines? How come I wouldn't let them watch violent movies, and television shows? How come I wouldn't let them have coffee?

I could have fed them some line about cutting out some of the amenities to save money, but that wasn't the truth. So I gave it to them straight. Take coffee, for instance. I told them I was well aware that they liked their coffee. And I didn't want them to like anything about my jail. So I wouldn't let them have coffee. And maybe not being able to drink coffee, as well as missing all the other things they liked, would make them hate my jail so much they would decide that they were never coming back. Maybe they would get a regular job, and start building a decent life for themselves. Or maybe they would just leave the county to get away from my jail. I didn't care. Whatever motivated them was fine with me—as long as the result was a decrease in crime in Maricopa County.

I took a break from the debate, and returned to the adjacent Estrella Jail to inspect the high-security jail pods where the problem inmates were held, and then moved on to the women's dormitory where 100 females were held. At each stop, the questions were pretty much the same, and so were my answers: No. No. No. Too bad. You don't like it? Then don't get sent to jail.

Back out in the yard, the rest of the evening went pretty much along the same lines through dinner and up to lights-out—the inmates angrily accusing my department and me of one or another misdeed; my more or less calm reply; the reporters capturing the moment for posterity, and the guards looking on nervously.

Incidentally, dinner arrived in a plastic bag. The main course was one of my jail's famed bologna sandwiches. I can't say it was delicious, but I was hungry, and I did eat and digest it.

Finally, it was 10:30 P.M., bedtime, and frankly, I was ready. I was tired of arguing with inmates who denied they'd actually committed any crime. They maintained, against all evidence, that they were either dupes or innocent bystanders. They had somehow also gotten the impression that society owed them something other than punishment for their crimes.

I thought I was getting a bottom berth—the tents only held bunk beds—but a pushy reporter actually had the gall to beat me to it. As consolation, the reporter got what he deserved, at least in psychic terms. Apparently, one of the cons had made the wrong bet on my sleeping arrangements, because the journalist stretched out to find that he was staring up at a brief message intended for me, inviting me to enjoy sexual relations with an unidentified party, scrawled in black ink on the bottom of the bed above him.

Finally, it was lights-out. But the talk was far from over. The insults were only starting. The slurs and threats came crawling out of the dark from my bunkmates.

Now I've spent my professional life around some miserable lowlifes, but this was kind of shocking even to me. Not that I expect or want these guys to love me, but this was something else. This was new, uncharted territory for me, distinct from the old world where the law might have been hated, but it was also feared and respected.

There was neither fear nor respect in that tent, not on that night. The comments were virtually indescribable: venomous taunts, vile threats, directed not only against me, but also against my family. The kind of talk that a normal person would have trouble even imagining, but which seemed to flow effortlessly and endlessly from the minds and mouths of the inmates. One sick, spoken idea from one con prompted or perhaps excited another to come up with something even more grotesque.

But don't take my word for it. Here's what the *Republic* had to say, as subsequently recorded by my increasingly nervous reporter friend in the bunk below, a bunk that suddenly seemed much more vulnerable and much less desirable.

"Insults so personal, so crude, some even made inmates gasp.

"Threats, obscene suggestions. And, apparently for variety, animal sounds.

"'Mooooo. Arffff, arffff. Cawwww, cawwww.'

"Venomous talk of Arpaio's family, his manhood, his intelligence, his competence, his honesty..."

And the newspaper had a couple of specific examples. Here's one—the least offensive one:

"'Maybe I'll go get a piece of rebar out where it holds the tent down...' Then a grim laugh. 'I could hit the old sheriff in the head with it while he sleeps.'

"His laughter was joined by a chorus of cruel cackles from the twenty prisoners in the tent."

For the first time, I seriously considered that this might be as bad a notion as some had suggested. More than bad—flat-out dangerous. Criminals are basically a cowardly and brutish bunch, and brutish cowards are most dangerous in the shadows, in the dark.

The vicious whispers continued for a couple more hours, and then slowly died out as the inmates grew bored and fell asleep. But I stayed awake, just in case.

And as I lay on that thin mattress on that cold, black night, with nothing to do but stay alert, I couldn't help but think about all the other cold, black nights I had spent in strange places, distant lands, waiting for drug dealers, murderers, human vermin of all kind, bluffing and dealing and duping the bad guys, making them crawl out of their hidden holes into the light.

It was 4:30 in the morning in the tent. Wake-up time. Rise and shine. I had barely slept, keeping one eye open, a habit I had picked up long ago.

As we walked to the dining hall for breakfast, the inmates displayed none of the viciously aggressive bravado that had marked last night's whispered threats. I took a tray and soon had some scrambled eggs, two slices of white bread, three potato nuggets, a handful of raisins, and a half-pint of skim milk. Let me tell you, the food in jail is as bad as you'd expect, which is exactly as it should be. I'm sure you won't be surprised when I tell you I didn't come close to cleaning my plate.

I really wanted a cup of coffee, but, of course, I had eliminated java from the menu.

On the other hand, unlike my dining companions, I was going to be out in a short while, and I could have all the coffee I wanted—which is also exactly as it should be.

The reporters I had brought along were quite pleased that they had come and gotten terrific stories, and *were probably even more pleased that they were leaving.*

I wasn't as pleased. The experience had bothered me. On the practical level, I wasn't worried that the cons had threatened me, or, even worse, threatened my family in the most degenerate terms imaginable. I knew it was all just talk, and knew nothing would ever come of it. After all, crooks are more often than not stupid and lazy, which has a lot to do with their being crooks, and even more with their being in jail.

No! What troubled me was how criminals had changed in the course of my career. When I was a young patrolman on the mean streets of Washington, D.C., I was assaulted *nineteen times* in one year, a total that earned me the number-one rating in that dubious category.

So violence, actual or promised, never fazed me. It was the very *nature* of the violence that was disturbingly different. The level of savagery has escalated beyond all rationale and predictability. The proof can be observed at every level of society, in virtually every arena. Kids once settled scores on the playground with their fists— now they carry guns and murder their enemies. A driver once would curse at someone who cut him off on the road—now we have "random freeway shootings." Muggers once simply mugged—steal the wallets or bags and run—now they steal and then beat and slash and rape and kill, just for fun. Even organized crime has gotten more barbaric. The mob was known at one time for only whacking their own, and never harming innocent civilians, cops, and journalists—now the criminal syndicates from Latin America and Asia and the former Soviet Union go out of their way to annihilate whole families, and anyone else in the vicinity, just for the hell of it.

And that night in the tents, the inmates had demonstrated precisely the changed situation, with their crude, even cruel scorn. They had no fear or respect for anyone or anything, nor for any of the institutions and values that most citizens instinctively esteem and love, from God to the family. The sad truth is, they don't even respect themselves, having abandoned the most basic of normal, decent feelings and attachments—at the bottom line, too many of these cons don't even value their own lives.

And a person whose own life no longer holds any value even to himself is not only especially pathetic but also especially dangerous, both to himself and to every member of society.

That's why I thought you should know about my little overnight adventure. It's one thing to hear inmates speak with reporters, displaying their best behavior for the cameras, and it's a whole other story when the cameras are gone, and the lights are literally off.

That's what crime is all about; that's who criminals really are—cowardly and stupid, contemptuous and vicious. Don't let anyone—the lawyers, the media, anyone—tell you differently.

That was enough pondering about the criminal justice system for one morning. Some matters were more pressing than others.

I *really* had to get home and have a cup of coffee.

CHAPTER SIX

And That's Not All

Ⅰt was a beautiful day. Perfect weather. Sunny, not too hot, not too cool, the temperature lingering at seventy-eight degrees. A November day like you'll only find in Arizona. Perfect.

Too good for criminals, you might say, but they were free to enjoy the sun and the air, same as anybody else, here in the tents, or to be more precise, here *outside* the tents.

Like I said—too good for criminals.

But did they appreciate it? Did they appreciate that my setting up the tents gave them the opportunity to soak in this beautiful day?

What do you think?

"Hey, Joe," a voice called, hidden somewhere in the shadows of the tents, "when are you going to spend the night in my tent?"

But meteorology and conversation are not the reasons I'm relating this story to you. No, I was visiting the tents because I was escorting a group of visitors (trailed, of course, by crews from several TV and radio stations), who had traveled some distance for this opportunity. My visitors included a sheriff, an assistant district attorney, an assemblyman, and a political activist. The sheriff was

The work of good government is never done

71

from Arkansas, and the others hailed from California. They had journeyed to Phoenix to see how the tents worked. They already knew a lot about the tents, enough to be very interested in applying my methods to their own jurisdictions.

My guests definitely liked what they saw. They liked the tents, the food, the clothes, the programs, the overall attitude of the officers and the inmates. Including the inmates in that positive assessment, I am referring to the grudging respect that the inmates invariably granted my guests, as well as their sheriff and warden. Oh sure, the inmates could be unpleasant enough when they were out of sight of the detention officers, such as when I spent nights in the tents. But that almost has to be expected from many of the cowardly punks who choose the sick life of crime.

Here's a small example of sick: Just the other day, a photographer came by to take a few pictures—some of the pictures used in this book, in fact. Before we went inside, I was speaking with her and her assistant. We were standing about thirty feet from the fences and barbed wire.

Many inmates were lounging on the other side of the fence. As the photographer and the assistant were both attractive women, some of the inmates were shouting out their usual crude remarks. A guard ordered them to shut up, theoretically asking how they'd like it if somebody was talking like that to their mothers.

That was good for about a minute.

We continued speaking when suddenly I heard a thump, and the photographer looked stunned as she realized that she had been struck in the back of the head with a rock. She couldn't understand what had happened or why, but I knew. The inmate who had thrown the rock from somewhere inside the compound wasn't aiming at the photographer—he was aiming at me.

It wasn't the first time a stone had been hurled in my honor. Not too long before, a projectile had smashed the windshield of my car while I was walking through the tents.

This time somebody had decided to take the direct approach and try to knock my head off. Of course, in attempting to injure their warden my would-be assailant didn't care who else might get hurt. Ponder for a moment what kind of person would do something like that.

Thankfully, the photographer wasn't badly hurt, but it could have turned out very differently. Nobody was willing to admit to the deed, so we gave the inmates an ultimatum: Either the offender was handed over to the detention officers, or every inmate in the yard would be punished for the attack.

As you might guess, the rock-thrower was promptly given up by his fellow inmates and sent to lockdown.

So when you think about the poor inmates, remember this brief, isolated incident, not to mention the one hundred fifty assaults on detention officers in our jails this year alone.

On the other hand, returning to the visit from my distinguished out-of-town guests, the inmates were more often than not downright friendly when you stood face-to-face with them in the light of day, and so it was on that day. In fact, one tent dispatched a representative to ask me to stand with the prisoners before their tent and have a picture snapped, as if we were old buddies at a class reunion.

I stood for the picture, considering it a reasonable request, but I didn't smile.

My guests were happy and excited. They were ready to move forward with their plans, to inform the people, and, at the same time, press the politicians and bureaucrats to make dramatic changes. The California assemblyman wanted to know if I would fly to Sacramento, and testify as to my experience with the tents and relay what I thought about the entire American penal system.

So when people wonder if there will be more tents around this country, the correct answer might be affirmative, particularly if you live in certain parts of Arkansas or California. Then again, you might have to move to my patch of America to see any real changes. The issue remains in serious doubt. I can't say for certain; after all, I only work for the citizens of Maricopa County, Arizona.

What happens where *you* live depends on your elected representatives, politicians, and law enforcement officials. It's up to all those people to do whatever it takes to keep the public safe, to exact appropriate punishment and real justice from criminals, and to use the jails and prisons not only for storage but also as an active tool in deterring crime. All this is your representatives' job, but it is each citizen's job to make sure that our officials enact and carry out our wishes.

It is also their job to do so with financial prudence and scrupulous care. Over and over you have listened to me talk about how much money this program or that measure of mine has saved, from cutting out coffee to utilizing the posse. Over and over, I have laid out the facts, penny by penny, dollar by dollar. Perhaps it is getting monotonous or dull; perhaps it seems pedestrian or petty. What difference does $10,000 make, $100,000, or for that matter, $1 million?

Well, I'll tell you why I keep talking about money. Because that is taxpayer money, *your* money. And any money I don't absolutely need, the more taxpayer money remains in the kitty to be spent elsewhere. And that is not some frivolous *elsewhere*, but on schools and roads and hospitals and housing, or maybe even on more police. In other words, the money should be spent on the most deserving members of society, rather than the least.

And, if there is some extra dough lying around, the money could even be put back in the taxpayers' pockets, and let the citizens spend the money any way they see fit. Returning money to the people—now *there's* a radical idea.

So now you understand why I keep harping on each greenback I save. These are not imaginary dollars, collected by the government only to evaporate in thin air—though it often feels that way. If we are ever to make government responsible and accountable, then we must demand that government forego the usual slogans and campaign demagoguery, and make authentic, exact choices, choices we can see and comprehend, count up and calculate.

Simply promising to cut taxes is not good enough *if it is not good enough*. Government must be creative and smart. The truth of any government, of any big enterprise, is that we can always do a better job. There is always fat. There is always waste. There are

Sheriff Joe announcing the opening of Tent City Jail

Inmates at work

Sheriff Arpaio and Len Sherman, coauthor and a new posse member

The helicopter wing of the posse

Gordon Holm, left, and Bud Munzer fly for the Sheriff's Posse

Aerial view of Tent City

Joe and wife Ava at a parade

With Phil Donahue
shortly after television
appearance

The sheriff
and the
Phoenix
Suns' mascot
wearing pink
shorts

Sharon and Ed Arnold, posse members on horseback

Bullet holes in red Cadillac when Joe was almost murdered near Vienna, VA. Note hole in windshield and two slugs in metal tray behind driver's seat

Joe, fourth from left, with Turkish police and 450 kilos of opium

Joe as a rookie cop in Washington, D.C.

Member of Sheriff's Posse watches over chain gang

Tent City

always stupid or selfish or sordid choices made. The work of good government is never done. Where are our tax dollars going? Where would they be better spent? If you need to spend more money on a particular program, which other program can we cut?

Apparently, nobody thought of tents before I did. Apparently, nobody thought that instead of spending forty or fifty or two hundred or five hundred million taxpayer dollars on a new jail, let's try something different. I didn't invent tents. The army has been using them for a long, long time, and so have outdoorsmen and the Red Cross. Tents were there, waiting to be used. All it took was somebody stopping to think and doing something.

And while the tents are terrific, I haven't rested on my laurels. We've implemented other programs, other proposals. And we're not about to quit now. We're going to keep seeking more programs, different plans, new ideas—anything that will work. Because that is our duty as public servants.

Having said all that, let's step back and take a broad look at our criminal justice system. We all know that something is seriously wrong with the system at many levels. Both prosecutors and public defenders are often so ridiculously overworked that both sides have a stake in never bringing any case to trial, which is why the court system has been turned into a game of let's-make-a-deal. Then, once the accused is sentenced and placed behind bars, this newly processed inmate can be pretty sure he'll get out on some form of early release or parole.

On the plus side, in Arizona and some other jurisdictions, a truth-in-sentencing law has been passed, which means that the inmate will have to serve at least a majority of his time. That's a step in the right direction—one step in a long, long journey that has no finish line in sight. The plea bargain game will continue to be played until the system has enough judges and prosecutors and jail cells to meet the increasing demand.

On the other side of the prison bars, poor defendants frequently receive inadequate representation, while the rich can stall and frustrate the system, eventually winning simply by outspending and outlasting the prosecution. In certain high-profile cases, we have seen the news media actually become a force in pushing the matter in one direction or another.

Of course, once somebody breaks the law and steps outside the community's boundaries, once somebody ends up in court, it's already too late. Family, school, church, all our institutions—they are primarily responsible for preparing our young people to join society. It's called the socialization process, and it has to do with love and security and education and fairness and opportunity and hope.

Obviously, we have to do a better job of socializing. And we have implemented some ideas that are geared toward that result. For instance, we are the only jail system in the country that has sponsored a National Institute of Justice program that attempts to foster better relationships between mothers who are incarcerated and their young daughters through the Girl Scouts. A Girl Scout troop has been organized for girls between the ages of eight and twelve, which meets inside the Maricopa County Jail every other Saturday. The members and their mothers engage in activities such as arts and crafts, while also discussing such serious issues as teen pregnancy prevention and drug abuse, individual responsibility and family ties.

The goal is to build solid links between mothers and daughters that will transcend the jail's walls and lay the foundation for a stronger, more supportive, more loving relationship. Considering that from 1986 to 1991 the female jail and prison population has risen by 73 percent, and that some 80 percent of those women are also mothers and frequently single parents to boot, not many programs could be more important in the battle to break this vicious and accelerating cycle of despair and waste.

So we do what we can. However, socializing is not my primary jurisdiction. I'm a cop, which means by the time I get involved, the situation has gotten out of hand. I step in and arrest them and lock them up. I deal with people who don't want to be held responsible for their actions, who want to break the rules of society and pay no penalty.

At this stage, I take over the socialization process. I interpret that responsibility in the manner I have already described, i.e., making certain that anyone committing a crime will be arrested and dispatched to my jail, and then making it so tough in that jail that no one would want to be there.

If love and education and encouragement constitute positive reinforcement, then my work can be called negative reinforcement. The former approach is clearly preferable, no doubt, but the latter works, too. Negative reinforcement has its place.

Let me give you an example. I was at a banquet just the other day, and a woman came up to me and said she had a story I should hear. She said her son is a Phoenix police officer. He arrested two people on some beef, and informed them they were going to jail. Now these were not virgins as far as spending time in the pen was concerned, so they knew what to expect. And knowing that, and learning of their impending fate, their faces dropped, and they begged the officer, "Please don't put us in Arpaio's jail, put us anywhere else." That is the word the lady used—"begged."

The mother of our Phoenix cop told me this story with some glee, because she liked the idea that bad guys trembled at the thought of going into the Maricopa County jail system. And, to tell you the truth, I enjoyed the story just as much, because that was what I was aiming at—a profound aversion to going to one of my jails. Now, whether my jails really deserve the mean reputation they have gathered among malefactors, or whether it's a combination of media hype and jailhouse rumor (because nowhere do rumors spread faster and wilder than in the pen, particularly about the pen), well, that's another story. What is absolutely true is that the word is out: Do whatever you can to stay out of Sheriff Joe's jail. Move out of town. Stay at home. Go straight. Go back to school. Take a correspondence course. Take up bird calling. Watch soap operas on the tube.

Don't go to jail.

Criminals hate this place. They also hate the sheriff who put them there. I expect them to hate me, that's par for the course, but I tend to think they hate me a little more.

The price of fame.

I can live with that.

Back in the old days, everybody knew how tough Alcatraz was. Nobody wanted to go to those prisons. Today, maybe the Maricopa County jails have become the Alcatraz of Arizona. That might not be such a bad thing.

Sure, we'll be facing some difficult decisions in the days ahead. Our constantly rising population will bring an increase in crime as well, and we'll arrest and lock up more criminals. I'll rely on the tents as long as possible to handle the new prisoners, you can bet on that. However, as I've mentioned before, I can only place sentenced people in the tents. Those awaiting trial must be placed in a hard facility. Since the court system is so backed up, my already overused facilities will be strained beyond all tolerance, and the county will eventually have to build another permanent structure type of jail.

Unless, of course, the rules change, and I'm allowed to put people awaiting trial in the tents, though that decision is out of my jurisdiction and out of my hands. We'll just have to wait and see what happens.

Whatever happens, I'll be ready, and ready with a few surprises. Because the fight is never over, and nothing ever stays the same. Change is inevitable, and law enforcement has to change with it.

PART II

The Posse

CHAPTER SEVEN

Actions Speak Louder…

It wasn't what you'd call a fancy venue—just a place near the airport. The bar was up front, with pictures of airplanes on the walls, and a baseball game on the televisions. In the back of the restaurant was another room, where tables were set up in anticipation of our meeting.

This is as good a spot as any to introduce you to the posse. I could begin this discussion in many different ways, going down a lot of avenues. But nothing could better serve to explain the underlying reality and importance of the entire posse concept than a recent gathering of the Air Posse.

A lot of people ask me what the posse does. The truth is, the posse does a lot of different things, and I'll explain them all. But first, I'd like to start by letting this one incident speak for itself, in the words of several of the participants.

The larger posse consists of forty-seven separate units. Some are organized around a function. Thus, we have a Search And Rescue Posse, a Water Safety Posse, a Medical Rescue Posse, and a Crime Prevention Posse. Other posses are set up around areas or neighborhoods, such as the Sun City Posse, the Desert Foothills Posse, the Southwest

The Air Posse is vital to search and rescue

Phoenix Posse. Several posses are a combination of both locale and purpose. Consider the Buckeye Mounted Posse, Chandler Mounted Posse, Maricopa Mounted Posse, Scottsdale Mounted Posse, Mesa Mounted Posse, and the Mesa Southside Posse—well, you get the idea.

The name of the Air Posse says it all—the group consists of pilots and their planes. Thirty-five airplanes, in fact, maintained completely at their owners' expense, owners who volunteer their time and equipment for the benefit of the Sheriff's Department. Let me stress that point. The Air Posse, same as every other posse, costs the taxpayers of Maricopa County absolutely nothing because whatever uniforms or cars—or airplanes—or virtually all other equipment used by the posse members are paid for by the posse members. So the owners of those different planes, from two-seaters to much larger craft (including a few small jets I haven't yet figured out how to use), even pay for their own fuel.

Bullets are the only exception. The Sheriff's Office supplies bullets during weapons training, and then, upon graduation, carefully distributes rounds to each qualified posse member, keeping exact records of who receives how many bullets and in what caliber. In this way, we are able to accomplish two critical goals. One, we can ensure that no weapons are loaded with either improper ammunition [for example, old reloads and wadcutters], which can result in that gun not functioning properly or even blowing up, or with illegal ammunition, such as armor-piercing bullets, which can result in illegitimate physical destruction. Two, controlling the bullets helps us maintain careful control over the disbursement and employment of all firearms sanctioned by the department.

Besides, despite budget cuts and restraints, we can still afford to provide a handful of bullets for our volunteers, even if we cannot afford to assist them with anything else.

So here we were on this night, about sixty men and women, posse members and their guests, assembled in this back room, a dais at one end and the other tables filling the rest of the space. The posse had come together to celebrate a job well done. But it was much, much more than that; it was a job that turned into nothing less than a lifesaving triumph, a triumph worth hearing in detail.

Each posse has its own volunteer commander, and James Stark is the chief of the Air Posse. He rose from his chair to spell out the evening's agenda. "Tonight we have a rare opportunity," Stark said, "to get everyone together and debrief. Al Schoenstene is my hero in this, because he was the brains, and we were the legs."

Schoenstene is the deputy in charge of coordinating all search and rescue operations for the Sheriff's Office, a job that puts him on call twenty-four hours a day. But we'll get back to him and his role in the story later, because the debriefing was proceeding in chronological order, and that meant that Joseph Thompson would lay out the situation. After all, his actions had unintentionally set everything in motion.

Joe Thompson is a rugged-looking man in his fifties, and the whole predicament clearly held some embarrassment for him. Nonetheless, he rose from his seat beside his wife, Vivian, and spoke frankly.

"I've been running around the backwoods of this country for at least thirty years," Joe said, "and I've been in a lot worse places, but I haven't been in more trouble."

He recalled that he and Vivian—and their dog—had left their Phoenix home on a rock-hunting expedition. They had driven north in their truck, toward Prescott, somewhere north of Maricopa County and into Yavapai County. The date was July 25, 1995. It was supposed to be a day trip.

The terrain was relatively difficult, part rock, part forest, the roads running up and down the mountains and canyons. Not the sort of roads many people used.

After a while, Joe realized that he wasn't on the road he expected to be on, that he had switched onto another road. Thompson wasn't too worried; he was still heading in the right direction.

"I didn't pay that much attention because I knew I was very close to Prescott. And when my truck broke down, I wasn't worried—until I got five miles down the road, and there wasn't any civilization. So at least I was smart enough to come back and stick with the truck. Well, what went through my mind?"

Joe sighed and briefly looked at the ground before continuing. "This is the first time I've ever gotten an award for being stupid," he said ruefully, earning an appreciative chuckle from the crowd. "I felt very, very dumb—the comedy of errors that happened. It was just weird, the way everything went together. We just sat there with the dog between us for three days, pawing us every hour for a drink of water."

Out in the wild, the situation can go from good to bad to worse in a moment, and that was what had happened to the Thompsons. The almost parallel but wrong road, the truck breaking down far from anywhere—the comedy of errors Joe had mentioned. Joe and Vivian knew they were in trouble, and that wasn't all.

"I'm really not one of those who gives people messages, letting them know where I'm going, and when I'll be back," said Joe.

Fortunately, Vivian had told their kids, so Joe and Vivian knew the family would realize they were missing. However, they also realized that the police wouldn't do anything for forty-eight hours. That was standard policy in missing persons cases.

"I understand why they do it," Joe said, "but in this country, forty-eight hours—you're dead.

"So I spent a lot of time thinking," he continued—"'gosh, I know the police aren't going to do anything for forty-eight hours, which means it's going to be at least Thursday before anybody even considers looking for us.' By Friday afternoon, I put my head down for the last time. It was all over."

Joe paused for a moment. "I just thank God for an organization like this. I hope nobody's here from Yavapai County, because I don't think Yavapai County knows we're lost yet. I heard some stories about the family calling up Yavapai County authorities and saying, 'How's the search going?' And they say, 'What search?'"

That little exchange garnered Joe his second laugh. Now it was time for the next part of the story, which meant Joe and Vivian's daughter, Joyce, speaking.

"I kept calling Yavapai County, and they kept saying, 'If we hear anything about an accident, we'll let you know.' I don't want to trash anybody, but Yavapai County told me they'd start a search in the morning. I called the next morning, and they took all the information again, and they still didn't do anything."

The situation was quickly becoming even more frustrating as local police descended on the Thompsons' home in Phoenix, searching for what the family knew they would never find.

"The police were in the house," recalled Joyce, "looking for a suicide note, looking for evidence of foul play."

Imagine! Your parents are missing, and the cops, instead of throwing everything into an all-out search, are acting as though they believe that *you* might have had something to do with their disappearance.

But all was not lost because there was one more police agency in this confusing mix—the Maricopa County Sheriff's Posse.

Deputy Schoenstene was the first Maricopa County law enforcement official to speak to Joyce, and he wasted no time in activating the posse that same day. "When I talked to that young lady, I knew we had a problem. I had the Air Posse fly Thursday afternoon, but they came up negative. I checked where they were supposed to be, but found nothing. I sat down that night and went over my maps again."

Schoenstene wasn't discouraged, however. "We had people searching all the time, so I knew we had a good chance. I just didn't know how far they had strayed off their course."

Schoenstene phoned James Stark, not only the Air Posse's commander but also a pilot, and asked him to check some other areas. Jim immediately agreed to take a look.

Before Stark could take to the air, he needed to contact his observer. The pilot had his hands, and eyes, busy flying the plane and keeping on course. The pilot watched the sky; the observer watched the ground. It was a team effort.

Stanley Foster was ready for the call even though he and Jim had just completed a search, and Stanley spoke next. "Posse work can be hours and hours of boredom. Then, once in a while, we get something exciting. I got home about one-thirty in the afternoon, because I had started before it was light. Jim Stark was on the phone saying, 'I need an observer. Can you make it?' We met at Glendale Airport forty-five minutes later."

Jim and Stan had frequently worked together, sometimes in Jim's plane and sometimes in Stan's, switching pilot and observer roles. Now they were going up one more time.

"I don't know what the temperature was at that time," Stan said, "but I know it was over one hundred fifteen degrees. We went toward the east, checking our grid for about two hours, finding nothing. It was extremely mountainous terrain, extremely rough out there. Very few roads. And we had finished our grid work, and we were on our way back, and then Jim said, 'Make sure you check out the Santa Maria River. We need to go and get a little closer at that area, because somebody might have had a notion or something.'"

So they headed over to the Santa Maria River, and then it happened—Jim Stark thought he saw something. It was just a white dot, but it was something. "I asked, 'Do you think that's anything?'" Foster said. "He said, 'I don't know, but we've come this far, so let's check it out.'"

They headed toward the dot.

"We made a sweep down there," Stan said, "which was in a canyon, which is a difficult place to maneuver. We saw it was a vehicle, a white truck, so we were on it now. Some rocks were on the top, which looked like a message of some kind."

In fact, Joe Thompson had collected some stones and spelled out, "HELP" on the roof, though the word was illegible to Stark and Foster. Regardless, the message got through.

"We knew they were in trouble," said Stan, "and we went down as low as we could go, to alert the people or wake them up. But nobody came out. So we climbed higher to establish communications. We got on the radio and got the helicopter. And we didn't know if anybody was in the vehicle until the helicopter came back on the radio and said, 'We've got two live bodies.'"

"That made our day," Stan concluded. "We went home screaming and hollering."

Though he was practically in a coma by the time he was airlifted out, his kidneys no longer functioning, Thompson was aware enough to know he and Vivian, after four days in the wilderness, where they barely kept themselves alive by drinking the windshield wiper fluid, were going to be all right.

"I had decided we weren't coming back," Joe related with some emotion, "and the most beautiful sight in the world was that chopper coming down beside the truck."

Deputy Schoenstene read the official citation in presenting Lifesaving Medals to Stark and Foster, which declared in part: "On July 25, 1995, Joseph and Vivian Thompson left the Phoenix area for a one-day trip to rock hunt in the Prescott area. However, when the couple failed to return the next day, anxious family members reported them missing. Due to the large area of the search, the ruggedness of the terrain, and the extreme heat this time of year, the Maricopa County Sheriff's Air Posse joined the search. On July 28, 1995, Posseman James E. Stark, a pilot with the Sheriff's Office Air Posse, and his observer, Posseman Stanley Foster, flew to Yavapai County in an effort to locate the missing couple. At about 1730 hours, they observed the victims' pickup truck in the area near the Sheridan Mountains. Their location was then radioed in, and the pair was rescued by the Department of Public Safety. The victims were found without water, and were very dehydrated. Had they not been located, they most certainly would not have survived much longer. The diligence and dedication to search the area and locate the victims saved their lives, and is in the finest tradition of the Maricopa County Sheriff's Office."

The Air Posse accomplished what no other agency, law enforcement or otherwise, was able to do: The posse quickly gathered together its members and resources and went out and did the job. The posse saved two lives.

The posse saved two lives using volunteers and initiative. But these invaluable resources were not thrown willy-nilly into the mix.

The posse had planned and trained for this sort of emergency, and so was able to execute with precision and achieve its mission.

The volunteers of the Air Posse received no reward for their remarkable success other than this night's recognition. But, of course, that is what volunteering is all about, working for no compensation other than personal satisfaction. A satisfaction of the deepest kind—the knowledge that one is making a real contribution to the community, that one is a vital component of society.

The Air Posse's dedication during those four excruciating July days earned each member a full measure of that deep degree of satisfaction. Such dedication embodies the essence of the posse concept.

You've just seen a lone example of the posse's work, but it is hardly atypical. We could have talked about the time the posse spent three rainy days and nights looking for a sixteen-year-old boy lost in the Four Peaks area, finding him just before dehydration and exposure finished him. Or we could have reviewed the case of the deer hunter who disappeared in the Superstition Mountains for the better part of a week—on purpose, it turned out—before we found him. Or we could have recalled the rather hairy rescue of two experienced mountain climbers who were seriously injured when boulders suddenly came crashing down on them, crushing and pinning them way up near the summit. Volunteers were helicoptered in, and prepared the climbers for an airlift. We could have discussed any of the forty-seven rescues the posse averages in any single year. Forty-seven rescues, frequently involving two or more human beings. Forty-seven rescues, sometimes involving up to 250 posse members, usually wrapped up within one day.

About half of the forty-seven posses have been involved in search and rescue efforts. The cost of one day's search can easily reach $5,000 or more. Though it has happened—rarely, very rarely, less than once a year, and usually when an individual is actively evading help in order to commit suicide—the missing are found alive.

So allow me to repeat a question I previously posed: What, in monetary terms, are those efforts—are those rescued lives—worth? While you're mulling that one over, let's move from this single case to a discussion of the entire posse, theoretical to practical, genesis to implementation to repercussions.

CHAPTER EIGHT

Volunteers Unite

Every month, citizens who wish to volunteer for the posse assemble at our training facility on Durango Street. After an introductory talk by the posse's director of training, Tom Wilmeth, the volunteers sign up, provide some basic information, and are fingerprinted. The information and the prints are checked to ensure that felons or other potential delinquents or lawbreakers do not sneak into the posse. After all, once accepted and trained, the posse operates in a law enforcement capacity.

Such power and privilege cannot be lightly handed to anyone, so each applicant must submit to an interview. The interview probes both common sense and a certain amount of psychological evaluation. In this manner, we are able to determine whether a volunteer's motives for joining the posse are reasonable and constructive, and if he or she will be an asset in what has proved to be an effective, reliable force.

The posse is about public service, not fancy uniforms

Anyway, I show up after some of the preliminaries have been completed, and offer a few words about the posse and their participation. I thought it might be useful to replay exactly what I recently said to one group of volunteers, so you can get an unobstructed, unadulterated representation of my view of the posse. I offer this without editing, apart from eliminating some repetition on my part—a penchant I have exhibited on occasion.

The auditorium was packed. A group of posse members in uniform sat in the front row. We also asked a handful of them to help answer any questions the new volunteers might have.

The rest of the hundred-odd chairs were filled by prospective volunteers, who had come to sign up or perhaps find out more before signing up. The crowd was the usual assortment, at first glance roughly mirroring the demographic mix of Maricopa County. There were a lot of white faces, to be sure, but also Hispanic, black, and Asian. The ages ranged from young to old, heavily male but a scattering of females. Some wore suits and ties, briefcases by their sides, wingtips on their feet, while others were dressed like mechanics or college students or cowboys.

A few appeared curious or unsure, but most were simply eager. By this time, most people in the county had heard enough about the posse to have formed a definite opinion, and clearly the majority of these volunteers had formed some unequivocally positive opinions.

I vaguely recognized a young woman seated in the front row. She was in her late twenties, pretty and blonde, quite serious, and in uniform. I turned to her and said hello, and then admitted I couldn't quite place her. The young woman quickly reminded me where I had last seen her.

"On *20/20*," she said.

The lightbulb clicked on. "Yeah, that's right," I said. "You were on Van Buren Street."

Van Buren Street is Phoenix's version of Forty-second Street, at least as far as prostitutes and drug dealing are concerned. Not long before, I had mobilized hundreds of members of the posse, and shut down the various nefarious activities, at least for a while. The ABC newsmagazine program *20/20* had tagged along, filming a story on several of our innovations, including the posse. The reporter had interviewed a handful of the volunteers, including this woman.

"You see that?" I announced to the room. "You join the posse, and you get on all these national TV shows. You get known around the world. Isn't it great?"

My question was greeted with widespread laughter.

"So why'd some of you show up?" I asked.

A young man wearing a baseball cap raised his hand. "Because of the coffee," he said loudly and happily as others applauded. "Because you took away the coffee. I'm waiting for you to take away some more stuff."

"Jesus, we're down to thirty cents a meal!" I said with mock outrage. "What do you want? Tell me how to get down to twenty-five cents, I'll be happy."

Amazingly, I had met some people who had actually moved from other cities with the express purpose of joining the posse, and I asked this crowd if anybody hailed from out of town.

Another young man called out his reply. "Anchorage, Alaska."

This was one I hadn't heard before. "Yeah, but you didn't come all the way to join the posse." I paused for a second. "Did you?"

"Basically, yes."

This one surprised even me, but I went with it. "You see, there's an example," I said. "Alaska. You probably read about the posse up there."

"I saw you on *20/20*," the man said.

"Oh," I said. Strike another blow for television. "You're sure it was me you saw and not her?" I inquired, nodding at the young woman, to the general merriment of the assemblage.

It was time to get down to business.

"Anyway," I said, "I have a lot of respect for the posse. You know what it is? Volunteerism. People want to do something to help fight crime. That's why you're all in here. It's not for money, because you don't get paid. In fact, it costs you a lot of money to join the posse. You have to pay for everything except your bullets. Add up everything, and it comes to about fifteen hundred to two thousand bucks—if you want to be armed."

I didn't believe that everyone needed to be or should be armed, and I wanted to make that clear, as well as emphasize that joining the posse was not an issue of affordability. The posse was about public service, not fancy uniforms or spending money.

"We have many posses where you don't have to pay for anything other than giving your time," I said. "We have jeep posses, horse posses, lake patrol posses, medical posses, search and rescue posses. The thing is, we need your time, your effort, your energy, your equipment, if you have any. We have about twenty-five hundred posse members, with eight hundred armed. By the way, I don't carry a gun, so if I don't carry a gun, why should you all worry about it? And remember, I have 150,000 people who go through the jails every year who don't like me. And that doesn't include all their relatives and friends. That's a lot of people who don't like the sheriff. And I don't need a gun."

That seemed to register with some members of the group, who were perhaps relieved that the posse offered all kinds of opportunities, most of which didn't require weapons.

"We have one guy who's eighty-five," I said. "Remember the old guy on *20/20*?—Dick Williams." I turned to the young woman who had shared that television appearance with me. "Remember Dick? You were on, too. Remember he took three minutes to pick up that gun? That was three minutes of *our* TV time."

After the laughter died down, I made a more serious point. "They picked the oldest guy—the *oldest* guy—to put on *20/20*. I wonder what ABC was trying to prove." Many in the audience muttered to one another, pretty damn sure *they* knew what ABC was trying to prove. "Eighty-five years old and in incredible shape, if you saw the program. Dick's still on the posse; he just turned in his gun after that show."

Now for some posse specifics. "We've used the posse since I've become sheriff for special programs. We went to the malls on horseback, so you could do your shopping without getting carjacked. Then we went to Van Buren Street. A lot of people warned me not to use the posse to go after prostitutes on Van Buren. 'Oh, you're going down to Van Buren? Oh, that's very dangerous.' Well, we went down there and got rid of the hookers. Sent them back to Los Angeles. And nothing happened. I mean nothing bad happened. The only injury was one posse member hit his head on a door. And now they've returned, so we're going back.

"And then we went after graffiti. We sent out the posse, six hundred strong, the first night. They were hiding behind walls, hanging from trees, trying to catch these criminals—and they're not taggers, as they like to be called, they're criminals—and we survived that. And then we went after deadbeat parents." The crowd broke into applause at the mention of the deadbeat parents' program.

"We got one hundred fifty with the posse. Nothing bad happened there. Served the warrants and locked 'em up, where they belong.

"The next great operation is our drug crackdown. I spent thirty-two years fighting drug traffickers around the world. All you hear about now are my two years as the sheriff. Nobody talks about my background. But that's where I came from. I spent thirty-two years in the federal government fighting drugs, and I promised when I was elected to go after the drug traffic. It's taken a little while, because I wanted to get tough in the jails and put up the tents, but we're ready."

I paused for an instant and glanced over the audience. "Let me ask you a question," I said. "My gut tells me to forget about drugs, to stick to the bologna, because I get more headlines on bologna than I *ever* will on drugs."

That brought more laughs, but it was true. The media loved the bologna and no coffee and no cigarettes and all the rest. Regardless, the drug operation was going to be the real deal. We were training posse members to assist our regular deputies in a carefully plotted, no-holds-barred assault on drugs. It was a program I had been planning for a long while and was now close to executing.

But we'll get into that in more detail a bit later.

I returned to the bottom line, which of course was the fundamental need for the posse.

"We're short of deputies," I said. "Our cars have over one hundred fifty thousand miles on them, because the Board of Supervisors took away over ten million dollars from me. Ten million dollars. If it wasn't for the posse, we'd be having some big problems here in this county, because of the shortage we have of deputies and equipment. The posse is critical now, because of the budget problems. So we're going to use the posse to fight crime.

"And I'm willing to take the political risk, because if you guys go out and something happens—and I have great faith in the posse—but if they pull their guns, and by accident something happens, boy, I'll have fifty thousand TV cameras here. And there would be some people—a very small minority—dancing in the streets.

"But I'm willing to take the chance. We have to do different things. It cannot be business as usual. We're at war against crime, we've got to take those risks. I'm willing to take those risks. The sheriff's main mission, and the government's main mission, is to protect its people. And I'm willing to do that."

I had said all this many times before, but it still meant something to me, because it was still all true.

"I was elected by the people. They hired me, and if they don't like what I'm doing, they can vote for somebody else two years from now. Very simple. Go get another sheriff. Very easily done around here. Since 1919, not one Republican sheriff has been reelected in Maricopa County. So you know how to get rid of your sheriff.

"So back to the posse. We're going to keep building up the posse, because we need the posse. We need your help. I think the credibility of the posse has been increasing, because nothing's gone wrong, and we're doing things the people appreciate.

"And remember, I'm elected to serve the people, not the other way around. A lot of politicians seem to think the people should serve them. I'm here to serve the public.

"And that's why you can't get more into volunteerism than this. I mean, you can talk about block watches, you can talk about citizens on patrol with two-way radios. But boy, when you can go into this, you don't go much higher on volunteering to help protect the neighborhoods and protect the people. And I have faith in my posse, and that's the way it's going to be as long as I'm the sheriff.

"So, if someone screws up, we'll have to face that. But the posse will never go away! I'm not going to abolish an organization because someone makes a mistake. I will never do that. You don't abolish a police department because someone makes a mistake. This is one sheriff who's doing different things that are called controversial. But I'll tell you one thing—it's all common sense. You just have to have someone to bite the bullet and take the chance. You have a sheriff who wants to do that."

After the applause died down, I finished up. "So that's my little pep talk. It's all common sense. I want all of you to join the posse. I don't want anybody to walk out of here saying, 'I'm never going to work for that guy.' Because you do work for me when you get your badge. You don't get paid, but you work."

And that was it. As honestly as possible, that's what I think of the posse and its role in my department and within society. It's not just a program or a group or a fact. The posse embodies something fundamental and necessary in the American experience. It embodies Americans working and fighting and pledging their efforts and honor to the community. And no work, no fight, no pledge could be more deserving of effort and honor.

That's what the posse means to me.

The posse is an old idea, born in the Old West when the sheriff would deputize a band of local citizens to mount up and help him catch the crooks who had just robbed the stagecoach. I've adopted and updated the concept, making changes for the modern age.

Now, many cities have volunteer outfits, but they're generally untrained and unarmed, trotted out to man the barricades during the St. Patrick's Day Parade, and for other ceremonial—and harmless—duties. And that was basically the situation here when I took office, but no longer.

Today, the Sheriff's Posse in Maricopa County, Arizona, is an authentic, crime-fighting force. Two thousand five hundred men and women, (outnumbering my sworn deputies five to one), have taken the official course and gotten themselves deputized to serve as more or less fully functioning cops, wearing real uniforms, driving real police cars, et cetera. So many people have joined up that the posse has its own command structure, with forty-seven specialized units in all. The posse is so popular across the socioeconomic board that we found it useful to create an Executive Posse made up of lawyers, doctors, accountants, and other white-collar, professional types, not to mention the governor of Arizona, and the mayor of Phoenix.

New units are always under consideration. In fact, not too long ago the Sheriff's Office received a donation of four Vietnam War-era helicopters from the U.S. Army. And now, as we recondition them, we're soliciting pilots to form a Helicopter Posse.

A further word about expense, just so you understand what can be at stake. Posse members wear the same uniforms as deputies, and that can include a class "A" long-sleeved shirt at $73 each, brown jeans or wool pants for another $30 dollars or more, brown shoes or boots for anywhere from $90 to $125, and a sheriff's baseball cap for $14 more.

And that's just for openers. Put down another $45 for the basket-weave, outer duty belt, in marine cordovan leather, $25 for the inner belt, $8 for the four belt keepers. Let's keep going, with another $20 to $30 for a handcuff case, $25 to $40 for handcuffs, $15 to $20 for chemical spray, $15 to $20 for the spray's case, anywhere from $18 to more than $100 for a flashlight, $8 for a flashlight holder, $6 for a name tag, $6 for a whistle, $10 to $15 for a whistle lanyard.

Then there are jackets for cold weather and shorts for lake patrol, and short-sleeve shirts and polo knit shirts, in both cotton and polyester, and cowboy hats for both winter and summer, and bags to carry it all around, and other incidentals a posse member can elect to purchase, but, always remember, no one is prompted to do so.

And, of course, let's not forget the badge, identical to a deputy's except for the words "Sheriff's Posse" inscribed across the top of the star instead of "Sheriff's Deputy." A small distinction, not readily discernible to any onlooker in the heat of confronting an officer who is patrolling and acting and reacting. The badge costs $35.

If the volunteer chooses to become qualified with a weapon, the cost rises dramatically. A duty holster, depending on style and manufacturer, adds another $45 to $75, and an ammunition pouch is another $20 to $30. Then there's the sidearm, which must conform to certain standards set by the department relating to manufacturer, caliber, and operation. A firearm can run anywhere from $3 to $400 on the low side to $500 or $700 or much more, especially if the tally includes night sights, cleaning kits, carrying cases, et cetera. Each gun must be equipped with three magazines, and a magazine for a semiautomatic pistol currently costs between $20 to $90 dollars.

Though it's not required, we strongly recommend that anyone carrying a handgun should also be wearing body armor, known as a bullet-resistant vest. (Understand that there is no such thing as "bullet-proof," only bullet-resistant to different calibers.) If the volunteer wants to train to ride as the second man in a patrol car, or other such potentially dangerous duty, he should be protected to the same degree as a deputy. National studies show that 60 percent of police officers shot in the line of duty are shot with their own weapons. Thus, the vest should be capable of stopping a bullet equivalent to the caliber employed by your own handgun.

Body armor is not cheap, and can add another five hundred dollars or more to the total.

So right there, depending on what the posse member chooses to buy—and remember, you can purchase nothing and still serve in many capacities—were talking about a potential outlay somewhere between one and two thousand dollars!

And that's not necessarily the end of it. Some posse members have gone so far as to purchase and outfit their own sheriff cars, equipping these jeeps and sedans with police lights, sirens, and radios. Outfitting these vehicles does not grant the owner the right to patrol *ad hoc*, on his own, outside of regulations. It *does* provide the department with more tools in the fight against crime.

All those expensive acquisitions are not always used only by the purchaser. Some posses have chipped in and bought cars, used them for a year or two, and then donated or sold them at sharp discounts to law enforcement agencies.

So, you can see, a lot of money is involved—though essentially none of it is spent by the taxpayers.

Of course, not everybody likes the posse. The local ACLU chapter repeatedly contends that this is some vigilante squad, or even the beginnings of a police state, notions that are both deeply insulting and moronic. It is insulting to the Sheriff's Office, to the deputies who work with the posse, to the volunteers who give their time to train and assist the posse, and obviously to the members of the posse itself, decent men and women who give so much of themselves to help their community. It is moronic to believe that adult Americans are so stupid or naive that their desire to get involved and do something positive for Maricopa County can be so easily turned by some malevolent pseudo-*fuehrer* or conspiracy into an unthinking detachment of storm troopers.

A few have even wondered whether the posse is in some way tied to the antigovernment militias running around the countryside. On the contrary. The militias are grounded in the insane delusion that the government is somehow evil, and actively seek to destroy America. The posse exists to support the government's legitimate efforts to safeguard our community and our people.

All these nonsensical notions say a great deal more about the accusers, and about their lack of faith in their fellow citizens, and in the beliefs that have made this nation great, than they do about the posse.

The posse is not only entirely legal, it also is in the great American tradition of self-reliance.

Volunteerism is a vital part of America's heritage. Let's face it, sooner or later every politician tries to employ that spirit to his own advantage. George Bush had his "Thousand Points of Light," and Bill Clinton has his national volunteer corps. Bush's concept was nothing more than a slogan, and Clinton has the right idea, but, as usual with politicians, his solution is to throw massive amounts of money at the problem. The posse is the best way, in every sense of the word, that I know to make our communities safer, better places to live.

The idea for the posse didn't occur to me overnight. After working all over America, I was well aware that the police were inevitably shorthanded. However, budget constraints guaranteed that the police would always be a limited presence on the streets, and that was undoubtedly for the better. After all, I had seen enough in many years overseas to know that Americans don't want to live in a country where there's a cop on every corner, watching every citizen.

But that still left the issue of fighting crime unresolved. And then the answer began to dawn on me when I was heading the Drug Enforcement Administration office in Turkey.

It all started with the fact that I didn't have police powers in Turkey. Sure, I was with the DEA, but that didn't cut much ice with the local authorities, and it certainly didn't garner me any legal status under Turkish laws. In other words, I didn't have the right to arrest anyone.

Still, I had to get the job done, and in Turkey or Mexico or Peru or anywhere else, that meant working hand in hand, side by side, with the country's officials. In a very real sense, I was a posse man, with abilities and manpower but no authority. I had to make the situation work.

And, as a sort of protoposse man, I worked with everyone in the country, from the cops all the way up to the president, trying to get the army together with the national police, the judges together with the investigators, all the while everybody mistrusting everybody else. And then I'd have to go back to my own people, from the CIA to Customs to the Embassy, and fight with all those government agencies, each one scheming and struggling to take control over drug enforcement.

In Arizona, as the newly elected sheriff, I was faced with something of a similar situation. I did not have the resources to accomplish the difficult task ahead. So instead of complaining about it, or kissing up to some politicians who didn't understand my job, I took action—unorthodox, but perfectly legal action. And so, just as in Turkey, where I possessed police powers only when I was operating alongside the local cops, the members of the posse would possess official positions only when they were with my deputies, under their authority. Working in this manner, the posse quickly proved itself an invaluable arm of my department.

A reasonable solution, reminiscent of those old cowboy movies I watched when I was a kid, starring Tom Mix and Gene Autry and Roy Rogers. I remembered the sheriff swearing in the local *burghers* as posse men and saying, "Go after the horse thieves," and away they'd gallop. And I said to myself, "Why can't that work today?" Maricopa County has almost three million people. How hard could it be to find a few thousand able men and women willing to devote some time and energy to their county? The Sheriff's Office has hardly more than five hundred deputy sheriffs, responsible for keeping law and order in a vast area, much of it sparsely settled. I got deputies out in a car in the desert somewhere, not within an hour of backup if anything happened. So why not recruit some civilians, train them and use them to help out?

So you put together my experiences in Turkey with my childhood memories from those Saturday afternoon westerns, and you have the posse.

And the posse is here to stay.

CHAPTER NINE

On Patrol

We've already reviewed the size of the posses and their different capabilities. You've seen how the Air Posse responded to a crisis with magnificent results.

Now let's see some more, so you can acquire a more complete view of what different posses and their members do. And more is the word, because I don't leave all this carefully accumulated and nurtured energy and equipment lying around unused. No way.

There's just too much to do.

It all begins with Enforcement Support. The posse assignments are decided and disseminated by this office. Once it is resolved which posses are required, and how many posse members have to be assembled for duty, the call goes out. Down from the top, the individual posses are contacted through each posse's operations officer, whose responsibility is to ensure that the posse's members are alerted.

The sheriff signs a pair of his famous pink shorts

Chief David Hendershott describes the posse as a "manpower chunking machine," particularly when the posse is deployed like an invading army during drug operations or chase-the-prostitutes-away campaigns. Take my word, it can be a daunting sight, as hundreds of uniformed volunteers swoop down to clean up the town. Imagine such a vision in your own town—hundreds of cops appearing at once to sweep the criminals from the sidewalks. No other police department in this country can afford that kind of massed approach on a regular basis. We can, because concerned citizens are willing to pitch in and participate.

Our mall program is a terrific example of this. Greater Phoenix is dotted with shopping malls. During the holiday season, the malls are jammed, as people rush about buying gifts. Unfortunately, where there are jammed malls, and people rushing about with gifts and spending money, there are thieves. Thieves who rip off shoppers, thieves who rip off stores, thieves who rip off cars.

The problem reached critical mass, at least as far as the media, and thus the public, was concerned, with a couple of carjackings in malls during the 1993 Christmas season.

The cry went out to the powers-that-be to do something, and you know that the powers-that-be tend to listen when the electorate is sufficiently upset. Soon enough, the governor was on the other end of the phone, asking if my department could help.

Could we help? Two days later, the Sheriff's Office was patrolling the malls.

That, however, is only the start of the story. The *background* of the story goes like this. Just because the governor was on the line didn't mean that law enforcement, from the Sheriff's Office to the Phoenix Police Department to the Department of Public Safety, wasn't more than a bit overloaded and undermanned—too many crimes, too few officers, too little money. In other words, just because it was time for Old Saint Nick didn't mean the regular emergencies and dilemmas facing law enforcement paused to converge on the malls. The cops were preoccupied with trying to handle their already full plates.

I believe I've already mentioned, once or twice how the county Board of Supervisors cut my budget and left me shorthanded and shortchanged. So if I was going to respond to this problem—and I was going to respond, come hell or high water—I'd have to find a different way. A way around the anticipated. A way around business-as-usual.

All of which led me straight to my posse.

The posse began patrolling malls throughout Phoenix on November 20, 1993, and continued without suspension through-out December 31. More than seven hundred posse men and women volunteered for duty. They patrolled on horseback, on foot, and in cars. (The Mounted Posse attracted most of the national attention. Something about horses and deputies and the West is just about irresistible to the media.)

To cut to the chase, the program was a tremendous success. The proof is in the statistics. Let's compare December 1993 with December 1992:

- Auto thefts decreased by 88 percent
- Burglaries from autos decreased by 87 percent
- Vandalism decreased by 75 percent
- Assaults decreased by 72 percent

Not too shabby, if I say so myself. In addition, deputies and posse members assigned to the malls participated in 36 arrests, 315 assists to other law enforcement agencies, 434 investigative stops, and 443 motorist assists.

More arrests probably could have been made if we had con-centrated on undercover operations. But the primary goal wasn't to nab crooks after they'd committed a crime, but to scare them away from even trying. After all, this was the biggest holiday of the year, and as I said at the time, "We are trying to keep a merry Christmas from being stolen from Maricopa County families. When the gifts are gone, or someone is hurt, Christmas is going to be kind of bleak, even if the culprit is in jail."

Those seven hundred-plus posse members worked 12,448 unpaid hours. Calculated at the basic rate of pay for deputies, those hours would have cost the county a cool $248,960—if anyone had gotten paid, which, aside from a few sworn personnel coordinating the detail, they did not. That's a quarter-million dollars' worth of law enforcement, courtesy of concerned citizens.

You know what the increased security meant to the malls. It meant more shoppers, and thus more sales. It was good for the people, good for business, good for the economy.

After that performance, you can be sure that the merchants and public were clamoring for a resumption of the mall patrol when Christmas rolled around again. However, my department's 1994 budget was still being severely squeezed by the Board of Supervisors, and I didn't have any money remaining to pay even one deputy to oversee the detail. The entire program was in serious danger of being just a memory.

As is my wont, I didn't keep the problem a secret. I said we were perilously close to losing the mall patrol.

Arizona responded immediately and generously. Financial support came from a slew of major companies, including Volvo International, Ray Korte Chevrolet, and Courtesy Chevrolet Leasing, as well as several of the large malls hoping for our help. The governor pledged twenty thousand dollars in financial support. The U.S. Army donated equipment.

Sixteen hundred shifts were manned by posse members, and the results were impressive. From the road (motorist assists, car accidents, traffic citations), to the street (public assists, arrests, investigations), the posse was everywhere. In fact, the program worked so well that virtually no notable criminal activity was reported in the eleven malls patrolled by the posse.

And not all the benefits were of the crime-fighting kind. Posse man Robert McCollum was patrolling the Superstition Springs Mall in Mesa when he was contacted by mall security, and told to come in a hurry. It was December 17, 1994, about 9:30 P.M. An infant was not breathing and they needed help.

Mall security had called the right guy. Robert McCollum is an E.M.T., (emergency medical technician), and he grabbed his first-aid bag and went running.

Robert found a seven-month-old girl turning blue, a sign of oxygen deprivation. He determined that her airway was clear and inserted a small tube. As another man performed chest compressions,

Robert gave the baby two breaths of air. The child began breathing on her own, her respiration quickly becoming strong and regular.

The Mesa Fire Department arrived a few minutes later, and took the baby to the hospital for evaluation. The doctors discovered that the infant had suffered a febrile seizure, which tightened the throat muscles, preventing the passage of air into the lungs. Robert's fast and certain response probably saved the baby's life. For his actions, Robert McCollum received the Maricopa County Sheriff's Lifesaving Medal.

The mall patrol has quickly established itself as an integral part of the holiday season. It is hard—no, impossible—to imagine that any future sheriff or politician would be inclined to forego the mall patrol. The people want it. The people deserve it.

Why? You know why. Because it works.

Another mass posse detail can be found on Van Buren Street, where an ongoing battle is under way. It is a battle familiar to every city in America—well, every city in the world—since humanity first crowded together in close living arrangements.

It's all about the battle against prostitution.

Van Buren Street used to be a major thoroughfare from the airport to downtown Phoenix. As Phoenix has grown, parts of Van Buren have fallen on hard times. In fact, Van Buren turned into the city's "red light district," our local version of New York's Forty-second Street. Prostitutes occupied street corners in increasing numbers, soliciting passing motorists and pedestrians. With prostitution came drugs, and then muggings and robberies; the street only got more lawless and dangerous.

This was hardly a sudden development. Van Buren had been spiraling downward for years, as law enforcement contended with more pressing problems. This "victimless" crime stayed way down on the list, until one day it was clear that prostitution, bringing so much other crime and danger in its wake, as well as devastating legitimate businesses and residents in the area, was suddenly not so obviously "victimless" after all.

From the day I was elected to office, I was determined to do something about this. Not that it would be easy. As we all know, prostitution is an especially difficult crime to eradicate—not for nothing is it the world's oldest profession.

I needed a lot of manpower to press the attack, a lot of manpower not for just one big push, but to keep pushing over and over. Lock 'em up, and we all know they'll be kicked loose soon enough, so we have to lock 'em up again and again and again, until they get the idea that this isn't a profitable proposition any longer. But the rub is, while we're doing this, we can't neglect the car thieves and crack dealers and homicidal maniacs, so there goes our concentrated manpower assault. (And then there's the ever-present rub of attempting to figure out some method to pay for any large-scale program, however worthwhile.)

Enter the posse.

Only the posse was capable of supplying trained men and women in sufficient quantity to make this work. Now remember, I could plan the attack, but I couldn't quite so simply order the troops forward, because these troops were all volunteers. So I did what I had to do—I asked the posse to help. And, yet again, the posse said yes.

I decided to restrict the operation to armed posse members. Given the uncertainties facing the detail, the uncertainty of whom we might confront, and how they might react, I thought it was the prudent way to go.

All volunteers were provided with some special training, from surveillance techniques to blood-borne pathogen instruction. They were instructed as to our strategy and our goals.

I had no intention of keeping this operation secret. I wanted the prostitutes forewarned, giving them the chance to leave town. Locked up or gone for good—either suited me just fine.

The Maricopa County Sheriff's Office and the Phoenix Police Department worked hand in hand to plan and implement the project. As is usually the case, cooperation between the two agencies was exemplary.

Operation Zero Tolerance commenced at 6 P.M. on April 4, 1994. Posse members in full uniform worked in teams of two, patrolling in marked cars, on foot, and occasionally on horseback, along with sworn county deputies and Phoenix police officers. More than five hundred posse members would eventually participate, essentially flooding the area day and night.

The results of Zero Tolerance were not long in coming. According to Phoenix Police stats, the number of police "calls for service" in the area of Van Buren from Seventh to Forty-fourth Street was reduced by nearly one-third, from 249 calls to 181 calls, within the very first week. In that same week, vice-related calls dropped from thirty-four to just four.

Perhaps most tellingly, it was not uncommon to view as many as forty-five prostitutes at the same time along Van Buren before the operation began. Since April 4, no more than three prostitutes could be counted at any one time. Most nights, absolutely no prostitutes were seen on the streets.

The program continued until June 6. The sixty-day operation yielded some mighty impressive facts and figures. Top of the list— Phoenix PD found that calls regarding prostitution were reduced by an amazing 91 percent. Just as significantly, overall service calls, related to all crimes in the area, fell by 17 percent, concretely demonstrating the close connection between prostitution and other criminal enterprises.

Businesses on Van Buren thrived, tourists were no longer harassed, residents felt safer.

While Zero Tolerance proved an unqualified success, it was not a permanent solution. That's the nature of this particular beast. The fight is endless. But society has wisely determined that this abuse of women, as well as all the other problems that are part and parcel of this tawdry trade, is a fight worth pursuing, so pursue it we did and shall.

Zero Tolerance had put a serious dent in the streetwalking traffic, and it took some time for the pimps and prostitutes to recover and regain their stride. And each time the criminals came back, so did the posse.

In fact, I called out the posse to Van Buren Street four times within eighteen months, and four times the posse responded with enthusiasm and alacrity. While the posse achieved its aims during each round of this ongoing operation, it was clear that a more enduring answer was required.

To me, that answer was pretty obvious.

"Prostitution has plagued this street for too long," I declared on September 10, 1995. "And the solution may be to create a neighborhood sheriff's posse."

The president of the Van Buren Civic Association, Barry Shemer, pronounced himself delighted with the idea. "Everyone, from the Sheriff's Office to the Phoenix Police to Van Buren Street residents, is sick of this problem. Maybe a local posse, properly trained, will do the trick."

As I am writing this, the Van Buren Posse is in the preliminary stages of formation. Starting a new posse is never a simple matter— volunteers must step forward, officers selected from the group, posse members trained, duties determined, schedules fixed. It is far from an overnight process, but then that's the tried-and-true formula that has to be followed to the letter if a new posse is going to be successful.

Given the outstanding record compiled by our many different posses, the public can expect no less from the Van Buren Street Posse.

One more total posse effort I'd like to describe was named Operation T.A.G.—Operation Take Away Graffiti.

Graffiti is another crime that has grown into a nationwide blight. For some time, it was fashionable to think of graffiti, or tagging, as either the pained cry of misunderstood youth or a new type of art. That's right, art, legitimate art, no different than the paintings hanging in museums and bought and sold at Sotheby's.

It has taken awhile, but all that hogwash has pretty much faded away. Partly because we have learned that graffiti is frequently a sign of gang activity. Partly because we have learned that graffiti hastens the physical and social decline of a building, a block, a neighborhood. Partly because we have learned that cleaning up the graffiti mess has cost us billions of dollars.

Let's briefly delve into each of those factors. It's been forty years since Hispanic gangs began creeping into Phoenix. More recently, a number of black and Asian gangs have migrated from California. The latest entrants in this dubious category are Anglo gangs, staking their own claims to a piece of the territory. All these gangs compete for turf violently and symbolically, employing both with extreme fury. As they deface structure after structure, they physically show, physically *prove*, to decent citizens that law and order can be fragile concepts, that civilization is an illusion. Studies have demonstrated that once a broken window in a building is allowed to remain unrepaired, then another window will be broken, and then another and another, until the entire building is given over to ruin. In other words, the rot must be stopped as soon as it is discovered, or the corruption can quickly become overwhelming and fatal.

Now attempt to add up the cost in cleaning and repainting and lost business and destroyed neighborhoods, and the count rapidly rises into the billions.

None of that is acceptable.

However, at the same time, tagging is not like carjacking or murder in presenting an immediate danger that demands an immediate police response, all other problems pushed aside. Graffiti is also a tough crime to stop. The usually young offenders move within a closed society, singularly hostile to outsiders. They customarily work at night, work fast, very often in out-of-the-way spots, and that makes them most difficult to catch.

For these reasons, graffiti ranks low on law enforcement's list of priorities, and that means it might as well be off the list. Hence, when I decided to attack this problem, I knew I was not only trying to crack a particularly tough nut but, as was par for the course, without enough deputies. Par for the course, it was improvise and adapt. And improvising and adapting to me spelled posse.

As I told the press, "This is a law enforcement effort—not a cleanup and paint program. Graffiti is a serious public concern in cities everywhere. Our local police can't spend the time and resources it takes to catch these hoodlums in the act. But my posse can and will."

The mayor of Phoenix, who had asked us to concentrate the first phase of the operation in his city, added a few encouraging words. "Graffiti is more than just pain on a wall. It steals the soul of a city, holds our neighborhoods hostage to gang warfare, and destroys the value of people's property. So we are grateful to the sheriff and his posse that they are willing to help."

Operation T.A.G. was launched the night of March 24, 1995, though preparations had been in the works for some time. A Graffiti Hotline had been set up so these punks with spray cans could call in and inform on one another, as they were always happy to do for a few bucks. To help us out, thirty-five cell phones were donated by Bell Atlantic; twelve cars were donated by Courtesy Chevrolet Leasing; twenty-eight night scopes were donated by Litton Industries, the Salt River Project, and the Arizona Public Service.

More than six hundred posse members assembled to hit the streets that first night. Twenty-five surveillance teams of twenty volunteers each, overseen by a deputy or reserve deputy, were placed in preassigned positions. The rest of the posse was allocated as needed.

"Graffiti is tied to gangs and drugs," I warned the criminals through the media. (Though they liked to call themselves taggers, I preferred the more precise word—criminals.) "So any violation of the law that we come across, we will act upon from criminal damage to concealed weapons to narcotics."

The effect of the posse deployment was remarkable. From the first night, graffiti instantly and precipitously dropped.

Graffiti virtually disappeared from most locations and remained just an ugly memory for the duration of the operation. The detail waxed and waned, as volunteers came and went, as their enthusiasm fluctuated, and schedules permitted. Nonetheless, by the middle of June, the posse had donated nearly fifteen thousand hours of surveillance work. Fifteen thousand hours! While arrests were few, the aim had been accomplished. Paint crews that ordinarily received dozens of phone calls reporting new graffiti, now received perhaps one or two calls. The long-term effect of the operation was an average drop of 70 to 80 percent in graffiti throughout Phoenix.

While there is no doubt that graffiti reappears when the posse fades away, the result is worth the effort. Maybe—probably—we can never stop it, at least not by police maneuvers. Fundamentally, graffiti is not a law enforcement issue, it is an issue of parental control, of familial values and community sanctions.

Still, while we wait for society to figure out what it's doing wrong and then actually do something about it, law enforcement has to play its part. So the posse will continue to go out at night, seeking to raise the price of vandalism, attempting to break the cycle of one gang besting another, determined to protect public and private property and restore a measure of sanity and decency to our streets.

The Sheriff's Office is no different than every other law enforcement agency in the country. Whether salaried or volunteer, we are all public servants. We all take an oath. We do what we can.

Speaking of another problem that falls outside the normal purview of the Sheriff's Office, a problem that exemplifies a wound deep within our society, we arrive at the "Deadbeat Parent" posse program. It begins with a 50 percent national divorce rate and the dissolution of the family, and ends with parents abandoning their children physically, emotionally, and financially. As hard as it is for most of us to comprehend—that a parent would neglect a child in any manner—it is both infuriating and depressing to realize that increasing numbers of children and their caretakers are left without the support ordered by the courts.

They used to be called "deadbeat dads," but we had to change the name, and not only to be politically correct. No! The sad fact is that nowadays women are deserting their children and responsibilities just like men. So our program is entitled in gender-neutral fashion.

The ball gets rolling when the court issues an action against a parent who has failed to pay child support. The order goes to the Warrants Unit of the Sheriff's Office, which, along with posse members, commences a background investigation of the delinquent parent. The examination is thorough. They check on the offender's friends, place of work, motor vehicle department record, possible criminal history, et cetera. They check everything—not only to know where to find the suspect—but also to know what the officers are going to confront when they make the arrest. This preparatory work is slow but invaluable.

On the day of a major operation, teams of deputies, reserves, and posse members are assigned to different sections of the county. Each team is responsible for several warrants located within its section. This detail is always popular with the volunteers, undoubtedly because of the nature of the task, undoubtedly because many of the volunteers are parents themselves. It is not uncommon to find one hundred fifty or more posse members showing up to work on the days the warrants are served.

This operation generally gets under way early in the morning, in the hope of catching the suspect at home, unaware. Once taken into custody, the team transports the prisoner back to a central processing and booking area, established just for this duty, and then goes back into the field to arrest the next deadbeat.

In a Happy Mother's Day gift from the Maricopa County Sheriff's Office in May 1995, Operation Pay-Back was a week-long sweep that garnered almost a quarter-million dollars for the families that needed and were owed the funds. Every time the department organizes a sweep, we rack up between twenty-five and sixty arrests in each twelve-hour period.

On two occasions, I set up the processing center in a mall parking lot, just so the deadbeats would be booked in public and in front of the TV cameras for all the world see, before being taken away to jail. Shame can be a most effective tool.

The Sheriff's Office and the posse perform many important and popular services for the community, but I would be hard-pressed to think of any that I consider more worthwhile than helping these needy families.

I could fill a volume talking about posse programs and operations. We could discuss the Attack of the Tumblin' Tumbleweeds, in which hundreds of tumbleweeds were rolling across the landscape around Sun Lakes, creating a serious fire risk and traffic hazard. The local homeowners association and Sun Lakes Fire Department possessed neither the manpower nor the money to deal with the predicament.

"We didn't know where to turn for assistance with this problem," the fire chief said. "No one around here had the resources."

Then somebody thought of us, and the call was made. And in no time, forty inmates, guarded by members of the Sun Lakes Posse, were out in force, cleaning up the area. And just like that, the problem was gone.

In somewhat similar fashion, thirty members of various posses and fifteen inmates helped clear away trash from Lake Pleasant one weekend. Assignments like these are not exciting or "sexy," but they are meaningful, especially to the people who live near or frequent the damaged areas.

And we've barely even mentioned the long list of other law-enforcement-oriented duties that many posses regularly perform, such as neighborhood patrol, extradition service, traffic control, prisoner transport, fingerprinting, lake patrol, communications, jail facility detail, parade patrol, crime scene security, mail run, maintenance support, computer processing, logistical support, administrative assistance, et cetera.

Then there are fairly exotic details, such as the posse members who have received special training from the Secret Service and serve on a multiagency task force, 130 persons strong, protecting officials and dignitaries, including the President of the United States, when they visit Arizona.

Even the Special Investigations Unit, the department's most classified bureau, which deals with such matters as organized crime, terrorism, intelligence and homicide, is happy to take advantage of posse members. To become involved, posse men and women must first pass a more stringent security check. Once accepted, they undergo intensified training in different areas. (Because of the time and money that must be invested to adequately train a posse member to work with Special

Investigations, the volunteer must be prepared to devote a fairly considerable amount of energy to this task. This, of course, differs from all other posse members, who more readily come and go as they please.)

Once a posse member is inside Special Investigations, they work side by side with the detectives, pursuing all sorts of cases. In fact, on rare occasion, a posse member might even go undercover. One such case resulted in the infiltration of an organized crime group and led to several important arrests. I cannot reveal any more about that case without jeopardizing our undercover operative.

As you contemplate all this, remember that the posse is made up of individuals from all walks all life. While the majority have led lives totally outside the realm of governmental or law enforcement work, others are retired cops or FBI or DEA agents eager to keep their hands in the game. Some come out of the military, where they might have served in a police or intelligence capacity. Still others have intelligence or private detective or forensic backgrounds. The background of the posse members is often a reliable indicator of how much time they wish to devote to the department, and also what sort of work they choose to do. Again, they are volunteers— the decision is always in their hands.

The point is, a posse member is capable of helping in many more ways than the average citizen might realize. Not every posse member chooses to wear a uniform and ride beside a deputy in a patrol car. The Sheriff's Office is a large organization, with a wide variety of needs. We are as grateful to those who handle the mundane chores as we are to those who go through the Qualified Armed Possemen training and go on patrol. In fact, most deputies, if asked, would say that they are most grateful to those who transport prisoners and take the patrol cars in for maintenance and carry out all the less exciting, less pleasant tasks, freeing the deputies to go out and do what they were hired to do—protect and serve.

You know, I have found that sheriffs in some communities are opposed to establishing posses in the mistaken belief that volunteers will somehow eventually replace them or the police. Nothing could be farther from the truth—the posse supplements and supports law enforcement's activities. Once this has been explained to those skeptical police officers—and that is a snap to accomplish—then they *always* enthusiastically embrace the concept. They come to understand that the volunteers only help the police do more policing.

Nobody becomes a cop to fill out forms and do administrative work. Men and women become cops so they can help the good guys and bust the bad guys. The posse makes it easier for them to do that.

CHAPTER TEN

How to Start Your Own Posse

I've talked about how the posse functions in the field and have provided examples of its capabilities and accomplishments. Of course, none of this would be possible if it weren't efficiently organized and managed. It starts with the sheriff, who sets broad policy and specific goals, and then shifts to the deputy chief of the Operations and Development Bureau, who directs the daily administration of all posse operations.

This is the first of several key roles in the organizational structure, and I promoted David Hendershott from captain to deputy chief because he was the right man for the job. Not only did he bring the expertise and experience gained in the course of a distinguished sixteen-year career to his new post, he also came armed with an undergraduate degree from Arizona State University, a master's in business administration, and is working on his doctorate in business administration. In an organization this large, every insight and edge helps.

Deputy Chief Hendershott's command is divided into two divisions—Enforcement Support and Training. Enforcement Support is in charge of processing the new volunteers, which includes

Posse training is a massive undertaking

conducting background checks. The accepted volunteers then begin training, falling under the jurisdiction of that division (which also trains sworn and detention officers). After training has been completed, and they are ready to serve, Enforcement Support takes over again, overseeing all posse assignments and posse business.

Initially, I am going to concentrate on the Training Division to give you some idea of what it takes to put a posse into the field.

Tom Wilmeth is the director of Voluntary Training, and coordinates the massive undertaking of educating and preparing posse members. And massive is precisely the correct word. Tom has a full-time staff of two detention officers and one civilian assisting and managing two hundred volunteer instructors. The latter teach and train and retrain the twenty-five hundred—and growing—posse members in a multitude of courses. To put it in raw numbers, our records show that just for the second quarter of 1995, the division logged 328,416 hours of posse training. Extend that typical quarter out for one year, and we're talking about more than one million training hours—exactly 1,313,664 training hours. That means volunteers spending all those hours training other volunteers, mostly at night or on the weekends.

The coordination required to handle all that labor is nothing short of mind-boggling. The overwhelming number of training hours and different courses is only the most obvious problem. The real complication begins with the fact that nearly everyone involved is a volunteer, and volunteers cannot be dealt with the way one deals with paid employees. Volunteers cannot be summarily ordered around. Nor, to be honest, can they be depended upon with absolute confidence. Volunteers show up when they want to, when they are in the mood, or unless something better comes along. So Wilmeth and his team must always have contingency plans ready, and be prepared to have extra or alternate instructors, or change the time of a class, or perform some other juggling act.

Wilmeth is well qualified to direct this never-ending traffic. Armed with a master's degree from Arizona State University, he ran the Bureau of Juvenile Education for the Arizona Department of

Corrections, responsible for some two thousand inmates/students. Before that, he served as the administrative aide to the governor of Arizona. Later, after his stint at Corrections, he filled the same post for one of my predecessors in the Sheriff's Office. In addition, Wilmeth has been a posse member for the town of Wickenberg for the past twenty-five years, serving at one time as captain of the posse as well as coordinator for the air search and rescue unit. In his other life, he has also been a successful entrepreneur. Put all those factors together, then you can comprehend how Wilmeth is able to supervise, bargain with, and cajole the disparate personalities, and cope with organizational demands that are at the heart of his job.

I point out Wilmeth's impressive résumé in order to demonstrate that you need the right person in the right job to make the system work, and finding that right person is not always easy—particularly since there are so many right people needed, from administrators to assistants to instructors.

And what's the result? What do all those training hours and volunteering and coordinating amount to? In a phrase, they add up to a lot of work. I've told you some stories—now take a glance at the compilation of hours worked by the posse members from January 1 through December 31, 1994, as submitted by the individual posses:

- Fountain Hills Posse, 19 members: 8,585 hours
- Scottsdale Search and Rescue Posse, 18 members: 5,054.8 hours
- Sun City West Posse, 309 members: 93,874 hours
- Gilbert Search and Rescue Posse, 40 members: 14,640 hours
- Executive Posse, 75 members reporting out of approximately 350: 19,155.5 hours

An interesting footnote: One hundred twenty-seven posse members worked more than 500 hours in 1994, (representing one full day's work each week for the entire year); 30 members worked more than 1,000 hours; 14 members worked more than 1,500 hours; and 2 members worked more than 2,000 hours. Of course, how much time a posse man or woman can donate to my department and the community depends on whether that member has a job or is retired, whether that member has children at home, and so on.

When we add up all those hours together, we have calculated that the posse members save the taxpayers a cool three million dollars each year. *Three million dollars!* A little while back, I posed the question, What's the result? What do all those training hours and volunteering and coordinating amount to?

Now you have some idea.

But it's more than that. While it is impossible to obtain a precise economic standard beyond calculating work hours, my office has concluded that last year posse work shaved an astonishing twelve million dollars from the taxpayers' bill!

And the benefits do not stop there. Perhaps the most important result of the posse labors are the indeterminate savings gained from crime prevention. Let me explain. A couple of Christmases ago, several carjackings occurred in mall parking lots. The press pumped the story up for all its worth, resulting in widespread alarm, causing the public to stay away from the malls, seriously hurting the shops during their most crucial selling season. By sending in the posse, we were able to flood the parking lots with a police presence. Instead of having the usual one or two deputies patrolling a few square miles, incorporating a handful of malls, fifteen department cars maintained a constant presence in the area. This overwhelming official presence immediately reassured the public and spooked any lurking criminals, which brought the people back to the malls, and saved the holiday season for the stores. How do we accurately calculate all the benefits that accrued because of the posse? Crime prevention, store sales, and, probably most valuable of all, reviving the public's sense of security, the feeling that the streets are once again safe—what is all that worth?

Security. Peace of mind. I can't put a dollar figure on that, but we all know it's worth quite a lot. Quite a lot indeed.

Once the administrators and the instructors are in place, the lessons and classes must be organized, and they must be sensible and on target. Once again, not a minute of any volunteer's time can be wasted or *perceived* to be wasted, or the whole group, *en masse*, will rise and walk out. Still, every essential point must be made by the instructors, and presented in such a manner that the knowledge being offered will be fully appreciated and absorbed.

The significance of all this is brought home to posse members by Tom Wilmeth in a short speech he delivers to each posse class. Tom tells them simple and straight, and there can be no doubt lingering in any of their minds when he's finished.

Tom starts by picking up a piece of chalk and drawing an umbrella on the blackboard. Then he draws raindrops all around the umbrella, some striking the covering, and others falling to the ground. Inside the canvas of the umbrella he writes "MCSO Policy." Along the handle of the umbrella, he writes "Posse Training." Finally, Tom draws a stick figure, who stands safely underneath the umbrella.

Then he puts down the chalk and turns to the class.

"That stick man is you," he says. "That stick man is every posse member. The handle is your training, and it's what holds up that umbrella of the Maricopa County Sheriff's Office (MCSO), policy and procedure. If you stay under the umbrella of the Sheriff's Office, and you do exactly as you've been trained, everything will be fine. Doing exactly as you've been trained means you don't go out cowboying on your own, you don't invent duties on your own, you don't flash your badge, you don't use a firearm that you haven't qualified with, you don't do anything we haven't taught you to do.

"Stay under that umbrella. Your training will keep you under that umbrella. Once you step out from under that umbrella, you're in trouble. Once you ignore MCSO policy, once you forget what you've been taught and what you've been trained to do, then you're on your own. Because you see those raindrops?"

Tom waits for the assembled posse to nod its collective head, just to make sure that everyone got the point.

"Folks, those raindrops are lawyers," Tom says, and the class invariably laughs, but it is always a quiet, attentive laugh. "You are protected and covered by the Sheriff's Office as long as you stay under the umbrella. When you go off on your own, we can't protect you. And if we can't protect you, those raindrops are going to hit you. You are going to be personally liable for anything that happens. You can lose your home—you can even lose your freedom.

"Now I don't expect any problems. I've been in the posse for twenty-five years, and we've never had a posse member involved in a shooting. We've never had a problem we couldn't handle. But it can happen—if you let it happen.

"We want to work hard, and we want you to enjoy doing it. Your training and MCSO policy will keep you safe on the street and in the courtroom.

"Okay?"

With that, Tom looks out over the audience, finished. And he can tell that if only one of the many messages delivered to the posse has really gotten through, this is it.

The classes provide the foundation, so let's examine them in more depth. In this way, you'll better understand which lessons the training is intended to instill. Then you'll better understand what it takes to be a posse member, and what the posse is all about.

Of course, this is not presented as a sort of shorthand guide to setting up a posse. Instead, this is a glimpse into the incredible amount of thought and effort required to organize a posse. The key is simple. The posse will only be effective and beneficial to the community if its initial organization is effective and judicious. Philosophically, every volunteer must be imbued with the law enforcement agency's policies and attitudes, ensuring that posse members fully understand their mission. Practically, various skills must be mastered by the volunteers, so they are capable of performing their duties satisfactorily and safely. Legally, every *T* must be crossed to avoid liability on the part of either the volunteers or the city or county.

That's a lot to ask, but too much is at stake—the lives of our volunteers, the deputies with whom they work, and the community they serve—to settle for less.

Law and Legal is a sixteen-hour course held over two days, and it is a requirement for all posse members who want to assist deputies in patrol situations. The course introduces volunteers to Maricopa County Sheriff's Office policies and procedures. It ranges from discussing justification of force scenarios and potential liability to uniform standards to prisoner control and transport to courtroom demeanor, and several other subjects in between.

It is imperative that volunteers understand the constitutional mandate as well as the powers and duties of the Sheriff's Office. It is imperative that the volunteers understand the criminal and civil demands and liabilities of Arizona law. It is imperative that the volunteers understand the role of the posses within the department. It is all imperative, because the volunteers will understand how to effectively and properly serve in the posse *only after* gaining a comprehensive grasp of department mandates and duties and liabilities and responsibilities.

Law and Legal isn't especially exciting. Rather, it is serious and exacting. But that is the nature of most police work, and it is no different when the posse is involved. The public has the absolute right to be assured that posse members are not cowboys or vigilantes, that they will always operate reasonably and legally, same as any sworn officer. So I shall begin with this particular course in order to establish a foundation for your understanding of the posse, before moving on to the more action-oriented courses.

Ethics is a relatively new part of the Law and Legal course, and it has quickly established itself as an essential area to understand. I begin here, because ethical considerations are at the core of the posse idea. After all, every volunteer joins the posse because of a desire to serve the community, a decision steeped in each individual's values and beliefs. How the posse translates that into action, the basis for how the posse serves the public, must be ethical behavior.

The point of this class can be summed up in a phrase—to explore ethics in order to familiarize the students with their personal responsibilities as posse members.

Our ethics course is different than an ethics course taught at a university. The university course is invariably centered around an examination of the fundamental meaning of ethics, and its intellectual development in human thought. The posse course is centered around an examination of how to act, what to do, how to initiate or respond to situations encountered while working for MCSO. More simply stated, the university course is philosophy; ours is practical.

The fundamentals are laid out so all the volunteers comprehend at the start what is expected of them. Now I'll lay them out for you, so we'll all be on the same page.

So here's the first proposition, as well as some questions and answers, that can serve as our opening consideration:

Consider these four steps to an ethical decision:

1. Collect as many facts as possible and understand the issues.
2. Evaluate the facts.
3. Decide, answering the following questions: Is the decision legal? Is the decision fair to everyone, or only to you? How will you feel about the decision later in life?
4. Follow through. Act on your decision.

Very direct, very forthright, very clear. Nothing complicated or controversial, almost a self-evident guide to behavior—at least in theory.

In similar fashion, here is a short list of ethical guidelines we provide the students:

1. Don't pass the buck.
2. Have the guts to stand up for what is right.
3. Find solutions instead of excuses.
4. Look for the ethical way.
5. View an ethical problem not as a crisis, but as an opportunity to do the right thing.
6. Ethical problems do not usually just vanish—*don't give up.*

From these broad ethical markers, we progress to specific instances, spelling out the official Code of Conduct for the Maricopa County Sheriff's Office. Though the Code of Conduct was written for sworn deputies, its policies apply to posse members as well.

Once again, many of the code's policies should be obvious, requiring nothing more than common sense. For example, under the section headed "Unbecoming Conduct and Public Demeanor," all department personnel, including posse members, are directed to "conduct themselves at all times, both on and off duty, in such a manner as to reflect most favorably on the office." Personnel are also ordered not to be disorderly in any public place, to perform their duties in a calm and firm manner, to foster harmony and cooperation among members of the department. Personnel will not subject any person or animal to cruel or unfair treatment, or neglect to take humane action when needed.

Of course, posse members are only permitted to wear their uniforms or display their badges when performing duties under the direction of the Sheriff's Office. Since the vast majority of volunteers work sporadically, special attention is paid in the classroom to alert posse members to be especially aware of their manner and behavior when in uniform. That means not drinking when on duty, and also not the night before. Nor should the volunteer finish his tour and then stop in a bar on his way home, still in uniform. The volunteer cannot accept any gratuities or rewards (including the proverbial free lunch), for performing his sworn duty. Nor can the volunteer abuse his position to avoid the less pleasant realities of life, such as flashing a badge to try to get out of a speeding ticket. Not only is it illegal, but it won't work, as several of our posse members can attest. By the way, not only did they get the tickets they deserved, they were also summarily drummed out of the posse.

The posse member also cannot chew tobacco or gossip or do a bunch of other activities that anyone with any common sense would know not to do when on duty.

The spirit and ideals that guide the Sheriff's Office's deeds and tenets are incorporated within our Code of Ethics, which all personnel must know and swear to uphold. I shall reprint the code in its entirety, because it is that important, particularly in this day when so many citizens have lost faith in the basic honor and goodwill of their law enforcement agencies:

As an employee of the Maricopa County Sheriff's Office, I pledge to uphold the Constitution of the United States of America and the Constitution of the State of Arizona, to obey the laws of the State and the United States, and the rules, regulations, and policies of the Maricopa County Sheriff's Office. I will never abuse the authority vested in me, and will honor and uphold the constitutional rights to liberty, equality, and justice afforded to all persons. I will be honest in thought and deed, in both my personal and official life, and will not allow my conduct to bring discredit, dishonor, or shame, upon the Maricopa County Sheriff's Office. I will never misrepresent myself, be untruthful, or take what does not belong to me, nor will I tolerate conduct on the part of any other employee of the Office which violates the principles of this Code of Ethics.

Those are not empty words, phrases to be mouthed and forgotten. I have spent my life upholding those ideals, living by those values, serving the public. That is why the overwhelming majority of police officers enter law enforcement, to do something good, to make a contribution. I demand no less from the posse. When they are working, in whatever capacity, posse members must be as dedicated and as honorable as any of my deputies. To settle for less would cheat both the posse and the public.

Of course, merely spelling out these ideas and lists does not an adequate lesson make, so we present ethical dilemmas in the form of videotape scenarios that we can work through and discuss.

The scenes show instances of fairly typical situations that law enforcement officers commonly encounter, and the *wrong* way to respond. These include a police officer who accepts a free meal from a restaurant, another officer who offers to forego handing a pretty girl a ticket for a traffic violation in lieu of "tutoring" her at home in the intricacies of the traffic laws, an officer who uses unnecessary verbal and physical force in dealing with a vagrant, an officer who steals office supplies from the department, an officer who pockets some money dropped by a dope dealer, and so on. Obviously, some of these situations are more serious than others, though none of the officers' actions can be condoned.

Ratcheting up the level of ethical wrongs, we then play a segment from CBS's *60 Minutes* entitled "Buddy Boys." The segment concerned a ring of corrupt cops in the New York Police Department, who became thieves and drug dealers and liars. Even after their convictions, many of the police officers somehow attempted to justify their actions, one going so far as to call herself a "victim."

We have more horror shows for our volunteers to view, including a network news report on a conspiracy among Miami police officers to murder witnesses and sell drugs. The story makes clear that the vast majority of cops regard their dishonest colleagues with revulsion. "I feel such an amount of anger I can't even explain it to you," said one Miami officer.

At the end of these scenarios and stories, the posse members have been exposed to the full range of ethical violations, from poor judgment to serious felonies. They must understand that serving as a law enforcement officer demands both common sense and a knowledge of MCSO rules and regulations, all considered within a solid personal and professional ethical framework.

Other parts of Law and Legal deal with different aspects of the job. For instance, one crucial segment reviews the permitted use of physical force in law enforcement situations. In short, the drill goes like this: The first level of force is simply the officer's physical presence, buttressed by verbal commands. Often enough, that can do the trick. However, let's say the officer orders a suspect to stand still, and the suspect instead runs away or takes a step toward the officer. In that situation, the next level of force can be applied, and that is physical restraint. Physical restraint does not mean hitting the prisoner, but rather, restraining the prisoner. If the prisoner fights or attacks the officer, then more force is applied until the prisoner is subdued. There are specific moves that are not allowed even at this level, such as the carotid artery hold, more popularly known as the choke hold. Posse members are not taught this potentially danger-ous technique, nor are they permitted to use it.

If this force level is neither sufficient nor appropriate, other measures are available. For example, if an unarmed but nonetheless large and furious man is charging a posse member, with the clear intent to fight, the posse member does not have to use each tech-nique, wait for it to fail, and then move on to the next. In other words, force does not escalate by the numbers. Obviously, that could never work in the real world, and would hopelessly handicap and endanger the law enforcement officer. The volunteers are taught to use the force demanded by the situation. In that case, a dose of chemical spray might very well stop the aggressor in his tracks without doing any permanent harm, while giving the volun-teer time to apply mechanical restraints on him. Posse members can only carry and use chemical spray and other weapons, such as a baton or stun gun, after they have taken and passed the class in that weapon, and they must learn the limits placed on that weapon's use. A baton, for example, should almost never be employed to strike above the shoulders. Some weapons, such as blackjacks, nun-chakus, and daggers, are always prohibited.

The ground rules for the application of deadly force—the final level and most serious type of force—are very clear. A law enforce-ment officer can use deadly force when that officer or other people are in immediate danger or face a threat of immediate danger. Deadly force can be used to stop an escaping, armed felon.

Breaking those rules will result in severe civil and even crimi-nal penalties.

Every situation must be viewed on its own, and the decisions taken will be judged according to what was reasonable and responsible in that specific situation. The key is employing the appropriate force for appropriate use. The instructor stresses that just because a situation is escalating in tension and possible danger, that does not mean that it cannot also de-escalate and become less confrontational, less dangerous. The posse member must remain in control of the situation and in control of his emotions and intellect.

Other lessons survey basic radio usage and patrol procedure, i.e., how to communicate with Central Dispatch by radio, how to conduct field interrogations, respond to emergency calls, and so on. Yet another lesson reviews officer safety and survival techniques, from self-defense to body searches to handcuffing to prisoner transport. (This is only a verbal review. Learning and practicing the techniques are reserved for the appropriate classes.) While none of these procedures is complicated or difficult—in fact, the point is to make all physical moves as simple and as natural as possible—they must be performed properly in order to be effective. So, when searching a prisoner, the first rule is to apply handcuffs. But simply having the handcuffs on is not enough. One hand should maintain a hold on the chain while the other hand pats down the subject.

The officer stands behind the prisoner. Never face a prisoner when conducting a search.

One side of the body is checked at a time, and the drill goes like this: Start at the head, work down the hair to the neck, check the collar, shoulder, arm, chest, lower back, all the way from the waistline from the belly button to the middle of the back. Check the front of the pants to the shoes, then the back of the pants, top to bottom, then the crotch. Change hands and repeat the procedure on the other side of the body.

Female prisoners can be just as dangerous as male prisoners, so they must be handled in similar fashion. However, male law enforcement officers must use an extra degree of care when patting down prisoners of the opposite sex. While male officers can check whether a weapon is secreted inside a bra by using two fingers at the center of the breastbone to pull the bra away from the chest, they must take care to let it back down slowly so as not to release it too abruptly. And male officers should not slide their hands inside any woman's legs, up her thighs. As you might guess, that just doesn't look right under almost any circumstances. Instead, the prisoner should be secured and checked, and held until a female officer can complete the search.

Delving back into the less exciting portion of the course, we turn to report writing and note taking. The report from the crime scene will serve as the primary explanation of what happened to all those people, including deputies, supervisors, county attorneys, judges, jurors, and reporters, who were not present at the scene. The basics must be covered, and they are the same on a crime scene as they are at any decent journalism school, summed up in the old newspaper catchphrase: "Who, What, Where, When, How, and Why." Be factual, accurate, objective, complete, concise, clear, and you probably won't go wrong.

From there we move on to courtroom demeanor. This covers how to act if called to court as a witness. How to prepare for courtroom testimony, how to dress and speak, how to respond to a hostile defense lawyer, and so on. Once again, while much of this is just common sense, it doesn't hurt to go over the particulars.

So that's the short version of sixteen hours worth of Law and Legal, a combination of discretion and reason, substance and rationality, values and honor, ethics and courage. The course might not always be overly interesting, and it is definitely not always thrilling, but the lessons are absolutely essential.

Many of the classes are not mandatory, but are rather specific to certain law enforcement situations. That's one of the beauties of the posse. The volunteer not only is able to choose where and when he wants to work, he also chooses which detail he wants to work.

Elective classes teach such diverse subjects as Lake Patrol Rules and Regulations, Environmental Investigation, High Risk Felony Traffic Stops, Street Survival, Gang Enforcement Training, and Narcotics Interdiction.

But of all the electives, one stands out as the most difficult of them all. It demands the most effort and the most dedication. This is it, the nitty gritty, the final and most arduous course, the class for those who want to get as close to having all the skills of a sworn deputy, and then have the opportunity to use them in the field. I'm referring to our QAP Academy, QAP being short for Qualified Armed Posseman—or Possewoman. This is our weapons class, where volunteers learn the proper employment of handguns, as well as develop a certain familiarity with shotguns.

Unlike some other classes, which are shortened versions of the regular classes, the QAP Academy requires *exactly* the same number of hours and demands *exactly* the same requirements and proof of skills and knowledge as the weapons class taken by any Arizona law enforcement officer, whether that officer works for the Maricopa Sheriff's Office or Phoenix's Police Department or Arizona's Department of Public Safety.

The reason is simple. A posse member has many choices. He can restrict his volunteer service to help in the office or in selected field operations, or he can go all the way and work as a second man in a deputy's car. Quite frequently, the posse performs in a support capacity, providing much of the logistical and administrative back-up to our operations. Thus, a posse member does not necessarily have to possess all of a deputy's abilities. The volunteer doesn't necessarily have to be that well trained in traffic control or gang intervention procedures, because he might choose never to place himself in a position to need or use such knowledge.

However, weapons present a whole different reality. Weapons are not like traffic control or gang intervention techniques or even handcuff techniques or hand-to-hand fighting. Weapons present life-or-death situations, no compromise, no second chances. To wear a handgun is to be prepared to pull it and use it, and the consequences can be forever. Given all that, there can be no compromise with each posse member's proficiency. And that proficiency must not only be in aiming and firing that weapon, but also in knowing when to draw it.

Hence, a posse member chooses to work under the same conditions as a sworn deputy, undertaking similar responsibilities and accepting similar dangers. Hence, he chooses to carry a weapon in order to fulfill those responsibilities and safeguard himself, his partner, and any other citizens in the vicinity. Hence, that posse member better know what he is doing, for everyone's sake.

So we have the QAP Academy.

The academy incorporates the requirements for all Arizona law enforcement officers, as determined and defined by the Arizona Police Officers Standards in Training, referred to as AZ POST.

These are far from casual guidelines. In fact, the lesson book utilized by our instructors is no less than ninety-six pages long!

In practice, this translates to sixty hours of weapons training and another twelve hours devoted to weapons retention (how to prevent your weapon from being seized by another person), and FATS, or Firearms Training Systems (an interactive video training system). The academy is conducted over a month of ten-hour weekend days, plus three weekday nights.

Before a volunteer is allowed into the academy, he must have successfully completed the following courses: Law and Legal, Emergency First Care, Traffic Control, Laws of Arrest, Mechanical Restraints, Chemical Agents and Defensive Tactics. All these classes, plus the seventy-two hours associated with the academy, total a formidable 129 hours. Not only does this provide a reasonable amount of training, it also weeds out those who are not truly serious about reaching this level of proficiency and responsibility.

The goals are laid out for the students on the first day, and they are specific and unyielding. They are important enough that I shall list about half of them for you. I shall also go through the other course lessons, so you will really grasp the intensity and depth of this course.

So, to begin at the beginning, with the course goals, the posse member will be able, by the end of the course, to:

1. Demonstrate the basic fundamentals of marksmanship—stance, grip, sight alignment, sight picture, trigger control, and follow-through.
2. Demonstrate the following shooting positions—standing, kneeling, strong and weak-side barricade, prone, and close quarters.
3. Demonstrate the proper use of a flashlight during nighttime firing sequences.
4. Demonstrate the ability to follow the range safety rules.
5. Demonstrate the ability to safely manipulate the weapon with the finger straight along the frame.
6. Demonstrate the ability to unload, make safe, and clean a duty revolver.

7. Identify the fifteen major components of a semiautomatic weapon.
8. Demonstrate the proper way to disassemble and assemble the semiautomatic pistol and magazine.
9. Demonstrate the proper clearing techniques for the four types of malfunctions.
10. Demonstrate the ability to clear a Class III malfunction, and fire one round within the four ring in nine seconds or less from the seven-yard line.
11. Demonstrate the two proper methods of reloading under tactical and stress situations.
12. Demonstrate the ability to safely load and unload department-issue shotguns.
13. Demonstrate marksmanship with a handgun by scoring a minimum of 210 points out of 250 points on the AZ POST qualification course.
14. Demonstrate night marksmanship with a handgun by scoring a minimum of 210 points out of 250 points on the AZ POST qualification course.
15. Demonstrate marksmanship with a shotgun on the approved seven-round course for a pass/fail score.
16. Demonstrate the ability to safely and effectively fire a handgun in the following combat conditions—timed, multiple targets and using various positions.

In addition, a written exam must be passed with a 70 percent score, and various tests taken during FATS and weapons retention must be successfully completed.

During the sixty hours, each posse member will fire fifteen hundred rounds of practice ammo, one hundred rounds of factory ammo, twenty rounds of birdshot, fifteen rounds of twelve-gauge 00 buck, and six rounds of twelve-gauge rifled slugs. Every student needs to have a duty gun belt, holster, eye and ear protection, knee pads, and, of course, his handgun. Each posse member supplies his own handgun, and is allowed to choose from a list of authorized manufacturers and calibers, semiautomatic and revolver. (The vast majority of police officers select semiautomatic weapons, citing superior trigger control and ergonomic grip angle, higher round and faster reloading capacity, and greater mechanical reliability.)

From the start, safety is stressed and stressed again. The four basic rules of firearms safety are: First, all firearms are loaded; second, do not point a firearm at anything you are not willing to destroy; third, keep your finger straight along the frame until you are on target and have decided to fire; and fourth and last, be sure of your target and beyond. They are hammered home throughout the course.

These are far from the only safety rules, which range from all handguns remaining in the holster until the student is instructed otherwise; all handguns are always pointed down-range; do not move off the firing line until ordered to do so; whenever handling a weapon that has been out of the student's control, even if only for a moment, immediately verify the condition of the weapon; all loading and unloading will be done on line, downrange, unless otherwise directed by an instructor, and so on.

The instructors also discuss firearms safety away from the range, particularly at home.

One way we ensure safety is to have, at a minimum, one instructor to every five or six students. Often we do better than that, and have twenty or more instructors show up to teach sixty or sixty-five students. During several aspects of the course, such as night shooting exercises, which obviously hold more uncertainties, and thus more danger, we strictly operate on the basis of an instructor for each student.

Next on the agenda, the instructors review the fundamentals of marksmanship, covering the stance, the grip, the sight alignment, and trigger control. The students then practice unholstering, aiming, and firing without ammunition, over and over again. This training exercise is known as "dry fire," and is critical to developing proper firearms technique, based on the recognition that a minimum of thirty-five hundred repetitions of the same movement is required for muscle memory to take hold and the action to be reasonably smooth and automatic. The students are urged to dry-fire their weapons each night for at least ten minutes.

The academy then calls for teaching correct clearing and cleaning techniques, culminating in students assembling and reassembling their weapons and magazines, identifying components and proper lubrication points, a minimum of three times.

The students are also shown how to inspect and care for ammunition.

At this stage, the progression should be evident, as the students move from safety rules to understanding the fundamentals of marksmanship to learning the proper care of the weapon.

The lesson plan moves on to the loading, unloading, and reloading of the handgun. Repeating each aspect of weapon care and use reinforces each lesson, and so it is with loading and unloading procedures. Every step is crucial, even something as deceptively simple and apparently benign as inserting or removing a magazine into a semiautomatic. The proof is found in the reality that more accidental discharges occur during the administrative (or regular, unhurried) handling of a weapon than during a tactical (or combat scenario) handling.

The shotgun follows on the schedule, and its application in law enforcement is explained. Capable of firing spreads of buckshot as well as heavy, powerful slugs, the twelve-gauge shotgun's advantages and disadvantages are revealed. Interestingly, the pluses and minuses are often mirrors of each other. For instance, the wide spread of the 00 buck pellets can help the officer control a crowd, but it can also injure innocent bystanders. The shotgun is serious business, and every posse member who is authorized to carry it must not only know how to load, unload, and fire it, but also must be fully cognizant of its destructive abilities.

On another topic, tactical issues are taught. Each volunteer must be aware of and be able to exploit the advantages of cover and concealment. Cover refers to anything that provides protection, and the posse member must know how to find and utilize cover. Concealment is for hiding, and has its own value. At the same time, the posse member learns about barricade shooting. This involves lessons of cover and concealment, as the students practice aiming and firing from kneeling and prone positions, including rolling over, from under and around barriers.

Multiple targets are also reviewed, and the underlying tip is straightforward: Shoot the closest target first. Though guns are seen as the overwhelming weapon, the raw fact is that if you are facing an individual armed with a knife and standing twenty-five feet away, he can most probably reach and attack you before you can draw your handgun from its holster.

The difficulties of night shooting are explained, from the thirty minutes required for the eyes to adjust to darkness to the eyes' reliance on peripheral vision in low light to the damage alcohol, cigarettes, fatigue, and other factors can have on night vision. Adaptation techniques are discussed, from keeping those orbs moving to refresh blood flow to the eyes to not staring at targets, to remembering that the tendency is to shoot low at short distances and shoot high at longer distances.

These hints take on added significance when one realizes that 60 percent of all gunfights involving police across the country happen in low-light situations. (Other key, related statistics: Most gunfights occur at a distance of twenty feet or closer, last an average of three seconds during which three rounds are fired, and 75 percent of the time the felon shoots first. Put those statistics together—the speed, the intensity, the uncertainty of the battle—and consider how frightening that moment can be, and how important it is to be trained to react instantly and effectively.)

In conjunction with this part of the course, the three prime flashlight techniques are rehearsed and drilled.

An absolutely vital aspect of the QAP Academy deals with mental preparation, and instructors expend considerable energy in highlighting these messages. The FBI studied deadly confrontations to determine those emotional and intellectual attributes that are key to surviving such incidents, and concluded that the following traits were indispensable:

1. Self-confidence in performance

2. Training

3. Effectiveness in combat (the ability to visualize victory)

4. Decisiveness

5. Perseverance under stress

The instructors repeat, as if a mantra, a two-word phrase that is the bottom line to surviving any fight: Never quit. Never quit fighting. Never quit surviving. Never quit living. Never quit. Never quit.

Anecdotal evidence has proved that a surprisingly effective tool in preparing to survive is application of the "What If" stratagem. Run through various possibilities and scenarios—two armed men jump you as you walk down the street, another car attempts to run you off the road, a mugger attacks you from behind, et cetera—and think about how you would react and win. See yourself fighting and winning, no matter what.

The students watch a video produced by the FBI dissecting a firefight that occurred between its agents and a pair of vicious criminals in Miami in 1986, a firefight that went horrifically wrong and resulted in the death of two feds. The video spares no details, and is meant to leave the viewer with no doubts about what it takes to respond quickly and efficiently and win. (In fact, videos are used throughout the course, illustrating a variety of classroom lessons.)

Posse members are also taught to be aware of their environs at all times, using a widely employed, color-coded system. This system is so simple and sensible that everyone, posse member or not, should give a moment to consider incorporating its lessons in daily life.

Condition white refers to a condition of complete relaxation, appropriate only when you are at home, safely locked in. Condition yellow means "relaxed alert," a general awareness that the world is not necessarily a safe place, though no specific threat menaces at that moment. Condition orange designates a specific potential threat, prompting you to consider tactical actions and legal ramifications. Condition red means that the fight is on.

Lastly and not inevitably, condition black spells panic. While the other conditions are a logical and sometimes inescapable progression, condition black is not, and can be avoided with training and forethought.

Further mental conditioning is gained through the FATS drill. A projection television screen fills up one wall, and various scenarios are played out before the student, scenarios that require the student to discern the level of potential threat and decide what action to take, and whether or not to use deadly force. The posse member is armed with a handgun that is keyed by laser to the screen. Pulling the gun's trigger causes the screen to record where the bullets hit, and mark the student's reaction time. Afterward, the student explains his reasoning, and the instructor evaluates.

Then there is the weapons retention segment of the course, which teaches techniques for responding to any attempt to take away the posse member's handgun. The techniques are elementary and sure, quickly learned and utilized.

The tests are conducted at the end of the academy session. If the posse member fails any part of the test, then he fails the entire test.

The posse member who passes all the tests cannot rest on his laurels. Same as any sworn deputy, every posse member must periodically requalify to ensure that his skills do not deteriorate.

After successfully completing the QAP Academy, the posse members are rewarded with a graduation ceremony, during which we review their accomplishments. After all they have given to the Sheriff's Office, and all they are going to give, they have earned this moment gathering applause and cheers from their families and friends.

As you can see through this brief review of just a handful of posse classes, this is no lackadaisical outfit. Standards are high, with old classes constantly being updated and new classes continually inserted into the curriculum. Posse members can take pride in their knowledge and skills, confident that they are capable of making a real contribution to the department in many different areas.

In many ways, having a posse is an all-or-nothing proposition. Volunteers need constant motivation to keep them volunteering. Everyone in the posse came to the posse already spoken for, to one extent or another, with days filled with work, family, obligations, hobbies, and the other realities that constitute real life. Finding the time to train and serve is not easy, and invariably involves sacrifice. To maintain the enthusiasm of so many people, from employees to volunteers to instructors, requires ceaseless planning and effectual implementation of those plans.

The posse existed before I was elected sheriff, but it was a mere shadow of the organization it has become. It is continuing to grow as more volunteers sign up. The bottom line is that the posse attracts increasing numbers of men and women because the public has seen that the posse works. It works in Maricopa County. Given the right motivation, preparation, and personnel, it could work where you live, too.

CHAPTER ELEVEN

Possibilities and Opportunities

The Sheriff's Office has an array of formidable weapons at its disposal: planes, boats, cars, technical contraptions, mechanical gadgets, legal machinations, psychological stratagems, on and on. But of all law enforcement weapons, the most formidable, the most effective, the absolute best, remains, as always, our law enforcement personnel.

The deputies serve as our front line, always ready, always willing, always reliable. But they are also precious few in number, even fewer now with the Board of Supervisor's substantial budget cuts. So we need the help of others, starting with the reserves. The reserves are volunteers who have undergone the full course of law enforcement training and are certified by the state to work as fully authorized deputies. When they are working, reserves are no different than deputies, possessing the same powers to investigate and arrest, able to operate on their own, without any direct supervision. In fact, they can supervise posse members, same as deputies.

We have proved the posse works, the tents work — Reserves are not compensated. Instead, they work for free, same as posse members. They have other jobs, and study to be part of the Sheriff's

Office on the weekends and at night. Most complete the rigorous training in about one year, sacrificing a lot to gain reserve status. About one hundred men and women are currently members of our reserve force. Reserves have demonstrated their value time and time again, and I hope to recruit more citizens to join their ranks.

Finally, of course, there is the posse, and we have talked a lot about what the posse does, and how it is organized. As you can see, this office has taken the posse idea pretty far, definitely a lot farther than any other sheriff or police department in the country has dared to go. And in going so far and daring so much, we have proved that the posse idea works.

But that's not the end of it. That's not the best we can do. That's not as far as we can go to accomplish all that we hope to accomplish.

The posse currently stands at about twenty-five hundred members, and we're closing in on one thousand of those having successfully completed the QAP Academy. Assuming I get reelected to another term, I'd like to see five thousand citizens in the posse, with two thousand of them armed. I think we can and will accomplish that.

But that's just the opening gambit in our continuing war on crime. I have some plans and ideas that will increase our ability to bring together all our possible resources in fighting crime. As you might expect, the posse figures prominently in these plans.

Let's consider just one proposal, after I first supply some background information: We have established a Sheriff's Posse Foundation, organized to offset some of the expenses that our posse members incur, especially gasoline, as they drive around the county on behalf of the department. (Don't forget, Maricopa County is as large as the state of New Jersey.)

The foundation hasn't raised very much money, though that has been changing lately with the phenomenon of the pink boxer shorts. (If you haven't heard about the boxers, I'll go into the whole affair in detail a bit later. For now, let it suffice to say that we had to change the boxers we distributed to the inmates in the jails from white to pink. The color caught the public imagination, and a market was created. The posse produced and sold slightly modified, slightly upgraded versions of the boxers to an eager population, and sold a lot of them.)

In any event, the foundation is starting to amass some funds. Let us assume, however, that the foundation, whether through private or corporate fund-raising measures, can build its kitty to a couple of million dollars. Instead of simply reimbursing the members for their fuel, the posse could purchase a number of properly outfitted cars. The posse could purchase other useful equipment.

But cars and equipment are only the tip of the iceberg, because the real innovation starts when the posse has the gear it needs in place. The real innovation, the real revolution in law enforcement, occurs when *the posse uses its funds to pay off-duty deputies to direct the posse on patrol.*

Follow my logic. Deputies are essentially on duty twenty-four hours a day. They never lose their authority, in uniform or out, whether investigating a case or out to dinner with friends. If an off-duty deputy witnesses a crime taking place and he makes an arrest, that is not a citizen's arrest. He's still a cop, and that is a *bona fide* law enforcement arrest.

So a deputy is a deputy is a deputy, no matter what. That is why shopping centers and stores and special events hire sheriff's deputies and Phoenix cops and law enforcement officers across America to guard their businesses, and patrol their byways, and direct their traffic. And the deputies usually perform this off-duty work in uniform, which is perfectly legal. But again, even though they are working for a private company (for which they ordinarily earn something in the neighborhood of twenty dollars an hour), the deputies remain fully authorized and empowered law enforcement officers.

Given all that, why can't the posse foundation hire the deputies, when they have finished their regular tours and are off duty, and have them direct posse operations? Why not, indeed?

Let's take this step-by-step. Step one: The posse members are employees of the office—noncompensated, to be sure, but employees nonetheless. Step two: The posse can work only when under the direct supervision of a sworn deputy. Step three: The deputies, even off duty, remain under my authority and control. Step four: Combine these forces, deputies and posse, both still under my command, give them their marching orders, and unleash them on the streets.

Imagine another ten or twenty or fifty deputies working for the department instead of a department store, managing the activities of one hundred or five hundred posse members, night in, night out, patrolling and protecting and serving. And let me stress again, because the deputies are working off duty, on their own time, my department will not be shortchanged in any form, neither in manpower nor effort. This will only prove to be an augmentation of our endeavors, a magnification of our policing abilities.

Allow me to anticipate a possible question: This would not set up some sort of backdoor police force or second department. The deputies and the posse would operate as they do now, in support of and in conjunction with the efforts of the Maricopa County Sheriff's Office.

One final reminder, so there is no mistake. All those law enforcement officers, deputies, reserves, and posse, paid and non-compensated, are still responsible to me. I am responsible to the people, to ensure the public's safety and security. Why not call on all those resources to do the best job we can, to serve the people as capably and as energetically as possible?

Of course, a host of details waits to be ironed out, assuming the foundation can one day afford to (and, as an independent foundation, chooses to) implement my plan. Perhaps the lawyers would find some legal questions that we would have to resolve. Perhaps some of the off-duty deputies' investigative range would be restricted. Perhaps we would have to make some adjustments in some unforeseen ways.

Okay. No problem. We can do the research, we can resolve the questions, we can make whatever adjustments must be made.

The fine points can be worked out, because the basic idea has obvious merit and incredible potential. If we are to win this war against crime, we must pull out all the stops, employ all our resources, and develop new ones. That applies in Maricopa County, Arizona, as well as every other city and county in this country.

The posse, as it is constituted under my direction and jurisdiction, is not a blanket solution for every city and town. Every community need not and probably should not exactly copy the Maricopa County posse model. The solution must be modified and adapted for each circumstance, each location.

While some counties have posse units, raised by the sheriff, most cities have auxiliary units, controlled by the police commissioner. Most auxiliary police do not have the authority that posse members have, because a police commissioner, usually appointed by the mayor or city council, retains very different powers and responsibilities than a sheriff elected by the voters. Thus, my posse members have broad police powers when acting in the proper capacity, while auxiliary officers generally act as civilians; i.e., if they make an arrest, it's a citizen's arrest.

Nonetheless, this is not to denigrate the efforts and effectiveness of auxiliary officers. And if the people and their representatives so resolve, the laws can be changed to increase the capabilities of these volunteers, to whatever degree is deemed desirable. In other words, a modified version of the posse, designed specifically for New York City, could certainly work there, just as the Arizona model could be successful in many cities and counties throughout the country. When you get right down to it, there's not much difference between patrolling Eighth Avenue in Manhattan and patrolling the desert outside Wickenberg, and that's from a cop who has worked the streets of Washington, D.C., Istanbul, Las Vegas, and Buenos Aires.

I hear it now. The posse in the Big Apple? Are you crazy? Hey, listen; walk down the street in New York, and count the number of private security types you see hanging out in every doorway, hardly trained, poorly educated, barely supervised. Is it crazy to think about substituting that ridiculous, private security mob with an organized, disciplined, regulated, controlled posse?

Well?

You know, so many places could really use the help. Los Angeles County, for instance—perfect site. Though most people don't know it, L.A. County already has a posse, but it's only formed as a search and rescue unit. It could easily be expanded.

Citizens' groups and politicians and sheriff and police departments from across the country write and phone my office every week, requesting information on how to organize their own posses. That doesn't necessarily mean that any posses will actually be formed.

In fact, I don't have much hope that many more posses will be set up, despite the letters and phone calls. Look, every sheriff and police commissioner has his own set of politicians and bureaucrats whom he has to deal with, fight with, live with. And what do most politicians and bureaucrats care about, first and foremost? They worry about risk. They care about liability. It's always "you can't do this, you can't do that, because we might get sued, we might be embarrassed." And that means we might lose our jobs, and our salaries and benefits and perks and privileges.

That's why we have a crime problem, because nobody wants to take a chance. Oh, say the right things, stand up straight and act tough, but don't actually *do* anything. Play it safe. Nothing will get better for the people, but nobody, meaning me, will get hurt.

I sure as hell have seen it in my own patch. For three years, virtually no Maricopa County officials have wanted to be part of what I'm doing, and you don't have to be a brilliant political analyst to figure out why. Bottom line: There's a better percentage in waiting for me to go down the tubes than for getting out front. What happens if a posse man shoots somebody? What happens if the tents fall down? What happens if the green bologna turns purple?

Even when politicos and civil servants and administrators aren't cowering in fear for their careers, even when they're willing to do something, it's usually something negative, something petty and destructive. Ego and jealousy, always powerful motivators, are especially potent in the self-centered, self-important, vainglorious political arena.

There is nothing inherently dishonorable about working in politics. Indeed, the profession should not only be honorable but also honored, for politics is all about managing the people's business, the business of serving society, of building society, of bettering society. However, because the stakes are so high, and so are the personal and professional rewards, politics frequently gives rise to corruption, and cowardice, and despair.

That's some of what I've learned during my term as sheriff—that's what I've seen and experienced, particularly when dealing with the more controversial programs such as the posse. Despite all the risks and backstabbing and jealousy, we shall keep building the posse, keep finding new ways to make it more efficient and productive.

The posse works in Maricopa County. Given the right motivation, preparation, and personnel, it could work where you live, too. Whether the posse will get that chance in other communities is far from certain. I guarantee that if the people demand its establishment, you will be seeing more posses across America. You'll also be seeing safer streets.

PART III

The Drug Wars

CHAPTER TWELVE

The Problem Only Gets Worse

Almost 70 percent of inmates doing time in America's prisons and jails have been convicted of violating drug laws or because of drug-related crimes. Drugs are not only illegal by themselves, they also account for an overall exponential growth in all criminal activity. Viewing narcotics as the center of a monstrous tornado, we know that it is not just the middle of the funnel that is so destructive, but the entire storm. Around the edges of the tornado, we see people steal, and even murder strangers, business associates, family, to get money to pay for drugs. Then, having attained the object of their desire, the evil is not done, for the very characteristics of some drugs cause men and women to become paranoid, confused, violent, psychotic.

Not long ago, you probably heard about the Arizona man who ingested crystal meth, a particularly dangerous drug, who calmly picked up his son, got in his car, drove some distance, and then, without warning, reached over and chopped off his son's head. Such a case of unprovoked, unreasoning violence is far from an isolated instance.

And then there is the other price that so many caught in this black whirl eventually pay. This is

A young Joe Arpaio, left, with fellow agents and seized drugs

the legal but perhaps even more pathetic cost, the cost of ruined lives, shattered families, wasted opportunities.

Drugs are everywhere, and so is the utter devastation they so frequently leave in their wake.

As a result of their pervasive reach into every dark area of American life, drugs require a few pages devoted solely to their attention.

Fortuitously, I have a special expertise in this area.

As we all know, and have known for years, the war on drugs is not going well. The Pentagon spends one billion dollars each year on drug interdiction. But that is just a drop in the bucket, one isolated if heralded aspect of our whole drug-fighting apparatus. The entire U.S. justice system spends more than twenty billion dollars every year on the various agencies and bureaus and departments that comprise the colossal, fantastic machine that generates libraries of papers and reams of policies, and implements hundreds of programs and schemes. And regardless of the direction or success of all the planning and effort, the money just keeps pouring into the machine and out again, devouring countless billions of taxpayer dollars.

And what has it all added up to?

We've all heard the figures, the endless figures, as politicians trumpet their "victories," sounding more and more like government spokesmen from the Vietnam War trying to prove that we were winning by announcing body counts. Still, I'd like to mention a few statistics, which provide a broad glimpse of where we really stand.

On the penal side: More than 330,000 Americans are imprisoned for violating drug laws. Two to three times that number are on parole or probation for the same reason. Because of the drug war, the United States has the highest proportion of incarcerated citizens in the Western world.

In one year, the FBI reported that 535,000 Americans were arrested for the possession, sale, or manufacture of marijuana.

On the other side: Law enforcement officials inevitably and annually claim that they stop somewhere on the order of a mere

10 percent of all drugs entering the country. Of course, this is a purely hypothetical assertion. After all, if we actually knew how much contraband was getting in, we'd obviously know how it was getting in, and where it was getting in, and we'd have a much better idea of how to stop it.

The drug lords earn an estimated fifty to sixty billion dollars a year.

Not quite two years ago, *Rolling Stone* magazine published a special issue devoted to the entire question of drugs. Though its writers and editors advocated the legalization of drugs, a stance I am firmly opposed to and which I shall explain a little later on, the issue was most interesting and informative. Interspersed through the several articles strung together were examples of the cost of our failed policy. I'd like to quote from a few of those examples to show the national disgrace and horror of where we stand on drugs:

From Portland, Maine: "Heroin, sold in heat-sealed Seal-a-Meal bags, is going for forty to fifty dollars for what police say is one-tenth of a gram. Skunk marijuana is easily found at one to two dollars a joint, two hundred dollars and up for an ounce. Blotter-sheet LSD is selling for three to five dollars a hit. Fly Agaric mushrooms, grown in Ellsworth and Bar Harbor, can be bought for three to five dollars for three to five stems. Colombia cocaine shipped from Lawrence, Massachusetts, sells for seventy-five to one hundred dollars a gram."

From Eugene, Oregon: "Possession of less than one ounce of marijuana—the state's fourth largest cash crop—is treated as a misdemeanor. Supplies are constant; so are prices at thirty to fifty dollars for one-eighth of an ounce. Black-tar heroin prices have dropped significantly in the past two years, from sixty to thirty dollars a gram, as the supply has increased. Methamphetamine is sold for as low as fifteen dollars a gram. LSD, called fry, is selling for three to five dollars a hit. Cocaine, say police sources, is in good supply at one hundred dollars a gram."

Birmingham, Alabama: "Local police say that crack has maintained an extremely high profile here. Dime-crack rock and twenty-cent crack, which sells for ten and twenty dollars, is widely available throughout the city. An 'eightball' of crack, an eighth of an ounce, sells for one hundred fifty to two hundred dollars. Marijuana, much of which is grown indoors, remains steadily available for forty to fifty dollars an ounce. Primos— marijuana joints or Blunts mixed with crumbled pieces of crack—are becoming popular. Blotter-sheet LSD bearing the image of Mickey Mouse sells for five dollars a hit. Methamphetamine shipped from California is easily found."

Salt Lake City, Utah: "Marijuana, half of which is grown in state, is in abundant supply. Prices have risen to twenty-five to forty dollars for an eighth of an ounce. Relatively weak blotter-sheet LSD and mushrooms can be found at some coffee shops. Methamphetamine, cocaine, and LSD are available at particular clubs. Cocaine goes for twenty to thirty dollars for one-quarter of a gram. According to local police, nearly 75 percent of all drug cases in the last year involved cocaine. Methamphetamine goes for about twenty-five dollars for a quarter gram. Brown-tar heroin sells for fifty dollars a chip."

The drug war is a failure. We can all agree with that.

What we probably all don't agree on is the predetermination of this failure. I say—I *know*—that the drug war could be vastly more effective and successful. I *know* that the major goals of the drug war could be attained. I *know* that the drug war could be won.

This is not a conclusion I come to casually. I base my beliefs on my three plus decades' experience fighting drugs, at home and abroad. I've pretty much seen it all, from the dirtiest dealings on the street to the vastly more sophisticated, though no less dirty, thievery and betrayals, and all-around vice and corruption found at the highest levels of privilege and power. I've seen it spread, and I've seen it defeated.

I'm going to call upon what I've seen, and what I've discovered in the course of my law enforcement career. In this way, I'll show you what has been accomplished, and what can be accomplished in the future, given the right motivation, training, and support.

As you know by now, this is not an autobiography. I made a conscious decision not to focus exclusively on my life and career.

Sure, after all these years I have compiled a long catalog of exciting war stories, with desperate shoot-outs, international conspiracies, and narrow escapes. But the point of this book was and remains how we can fight crime, how we make this a prouder, happier, better country in which to live. At this stage, to further this objective, it is appropriate and useful to briefly run through some of those war stories.

So this is how I fought crime. And these are some of the lessons I've learned.

CHAPTER THIRTEEN

Lessons Learned

S o this is what happens when a plan goes wrong.

It wasn't a complicated deal as far as these deals were concerned. I was posing as the owner of a Pittsburgh pizza joint, who sold "pizza over the counter and marijuana under the counter," to quote a man known as "Big Joe." Big Joe and his buddy, "Little Joe," were happy to supply the Pittsburgh restaurateur with forty-five pounds of pot for four thousand dollars cash, of course.

Like I said, nothing complicated.

I met the boys in a Georgetown eatery where they had established something of a reputation in the Washington, D.C., drug community. The boys were aged twenty-one and twenty. The younger man—Little Joe—was the son of a fairly prominent Virginia public official.

One of my informants introduced us, and I played the role of the eager buyer. I responded, as my newfound pals would expect an out-of-town wholesaler to respond, with enthusiasm. We arranged to exchange the merchandise for the money.

Joe Arpaio, as a child, with his father

Done it a thousand times before.

I was the agent in charge of the Washington, D.C., office of the Bureau of Narcotics. It was 1968, and I had worked in a lot of cities, and a lot of countries, contending with a crew of desperate characters. These guys were nothing—small-time, small fry, maybe one step above amateurs.

So I drove up in a shiny red Cadillac (which we had seized from a drug dealer, and used to present the right front), and picked up both Joes one dark May night. I told them I had brought their money, four grand cached in a paper bag locked in the trunk, so they were happy. I forgot to mention that along with the dough I had stashed a fellow agent in that big trunk. I also forgot to mention that a second car of agents was following us.

We cruised into Virginia. It was nearing 2 A.M. The road was deserted.

Business as usual.

The Joes told me a "man driving a milk truck" had the dope, and we were meeting up with him at a lookout point on the George Washington Parkway just below Dolly Madison Boulevard.

Okay.

When we reached the spot, nobody was there, no milk truck, no milkman. Little Joe got out of the car, and walked to a trash can to see if the supplier had left a message. Little Joe returned with directions to drive toward the town of Vienna.

Okay. Drug deals aren't planned in a lawyer's office. (Well, *most* drug deals aren't planned in a lawyer's office.) Schedules aren't fixed. Things change. Problems arise; people adapt.

We drove on. We left the main road, and turned onto a dirt path, which was some unsuspecting soul's lonely driveway. I spotted my backup off to the side of the road, sitting in a car, angling in to park close by.

The Joes told me to stop the car. The driveway was very isolated, very dark, and very quiet.

I had seen this movie before, and it was not a comedy.

I said I was tired of this, and was heading back to Washington. However, before I could turn the car around, both Joes pulled out handguns, pointed them at me, and announced that they wanted the money. They notified me there was no marijuana. Surprise!

Big Joe demanded the keys so he could get the paper bag and the loot out of the trunk. Little Joe stuck the gun into the back of my neck. I handed Big Joe the keys, and he opened his door and stepped out. I knew I couldn't let him open that trunk. The agent hiding there wouldn't have a chance.

Little Joe ordered me to place my hands on the steering wheel. His gun was starting to make a dent in my neck. It was time to act.

I told him I was a federal agent, and used my best command voice to order him to hand over his weapon and tell Big Joe to come back. My words caused Little Joe to pause and consider. That was all the opening I needed. I had no intention of waiting for his decision, but whirled around and reached for the gun. I grabbed it, but Little Joe managed to hold on. We struggled for several moments, and then I lost my grip.

A bullet passed by my head and smashed through the windshield as I lunged for the door handle, and then more bullets ripped into my seat. I managed to push the door open, and as I fell out of the car and on my knees, I heard several more shots whistle past.

As I pulled my Smith & Wesson .38 with the two-inch barrel from my inside jacket pocket, I quickly calculated that Little Joe's pistol was empty. I turned toward the rear of the Caddy, because my first concern was for my fellow agent still locked in the trunk. Big Joe was ready. His handgun was aimed at me, and he pulled the trigger.

Nothing happened; the gun misfired. That didn't mean the weapon would necessarily continue to misfire.

I had definitely had enough of this. It's personal when they start shooting point-blank at you, whether it's at the back of your head or the front.

I returned fire before Big Joe could clear his gun and start banging away again. I shot at Big Joe six times and missed. In my defense, I was to the side of the trunk, and Big Joe was behind it, and I had to shoot high to make certain I didn't strike the car and hit my fellow agent.

Of course, I never was the best shot, as I might have previously mentioned.

Bang, bang, bang, bang, bang, bang. I should have hit the son of a bitch.

Six shots and I was done. I was out of bullets.

Where the hell was my backup? Where the hell was that second car? They had to have heard those shots.

I didn't drop my gun. I didn't put it down, because even though I knew I was essentially unarmed, I could see that the bad guys didn't know it. So I kept pointing my two-incher at the bad guys, and returned to that command voice.

Surrender, I severely counseled. You are surrounded. Other agents have encircled the area. You are surrounded. Surrender. Give up.

I kept talking because as long as somebody talks, and somebody listens, nobody shoots. It's really true. Most people have to stop and think before they can pull the trigger and fire. The two actions seem to be incompatible. (I'll leave it to you to consider whatever lesson might be lurking there.)

The pair of Joes hesitated. Mexican standoff. Bluff and counterbluff.

The agent in the trunk, hearing me shout that the scene was surrounded by feds, started to yell.

I kept talking. Sometimes the Joes threatened to kill the agent still locked in the trunk, sometimes they threatened to kill me. I just kept talking. I talked for twenty long minutes.

Eventually, the Joes gave up. They didn't have the stomach to keep going, to slug it out to the death. They were more scared idiots than hardcore killers, and they must have figured they had no way out, no guaranteed, clean way out, unless they wanted to keep shooting it out, and maybe get themselves killed—assuming I had bullets, of course.

I took their guns, handcuffed them, and got my buddy out of the Caddy's trunk. The poor guy was so angry at what happened, angry at the two Joes, angry at the missing backup, just plain angry, that he fired two shots into the air in a furious attempt to alert the backup.

Astonishingly, after everything that had already occurred, this worked. The agents arrived a few moments later, in a hurry.

(I found out afterward that the agents in the backup vehicle had inexplicably rolled up their windows, and were listening to the radio, which explained how they had managed to miss the entire shoot-out. Later in his career, one of those agents would become fairly well known as the head of the New York office. When he retired and wrote his memoirs, I seem to recall that he somehow omitted this incident from the tome.)

When examining the car the next day, I discovered just how close I had come to my final showdown. The red Cadillac punctured by bullet holes, through the windshield, the dashboard, all over. But one was especially interesting. You see, the Caddy was equipped with every luxury extra its former owner could buy, and that included a pull-down tray attached to the back of the front seats, similar to those found in an airplane. The trays were constructed of steel, apparently heavy-duty steel, because I found serious dents in the tray where bullets had apparently struck and been deflected. Without that tray, those bullets would have ripped through the seat, and struck me right in the back.

God, I loved that car.

The Joes were convicted of assaulting a federal agent. Each received a five-year sentence.

I received a nice letter of commendation from U.S. Attorney General Ramsey Clark, and a five hundred dollar cash award.

Case closed. Next.

I always wanted to be a cop. I'm not exactly sure what first prompted this wish, but that desire was always there, as far back as I can remember.

I was born on Flag Day, June 14, 1932, in Springfield, Massachusetts, to first generation Americans from Naples, Italy. My mother died in childbirth, and my father, busy day and night building a grocery store into two sizable stores, required help in raising me. I bounced from family to family until my father remarried when I was twelve.

I graduated from high school, turned eighteen, and joined the U.S. Army as the Korean War exploded—all on the same day.

After three years in the military, where I reached the rank of sergeant, I got out and set about getting my career under way. I longed to be a G-man, an FBI agent, and took whatever civil service exams the federal government was offering. At the time, that included tests for the Border Patrol and the Metropolitan Police Department in Washington, D.C.

I joined the Metropolitan Police Department in 1954. I was gung ho, to put it mildly, same as most young rookie cops, proud of that new badge, and eager to show my stuff. I walked a beat for over three years, a tough beat in a poor, black neighborhood. I learned a lot on that beat, some of the most important lessons of my entire career. I learned that the best police officers are not distant centurions, separate and removed from the community, watching for the bad guys from the warmth and security of a patrol car, suspicious of everyone and cynical about everything.

No, the best police officers know the good guys at least as well as the bad. The best police officers know that the overwhelming majority of men and women are decent, law-abiding folk, trying to do the best they can for themselves and their families. They not only appreciate the efforts of law enforcement, they want to support those efforts in any manner they can.

Unfortunately, a few police departments in urban areas have taken on the appearance of an occupying army in unfriendly, foreign environs, and have lost the confidence and trust of the citizens they are serving. Without that confidence and trust, a cop's job is infinitely more difficult and dangerous.

Back in 1954, the public's confidence and trust in the police was a given. Perhaps in looking back, we all tend to wax nostalgic, remembering the good and forgetting the bad. Perhaps the reality wasn't as cut-and-dried as I recall. Perhaps. But even if that is so, the street—almost any street—was a lot friendlier for the cop in 1954 than it is now.

I soon became a familiar face to the shopkeepers and residents of my beat, and they knew they could rely on me.

Of course, I'm not claiming that *everyone* was thrilled with the police. No way. Not for nothing was I involved in scrap after scrap, fight after fight. Not for nothing, as I mentioned much earlier, did I earn the title of most assaulted D.C. cop in 1957. In a tough neighborhood, part of walking the beat is establishing *presence*, proving who's boss on the street. It isn't sophisticated, it isn't taught at universities, but it is real.

Example: My partner, a trainee, even younger than my own twenty-five years, and I spotted a guy who appeared to be intoxicated. Public drunkenness being a crime, and one that was regarded with scant tolerance in those days, we approached. The brother of the inebriated man was also present, and he didn't take kindly to our displeasure with his brother's condition. In fact, they were both exhibiting "disorderly conduct," as the expression goes. Words quickly escalated, and then one brother jumped me, and a brawl ensued. I wound up in the hospital with head injuries. We gave as good as we got, and both brothers made their own trip to the emergency room, on their way to being booked.

But that wasn't the whole story. While we were fighting, a crowd quickly formed. Soon more than one hundred people had gathered to watch the proceedings. As usual with a crowd, emotions ran high and varied, some people cheering the brothers on, some mumbling unhappily, and others just standing quietly by, plainly upset by this unpleasantness.

One bystander was violently distressed, and urged the others to attack us. His exact words, repeated over and over, were "Kill the cop, kill the cop!"

The crowd didn't respond to his appeals. However, I did. He was also arrested, and charged and convicted of trying to incite a riot.

No backing down, not if you're facing a couple of belligerent drunks, or a hundred uncertain citizens. No backing down—that's the key.

I lived with my partner in the Woodner Hotel, which was a pretty nice apartment/hotel at the time. We were able to swing it by sharing the rooms, and the expenses.

My partner introduced me to Ava. Marrying Ava was both the luckiest and the smartest move I made in my life. You'll understand why, at least in part, soon enough.

My career took an unexpected detour on the occasion of President Dwight Eisenhower's second inauguration in 1956. A parade always begins the day, with bands and drill teams and marching units coming to Washington from around the country. I was accorded the honor of carrying the flag, and leading off the inaugural parade down Pennsylvania Avenue.

In the course of the parade, I met the sheriff of Clark County, Nevada, which includes Las Vegas. The sheriff had brought a mounted contingent from his department to participate in the parade. He took a liking to me, and urged me to leave Washington, and come out West. (His department wasn't hiring at that moment, but he was happy to introduce me to his counterparts at the Las Vegas Police Department.) It wasn't an unappealing notion. After almost four years on this tough beat, after four years of knocking heads with some pretty hard characters, I was ready to consider a change. Besides, I wanted to be a detective, and the promotion rolls were fairly well backed up. I reasoned that I would have a better shot at moving ahead elsewhere.

As a reserve officer in the Army, I managed to hitch a ride for free on a military plane. I took the test for the Las Vegas PD and passed. I was offered a job, accepted, and moved West.

I spent six months in Vegas. It was often interesting work because not only did Las Vegas have its own assortment of criminals, the lure of gambling and big money attracted fugitives from every state. I'd catch an out-of-state fugitive almost every day in Vegas.

Not only did I lock up the usual cons and crooks, I once stopped Elvis Presley. Elvis was on his motorcycle, a beautiful blonde holding on behind him, man, machine, and passenger all traveling at excessive speed. The year was 1957, and Elvis was in the process of transforming from star to extremely big star. He was also a charming guy, simple and sweet. Maybe because I was young and impressed by meeting Elvis, he talked me out of giving him a ticket.

That's not to say I didn't take him in. I brought him to the station, and the other cops crowded around, introducing themselves, getting autographs. While that was going on, Elvis asked if I would mind having a police mechanic take a look at his bike, which required a little tuning. For Elvis? No problem.

Later in his career, Elvis was widely recognized as a friend of the police. In fact, he gave away about twelve Cadillacs to cops he met here and there along his travels.

I like to think that one reason he liked police officers was because of the way I treated him back in Vegas in 1957, when he was young.

For the record, I never got a Caddy.

Even though I liked Vegas, I had not given up my dream of being a fed. Suddenly, the opportunity presented itself. I was able to get an appointment to the U.S. Bureau of Narcotics through the agent-in-charge in Washington, D.C., he was very close to the commissioner, who introduced me to the deputy commissioner, who interviewed me. The deputy commissioner looked me over, and got to the point: "You're Italian, right?" he asked. "You mind busting Italians, undercover?"

"No," I replied. "I can do that."

And that was essentially that.

Six months after arriving in Las Vegas, I departed for Chicago, where I received a special appointment to the Bureau of Narcotics. In those days, instead of taking the civil service exam, the bureau could appoint you under Schedule A, which was the fastest way of getting somebody in the department. You were a regular agent, but not really civil service, which also saved the constantly strapped bureau some money and some benefits, at my expense. I took the oath of office in Chicago instead of Washington, saving the bureau a plane ticket.

Despite all that, I didn't care. I had achieved my goal of being a federal agent.

The bureau had hired me in part because I was Italian, and the bureau was short of Italian agents. They expected me to work undercover, which I had never done. That was all right. I was willing to learn. I was willing to do whatever it took.

I was ready to go to work.

I found out something very quickly: I liked working undercover. I *loved* working undercover. I enjoyed fooling and outfoxing the dope peddlers. I had the knack.

I played a hundred roles, I had a thousand stories, I went into every neighborhood and bought drugs from all comers. In fact, I made so many undercover buys in Chicago that it was amazing I was never really recognized. I wasn't even recognized in the black neighborhoods, where I definitely stood out. I might hide behind a tree or wear phony glasses. I used whatever I had, whatever I could find. I made hundreds and hundreds of undercover buys from everybody—Italians, Irish, blacks, Puerto Ricans—everybody and anybody who thought they could play in the big leagues.

I was my own boss in the sense that I got my own information. An awful lot of police work is initiated and conducted through informants, who sometimes make the introductions, negotiate the prices, even do the deals. I used informants when I had them, and I made my own cases when I didn't.

In addition, many times one agent who developed a case through an informant might ask another agent to make the buy. An Italian agent in an Italian neighborhood. A black agent in a black neighborhood. That sort of thing.

I didn't accept that. I made my own buys. I bought drugs off every ethnic group. I walked in, told my tale, did the deal, made my bust.

One time a guy actually did catch me. I was helping other agents on a raid; the bust was made and we were doing the fingerprinting as part of the booking process. I fingerprinted this man, and five months later I was buying dope from him.

He looked at me and looked at me, but he couldn't quite place the face.

"You know," he said. "You look familiar."

I didn't exactly remember where I had seen his mug, because I had seen so many of them. But I knew he was nothing but another bum, and I decided to play with him.

"You know," I said, "you look familiar, too."

Well, we went our separate ways, and not too long after I made another buy from him. And he kept repeating, "Man, I know I've seen you somewhere before."

"No kidding," I said. "I think you might be right."

I realized the longer this idiot thought about it, the more likely it was he'd remember the cop who smudged his fingers with ink on the way to the joint. After all, criminals are a suspicious bunch, and they are often prone to resolve their disputes violently. I determined to knock him off before things got hairy.

So I did another deal, sucked all the information I could out of him, and nodded while he went into his mantra about knowing me, though not knowing where. And then I smiled and lowered the boom.

"You stupid"—well, I won't say what I said—"you know where you saw me? I arrested you! I fingerprinted you! Now we're going to do it again. You're under arrest. Again."

I worked the little guys hard, trying to get up to the bigger guys. That was the mission: clean up the trash on the streets, and shut down the operation at the top. Bottom to top, and back down again.

Along the way, I acquired a nickname: "Nickel-Bag Joe." I got that from starting with a measly nickel bag and leveraging it up to the big busts.

One afternoon in a Chicago suburb, called Melrose Park, I walked into an ice cream parlor to make a phone call to somebody about a drug investigation. I wasn't working undercover that day and so wasn't dressed for the part. Regardless, I started talking to this guy standing nearby who turned out to be a serious drug suspect and began negotiating a heroin purchase. The suspect was instantly on his guard, taking particular and unnecessarily derisive note of my shoes, which were typical of the type cops wore, calling me a "fed." I casually laughed, and sarcastically agreed that he found me out, that I was a cop. This had the desired effect of putting my new pal at ease, and it wasn't long before the dealer sold me a small, sample bag of heroin. (Of course, if the guy had taken a peek under my coat, he would have found a pair of handcuffs and my weapon to go along with the shoes.)

We met again and concluded a more substantial deal. This ongoing investigation led to the arrest of three major drug dealers, and the seizure of two kilos of pure heroin.

My new pal, the drug dealer, received a life sentence for his part of the business.

And the investigation I was calling about that afternoon in the ice cream parlor? It proceeded just fine.

Work the case, all the way, from the bottom up.

Going undercover means getting into the heads of the suspects, getting them to trust you, all the way.

I had infiltrated a Latin American drug organization operating out of Chicago, and had negotiated for a large shipment of marijuana. Having settled the deal, I was following the suspects, as per their instructions, to pick up the merchandise, located somewhere out of state. I was cruising along in a Cadillac, my favorite mode of transportation, driving down the Indiana Turnpike. Following at a safe distance were ten vehicles carrying officers and agents from the Michigan State Police and the Bureau of Narcotics. Everything was proceeding according to plan.

Then I noticed something. Or, to be more precise, I smelled something. And then I saw something.

My Cadillac had caught fire.

I veered off the road, the car now ablaze. The suspects were watching and also pulled off. They jumped out of their vehicle, and extinguished the fire. They risked their lives and helped save mine.

Maintaining my undercover pose, I called my backup and had them deliver another vehicle right to me, as though they were part of my gang.

I got in the new car, and the suspects and I resumed our journey. The trail led us to Fennville, Michigan.

A farmhouse waited at the other end of the line, a farmhouse containing ten Mexican-Americans and 150 pounds of marijuana. The bust was completed without complication. The seizure established a Michigan record at the time.

Drug fighting is not a racket for the faint of heart.

I had a meeting with two guys at their pizza shop, and negotiated for a very large quantity of heroin. After the men delivered two pounds of junk, we shut the investigation down and arrested them.

When I appeared in court to testify against them, the brother of one of the defendants made a motion in my direction that was the Mafia sign for death. To add the cherry on top of the sundae, I heard him say that he was going to "kill Agent Arpaio."

I arrested the son of a bitch on the spot. For threatening a federal officer, he was convicted and got two years' probation.

No backing down.

The lure of the drug business has proved irresistible to men and women in every walk of life. This includes those who should know better, those who have seen the terrible cost that drugs exact, those who have sworn to protect and serve. This includes cops.

I got wind of a Chicago police officer who was selling drugs. In an undercover capacity, I met with him and negotiated to buy heroin. He was a brazen guy. He had me call him at his police station and sold me the heroin in his squad car on three occasions.

While that might sound like a rash way to act, there was a method to his madness. He would turn on his lights and sirens in his car while we exchanged money for drugs and drive rapidly through the city streets, effectively prohibiting any attempts at surveillance.

Nonetheless, the investigation continued on pace, and I was able to identify the entire gang. It was time for the big finish.

I set up another buy with the officer. I also arranged with Chicago PD to radio their man while I was in the car, and instruct him to return to police headquarters. When he arrived, with me in the car, not to mention the drugs and money, he was arrested.

He wasn't the only corrupt law enforcement officer I put behind bars in my career. It's true what they say, you know—nobody hates a dirty cop more than another cop. It's a personal affront, a profound insult, a hateful and treacherous act.

If it were up to me—and it is not—they would receive the harshest penalties the law allows, and leave mercy to a higher authority.

I was always prepared to take on another case, no matter where, no matter when. One time, I was in New York City on a special undercover assignment, negotiating with a pair of Puerto Rican drug dealers, working in conjunction with bureau agents stationed in the city. There's always a lot of downtime in the course of any investigation, a lot of hours watching and waiting. During some of those long hours together, the New York agents told me about this pair of guys the entire local law enforcement community, cops, and feds, had been after for years and years, to no avail. These were major dope peddlers, operating under the protection of the mob.

We can't touch them, the New York agents declared. They're too smart, too cautious, too connected.

It was just idle cop chatter. But then there's nothing I like better than a challenge.

"Give me that number," I said. "I'll take care of this."

After some hesitation, the agents figured what the hell and handed me the drug dealers' phone number. I tucked it away for safekeeping and concentrated on the Puerto Rican case.

I pulled out that phone number when I returned to Chicago and started calling. I did it blind, without an informant, without any introduction. It wasn't easy. They were very leery, to put it mildly. "Who are you? Who do you know? Who sent you? Who gave you this number?" The usual questions.

I had an answer for every question. But even better than that, I had a secret weapon: Ava.

You see, I used to give out my home phone number to all the dealers I was working. That cooled off their natural suspicion and paranoia, because most prudent cops and Feds kept their private and professional lives separate, developing their cases from their offices. I worked my cases very aggressively. I worked day and night. I *had* to give out my home number. And that meant that I needed Ava to act on my behalf, because I wasn't always home to take that call.

This wasn't as simple as jotting down a message. Ava had to play a role to match whatever role I was playing.

I worked so many cases at once, and sometimes a different undercover name for each one, Ava had to keep a list by the phone to keep them all straight.

If somebody asked for "Gino," Ava had to remember that she was Gino's prostitute and speak accordingly. Usually, Ava played "my woman, my broad," as the expression was commonly employed in those days, and she played it exceedingly well. Some lowlife would get Ava on the horn and tell her about the deal or the meeting, and she would pass the information on to me. And sometimes I would have Ava pass messages back to the dealers.

My undercover work could get so hectic that Ava sometimes would play the game when she didn't have to. One day this guy called and asked for "Johnny." Ava couldn't recall me being Johnny for any ongoing case, but she went with it anyway, and said Johnny wasn't home and asked if she could take a message. "Just tell him I'm waiting at the filling station," the guy said and hung up.

So far, so good. Unfortunately, when she relayed the message to me, I had to inform her that Johnny wasn't one of my aliases, and the caller was just some innocent fellow looking for his friend Johnny. Ava says she still imagines the poor guy standing at a filling station out in the middle of nowhere, waiting for Johnny.

In any event, I was still working these New Yorkers, working for a long time to gain their confidence, and Ava also spoke to them and helped ease their concerns. Most cops will only go so far in making the case, and everybody on both sides of the law knows that. I went farther, and took the bad guys by surprise.

It took a few months, but I finally struck a deal. Not just a deal—I convinced them to bring the kilo of heroin in person to Chicago. In those days, a kilo was pretty substantial.

The two dealers drove all the way to Chicago in their brand new Chevrolet. I arrested them when they arrived. I took the drugs, and I took the Chevy.

The dealers flipped, meaning they cooperated, and the information they supplied resulted in the arrest of several major Mafia figures in New York.

And they said it couldn't be done.

Never back down.

I was negotiating with a local bail bondsman for half a kilo of heroin when the idiot got himself arrested on a robbery charge. No slacker, the bondsman was also a central figure in a Chicago Municipal Court bail bond scandal. In other words, he was definitely wrong.

Cut to the not too distant future. I was walking through the halls of the Illinois State Court when I happened to see the bondsman in court. He was appearing before a judge on the robbery beef. I stopped to watch, and discovered that the judge was about to let the guy off with probation.

Even though I was in the courthouse on another matter, I was duty-bound to interrupt. I approached the bench and apprised the judge of the drug deal I had had brewing with the bondsman. My testimony led the judge to impose a one- to ten-year sentence on this busy criminal.

Let's talk commitment.

February 20, 1960. One date I'll never forget.

I was working this dealer, who was operating on a street corner not too far from my home. I was angling to buy a sizable amount of heroin, and gave the dealer a down payment. He took the money and left, saying he'd soon return with the drugs. About four hours later, I saw the dealer come strolling down the street.

Very good, I thought to myself. Right on schedule.

However, fate in the form of a vigilant Chicago cop intervened. He spotted the dealer, who was already wanted, and arrested him on the spot. That might have been good police work, but it seriously interfered with my investigation, as well as losing the heroin I was supposed to be buying.

I was losing the heroin because the dealer hadn't returned with the dope. Oh, he had gone out and picked up the heroin, and he had brought it back, but he hadn't brought it back all the way. He had hidden it close by, a standard procedure in this business.

Not good enough.

I sidled up to the arresting officer when the dealer was busy being handled by other cops and told him who I was. The officer didn't believe me. Not that I could completely blame him. Since I was undercover, I wasn't carrying official identification.

Regardless, I was finally able to satisfy the officer that I really was a bureau agent. Once that hurdle was overcome, I succinctly explained my plan to him.

"Arrest me," I said. "Put me inside with him."

Simple and elegant, in its own rough-hewn manner. I would stick with this bum until I got what I came for.

I was handcuffed, driven away, and tossed into jail along with my dealer and other accused members of society. We were dumped into a holding tank, filled with a significant segment of the cons and crooks, rapists and murderers, perverts and depraved, who walked the streets of Chicago.

I stayed near my man, and we verbally went at it for a while, each accusing the other of causing this distasteful situation. Hey, that was the normal response of an individual faced with an unanticipated and unappreciated prison term: Blame somebody else, anybody else.

It took time, but eventually we agreed that this was just one of the hazards of our particular occupation.

Once we were on the same page, the rest was easy. I got the dealer to tell me where the dope was, the dope that I had already bought, the dope that was my evidence. He had stashed it in a garbage can.

Now I had to get the word out. But I didn't intend to blow my cover in front of all these lawbreakers and blow my chances of making more cases. So I couldn't walk up to the bars and announce that the jig was up, I had what I wanted, and it was time to get out and go home.

No way!

Instead, I managed to quietly get a message to the police, instructing them to have one of my bureau comrades pose as a bail bondsman and get me sprung from the stockade. This would get me out without raising the dealer's suspicions.

On the down side, this also meant that I would have to spend the night in jail.

When I was released in the morning, I went straight to the garbage can and recovered the heroin.

Case closed.

But that wasn't the end of the night's excitement, not on the night of February 20, 1960. In fact, the bust was the *least* of it.

You see, I went from that garbage can to the hospital right up the street, where Ava had given birth to my son, my firstborn, while I was in jail.

"Nickel-Bag Joe" worked hard and long and got results, sometimes big results. And Washington recognized and rewarded those results. I was the only agent in bureau history to have skipped a grade when promoted, jumping from grade nine to grade eleven. (The civil service classifications might not be sexy, but they are specific.)

But there was a larger reward in store for me, a very special, and exciting honor. After four years in Chicago, I was given a new assignment.

And it was definitely one of a kind.

Turkey in 1961 was the hottest spot on the planet as far as the drug trade was concerned. The country, located between east and west, was the center of the global heroin trade, and the heroin trade was probably at the height of its vicious influence and reach. It was the place where it all began, where the opium fields ran on forever, where the legions of farmers harvested their crops and sold them to endless hordes of buyers, who took the opium to labs in France and Italy, where it was turned into heroin, the purest heroin in the world, and shipped to the United States and around the world.

The Bureau of Narcotics was responsible for stopping this deadly trade, as well as all the other drugs that were washing through our nation. Two-hundred-plus agents arrayed against scores of drug cartels, thousands of criminal organizations, a numberless army of procurers and dealers, suppliers, addicts, users, and an ocean of drugs.

And as for Turkey, vital, mysterious Turkey, the axis of so much intrigue and misery? What resources did the government of the United States allocate to this critical, desperate battle? How many battalions of cops, how many shiploads of equipment, how much money, how much support?

You're looking at how much, at least figuratively. The bureau sent me. The bureau put me on a plane, dropped me off in Istanbul, and told me to go to work. Good luck, good-bye, keep in touch. Get it done.

I think most people expect that an American agent dispatched overseas is prepped and prepared in every manner possible, physically, intellectually, sociologically. Well, maybe agents are properly readied today, but not in my day. I wasn't provided with language instruction, cultural lessons, geopolitical background information. Not even a light dusting, a veneer of schooling, or grooming. Nothing.

Let me put it this way: Talking Turkey, I didn't know anything, and I didn't know anybody. I had hardly any resources at my disposal, just my trusty Smith & Wesson and a pathetically small roll of flash money. No support, no backup, no leads. I had no legal authority or power, I was just a stranger in somebody else's country. I wasn't even officially sanctioned to carry a gun.

The Bureau of Narcotics was so short of money, and ran such a bare bones operation, that my superiors refused to send my family with me. That's right. The bureau said it didn't have the money to put my wife and baby on an airplane to Turkey—not until I spent six months on my own in Turkey and proved I could do the job. That was the arrangement. If I could corroborate and confirm that I could cut it overseas, then the bureau would spring for the plane tickets.

And whether I could cut it was unclear for a time. In retrospect, if I had really sat down and thought about it, I might have become paralyzed by the enormity of the task, the paucity of my resources, the numbing isolation of my position.

Fortunately, considering the circumstances, that wasn't my way. I simply went out, and tried to make the cases. I talked with my Turkish colleagues, I walked the streets, I hung out in the seedier parts of town. I did what a cop does to get the lay of the land, to make the contacts that a cop needs.

And it was tough. Very tough. The bad guys didn't know me, and they weren't too eager to make my acquaintance. I didn't know who was reliable, and who knew what they were talking about. It was all hit or miss, trial and error, guided only by instinct and luck. A steep learning curve, straight up from zero.

As usual, I had to start pretty near the bottom, trying to get hooked into the mix, working my way up the drug ladder. I wasted some time and money with one jerk or another, each claiming to be connected, to be tied into prime sources.

I wasn't making the cases, and I was getting frustrated and angry. But there wasn't any other way to go. I had to keep looking and meeting and talking until I struck paydirt. It wasn't fancy, it wasn't sophisticated, but that's what police work, and particularly undercover work, is about.

But then I started to connect. I started to get into the mix. I met one, then two, then a few more informants and users and dealers. Small fry, maybe, but players to one degree or another.

I was building up my network of bad guys. I was getting acclimated to this very big neighborhood. My sixth sense, my special policeman's nose and ear and eye, was coming back in fine style. I was negotiating and buying. I was breaking cases.

This change of fortunes had a personal as well as professional impact on my life. As I got closer to the six-month deadline, and I gained some confidence and some success, I informed Washington that my son would celebrate his second birthday about a month before my trial period was up. In those days, a child under two flew for free, so if Ava and the baby got on that plane right away the bureau would save the cost of a one-way ticket. Just a reminder.

The speed with which the bureau jumped, you'd think I'd just been appointed director of both the BN *and* the FBI. Agents were immediately dispatched into the hills of Virginia to track down Ava and my son, who were off visiting her relatives. The bureau managed to find them, and hustled my wife and baby onto a plane and got them to Turkey just under the wire. They moved so fast Ava barely had time to pack. The bureau wouldn't pay to ship our furniture, or hardly anything, for that matter. But Washington had saved its ticket, and I had my family.

Getting my family over early had a very important side benefit. It saved my life, literally.

I was scheduled to fly to Beirut that night. I had a big case going, and I had to get to Lebanon. I hated to put off the flight— it just wasn't in my nature—but I wouldn't have skipped my family's arrival for anything.

And now for the kicker. The flight I missed crashed into the mountains, killing all aboard. I did take that same flight the next day, after getting my family settled. We flew over the wreckage of the downed turbojet.

That special set of circumstances did not happen once to me, but twice. Shoot-outs aren't the only way to die.

(People are always asking me why I don't have bodyguards or carry a weapon. They wonder why I'm not worried about the many lowlifes and reprobates who've been in and out of my jails, and have expressed a strong dislike of yours truly. From gun battles to undercover deals to plane crashes, I think I have an unusually fine appreciation of exactly who and what deserves worrying about.)

In any case, we had a gala reception for Ava and baby at the airport. When I say "we," it's because I didn't show up alone. Oh no. A caravan of high-ranking representatives from the police and the military escorted me right onto the runway, bearing tremendous bouquets of flowers. It was a terrific welcome.

Ava adjusted with remarkable ease to our new life. Istanbul wasn't anything like Washington or Chicago. Nor did we live the way our government employees lived in other postings, such as London or Paris. There was not much that was fancy about Istanbul, not in those days.

We lived in a small brick house in an American enclave located in the city, populated mainly by U.S. Army and embassy personnel. We didn't have a telephone in the house. Nobody in the neighborhood was wired for phone service.

Ava shopped at the army PX as well as local markets for food. Ava's friends were chiefly other Americans. Our son had a good friend, a little girl, who lived up the street.

I wasn't around much. I just came home to change clothes and get something decent to eat. I probably spent three out of four weeks in the boondocks, in the mountains of Turkey or Syria or Lebanon, in the border towns, in the valleys, in the fields, in the middle of nowhere surrounded by nothing but trouble and danger.

Like I said, it wasn't a fancy life. It was at least as hard on Ava as it was on me. But I loved it. It was good work, important work, exciting work. One day I'm meeting with the president of Turkey, the next day I'm shooting it out with the bandits in the hinterlands.

And Ava stayed behind to mind the hearth and home, and take care of our baby, cut off from family and old friends, cut off from anything that was familiar and comforting, waiting for me to return from God knew where, God knew when, God knew how.

It wasn't always easy. But we did it together. We were—we are—a family.

Back to business.

Death is always lurking. It is always there. You just never know who it will take next. You never know when or how. But it is always there, always waiting, always ready.

I had been investigating a drug ring for five months, working with the Turkish national police. It was a powerful ring that regularly shipped huge amounts of heroin to the United States, hidden in bales of tobacco. We had identified Kerim Ali Courtuk, age forty-four, a wealthy tobacco merchant, as the head of the group. Three other men were the other leaders of the conspiracy. These four comprised our primary targets, along with the extensive drug lab they managed.

Finally, the moment arrived when we were ready to move. I accompanied the police units as they surrounded the farmhouse, near the town of Samsun on the Black Sea, which operated as the group's headquarters. We approached quietly, carefully, guns drawn. These drug dealers were an unpredictable bunch, but ordinarily well armed, and there was no reason to take a chance.

Quickly the police captured the four ringleaders and a large heroin laboratory, along with 550 pounds of opium and thirteen pounds of heroin.

I immediately sat Courtuk, the top boss, down and started to interrogate him. We talked for a short time while the police rummaged through the farmhouse. After a while, I decided to continue this at headquarters. The Turkish cops led him to another room and evidently left him unguarded.

A few moments later, I heard a familiar bang. I ran inside to discover that Kerim Ali Courtuk, wealthy, successful, and a drug dealer, had committed suicide with a bullet to the head.

One month after wrapping up the case described in the opening pages of this book, the largest seizure ever made in Turkey, garnering worldwide publicity for the Turkish government, I landed in very hot water with the local authorities.

I was up in the mountains with a contingent of Turkish cops, approaching Afyon. It had been a typically rough ride to this place. Whether in my 1957 Chevy or the jeep I borrowed from the U.S. Army colonel who lived next door, they were all rough rides in the mountains.

We always brought gum with us because rocks would puncture the gas tanks, and we'd need something to cover up the holes. Gum wasn't necessarily the recommended material, but it was the best we had, and it usually worked, at least temporarily.

We'd drive three, four, five hundred miles into the mountains, risking my life and the lives of the Turkish cops and soldiers I usually had along just driving to the drugs. And then the real danger was only beginning, because once we arrived, the waiting would begin, the waiting for the dealers to show up. We'd be holed up in the middle of nowhere, at night, in the dark. And let me tell you, you don't know how dark the night can be until you've gone four hundred miles from the nearest gleam of electricity.

It was so dark that we'd only know somebody was coming when we'd hear the clanging of the bell hanging from the donkey who was ferrying the drugs in the far, far distance. (Because, as dark as it was, it was just as quiet.)

And then that clanging would get closer and closer until it was almost upon us. And we still didn't see anything or anybody, so we didn't know how many farmers and dealers were arrayed before us and how many weapons they were toting.

But it didn't matter in the end, because however many of them there were, I'd give the signal to leap out and grab the farmers and the drugs. Then the shooting would start, and the screams and curses, and we'd capture the opium as well as the farmers who didn't move quickly enough to escape. It was very exciting. I know that might sound a bit trite, but it's absolutely true. It was very exciting.

And then we'd drive all the way back to Istanbul, because we couldn't trust the local authorities in the mountains. I used to drive one, sometimes two nights without stopping, because hardly any of the Turks with whom I worked knew how to drive.

I'd bring army K rations, which were hardly a delicacy, because I didn't want to eat the local cuisine. Inevitably, however, I'd wind up giving my K rations to the underpaid, undernourished Turks, who craved the army fare, and I'd eat whatever I could scrounge from the locals. I'd bring whiskey, which I'd also hand over to my Turkish compatriots, and drink the native favorite, *raki*, which tasted like Italian *anisette*.

I told you it wasn't London or Paris.

Anyway, back to the story at hand. It was around 10 P.M., and the deal was about to go down. Seven Turks approached, as per arrangement, and delivered 224 kilos of opium via horse and wagon. I had my borrowed jeep and a truck. Inside the truck was concealed a group of national policemen.

I gave the signal, and the policemen came tumbling out. But the seven Turks chose not to surrender or flee into the night. A gun battle erupted, and two of the Turkish dealers were killed.

What is there to say? We were playing for keeps, all of us. It wasn't an accident that everybody on that lonely road outside of Afyon on that pitch-black night was armed and ready.

The bad guys and the good guys were well aware of each other's proclivity to shoot first, ask questions later.

However, the Turkish governor of the region had not been properly forewarned and advised of my investigation. The governor didn't like this, and decided to show who was the boss. This was a case of local politics and I had inadvertently stepped into it.

The governor started to make noises about foreigners and interference and murder and anything else he could think up. He wanted to use me, along with five Turkish cops, to cause trouble. Contrasting his important, very visible position with my sensitive, somewhat murky status, he could have caused quite a lot.

The Turkish governor didn't get to play his petty game for long. Between his political betters back in Istanbul and the American Ambassador, the pressure was applied from both sides. The governor quickly crumbled. The charges were dropped, and the press didn't get a chance to smear the story all over the front pages.

I can't say I lost much sleep over the whole business. It's not that I was glad the dealer had been killed. I wasn't. But it happened, and more often than on that one occasion.

Nobody was embarrassed. I went back to work.

That wasn't hard to do, because I had never stopped.

I spent over three years in Turkey, fighting throughout the Near and Middle East. I operated on my own, using my own judgment and discretion to get the job done. I received the Exceptional Service Award from the general director of the Turkish National Police, a Special Service Award from the U.S. Treasury Department, as well as a Superior Performance Award from Treasury. (Awards and commendations are one of the prime currencies of success for those in government service. In the course of my career, I received a score of such citations and decorations, including the Excellence of Performance Award from the DEA, the Extraordinary Service Award from the Office of Special Investigations of the U.S. Air Force, a Special Award from the attorney general of Mexico, a Special Award of Honor from the International Narcotic Officers Association, awards from police departments in Baltimore, San Antonio, and Arizona. Well, you get the idea. And not every award comes courtesy of some government—moving from one arena to another, I received the Barry Goldwater Award from the Young Republicans as their Man of the Year for 1995, and days later was named the Man of the Month for February 1996, by *Today's Arizona Woman's Magazine.*)

While I enjoyed unprecedented, and perhaps even extraordinary success, it was no cut-and-dried business. I had my false leads, dead ends, wasted efforts. I spent a fair amount of time cultivating a semifamous Turkish actor who claimed to be in with big-time drug dealers. In my undercover guise, I accompanied him on trips into the mountains, and wined and dined him at the Hilton Hotel in Istanbul, even letting him take a spin on the dance floor with Ava that night!

But it was a waste of time. He was all talk and no action. All that talk added up to nothing.

Hey, in this business, you had to kiss a lot of fast-talking, con-artist frogs to find a drug-dealing prince, so to speak.

Regardless, as part of an all-out government effort, directed from Washington, and implemented not only in Turkey but also across the U.S., we stopped the heroin trade.

It can be done.

It *has* been done.

My next three postings were all in the United States, which pro-vided a welcome respite, especially for my family, from the partic-ular inconveniences of foreign service. And so we were reunited with all the people and things we loved so much: family, friends, phones, paved roads, pizza, cheeseburgers, television, and all the rest that makes America so American.

The year was 1964. I was special agent-in-charge in San Antonio, Texas. The drug trade between the United States and Mexico was heating up, and the southern border—Texas, New Mexico, Arizona, California—was wide open.

The shutdown of the Canadian/New York end of the French Connection meant that heroin, as well as other drugs, was increas-ingly rerouted through Latin America and Mexico into the U.S. And so the war went on, fought on another front.

Item: A two-month investigation led to the arrest of a San Antonio man and the seizure of one hundred thousand dollars worth of heroin.

Item: Five men and women were arrested after a raid by feder-al, state, and local officers uncovered a large quantity of marijuana and barbiturates.

Item: Four and a half ounces of heroin, valued at thirty-five thousand dollars, was seized, and two men and a woman were charged with illegally importing and selling a narcotic.

Item: Fourteen were arrested in a multiagency raid that also netted a sizable amount of illegal drugs. It was the fourth large-scale raid in ten months in San Antonio, resulting in the capture of dozens of drug suspects.

Item: I personally led the raiding party which grabbed half a million dollars' worth of pure heroin, and an abundant quantity of procaine, a synthetic cocaine, as well as a tall stack of twenty-dollar bills, in the largest drug haul in the city's history.

And that was just the beginning.

In an undercover guise, I met a Mexican dealer in San Antonio, purchased a sample of heroin, and arranged to buy a considerably larger amount. Cutting to the chase, I enticed the dealer to personally deliver the heroin in front of the federal building, which housed the Bureau of Narcotics. When the dealer showed up, I arrested him, and brought him right upstairs to my office.

In a somewhat similar instance, I bought heroin several times from another Mexican national, entering into negotiations for a much greater purchase. A few days later, before the deal could be consummated, I was walking through that very same federal building when I spotted the Mexican in the lobby. He was filling out a civil service application for a job at a military base.

The dealer saw me and smiled. "Hey, man," he said, "you work here?"

Even though my undercover identity hadn't been blown, this was too close for comfort.

"Yes, I do," I said. "And you're under arrest."

Drugs were running rampant through the high schools and colleges. We received word that a trio of high school students, including the son of a local police chief, were selling marijuana by bulk through the city. Though I was thirty-five years old at the time, I took the direct approach, without benefit of an informant, and briefly went undercover at the group's high school. Before long, I had purchased several pounds of pot. All of the boys were eighteen years old at the time of their arrest.

The drug war kept expanding, and more and more troops and agencies were thrown into the breach. In San Antonio, the federal government was represented by the Bureau of Narcotics (BN), which of course was in the Treasury Department. But the BN was not the sole federal agency in town. In 1966, the Bureau of Drug Abuse Control was formed, under the jurisdiction of the Food and Drug Administration, a component of the Department of Housing, Education and Welfare (HEW). The BN focused on what were considered "hard narcotics," such as heroin, marijuana, morphine, and other opium derivatives. This new agency was charged with pursuing LSD, barbiturates, mescaline, amphetamines, and peyote-type drugs. Three hundred agents were recruited for HEW's latest bureaucratic addition, many of whom were BN veterans.

President Lyndon Johnson soon realized that this split authority didn't make much sense, and had the Bureau of Narcotics, by this time renamed the Bureau of Narcotics and Dangerous Drugs, absorb the Bureau of Drug Abuse Control. This merger, which only made sense, would lead to some problems as agents and administrators vied for position and power. The two directors of the individual agencies became associate directors of the new bureau, and an outsider, John Ingersoll, the police chief of Oakland, California, was brought in as the boss. As you might imagine, that properly set the stage for intrigue on a scale that would do a Greek tragedy proud.

I had a front-row seat to all this, because by then I was the agent-in-charge of the Washington, D.C. field office. While manning that post, I initiated an investigation into reports that a bureau deputy director based in Baltimore had gone bad. This fellow had joined us from HEW's Bureau of Drug Abuse Control, and he was something of a rival, who coveted my job. I had solid information that he was selling heroin out of his office. Because of the intra-agency tension the merger had created, my investigation had to be handled with the utmost discretion. The probe was classified as a secret mission by Commissioner Henry Giordano. Eventually, confronted with the evidence, the deputy director caved in, flipped, and implicated his confederates, some of whom were also agents.

Returning to the subject, on the federal level, we had my Bureau of Narcotics and this HEW entry. But the feds were also present through the good offices of U.S. Customs, the U.S. Border Patrol, and, of course, the FBI.

One more note: the Bureau of Narcotics and the Federal Bureau of Investigation had always had something of an adversarial relationship, embodied by the legendary founders of the two agencies, Harry Anslinger of the BN and J. Edgar Hoover of the FBI. Part of the fundamental and quite bitter dispute between the departments resulted from Hoover's decades-long insistence that the Mafia did not exist, that organized crime was a fiction. Anslinger knew better, because the mob was deeply involved in drugs. Hoover had his own political reasons for denying the existence of the Mafia, such as his overriding interest in pursuing communists, and other subversives. Regardless of his motivations, Hoover's intransigence, which forced a draining, wasteful battle between the agencies, inevitably hurt the national effort in the drug war.

Once again, back to the subject: In addition to the five federal agencies listed above, the Lone Star State contributed the personnel and efforts of the Texas Department of Public Safety, the Bexar County Sheriff's Department, and the narcotics squad of the San Antonio Police Department.

Anyone could seriously doubt that creating this huge agency stew was the most efficient way to fight the war. However, no one could doubt that there were enough drugs, not to mention dealers and buyers, to go around for every agency to legitimize its budget by grabbing a piece of the action.

Meanwhile, bureaucracy aside, I had my own battle to wage.

In April 1967, posing as an Italian drug dealer from Chicago, I traveled to Ciudad Acuna, a small city in Mexico. My target was a fugitive from America, and the bureau. I made contact with my man, and initiated negotiations, which quickly led to his capture by the Mexican Federal Police.

But the real fun began when I assisted my Mexican colleagues on another case involving a couple of other dealers. Still playing the same role, I made the approach and was soon accepting delivery on twenty ounces of heroin. The *federales* were on the scene, ready to round up the pair. One of the panicked dealers made a run for it.

He didn't have a chance. The cops had him in their sights and were about to shoot. I jumped up and tackled the dealer, who proceeded to hug me, thanking me for saving his life. Then I turned him over to the Mexicans, still in one piece.

The year was 1968. More of the same action in Baltimore, Maryland, where I served as Deputy Regional Director for the Bureau of Narcotics and Dangerous Drugs (BNDD).

Item: A twenty-eight-year-old third-grade teacher at a parochial school was arrested with five ounces of cocaine in her purse, with a potential street value of ninety thousand dollars.

Item: Thirty-five thousand dollars worth of marijuana was discovered in a house on a quiet, upper-income neighborhood. I spent six months undercover to reach this day. It began on the street, negotiating with small-time pushers and gradually led to larger and larger purchases, with bigger and bigger dealers, finally culminating in a five-hour arrangement and a walk through the door of this two-story frame house. After examining the merchandise, I managed to sidle up to a window and signal the police waiting outside to raid the place. Seconds later, it was all over. Five men were taken into custody.

In September 1969, in an attempt to stop the flow of drugs from Mexico into the U.S., the American government initiated Operation Intercept. It was controversial and bold, either a radical or ruinous concept, depending on which side one stood. The plan was opposed by many Americans and Mexicans alike, with a chorus of politicians and commentators on both sides of the border convinced that it would irretrievably damage relations between the two countries.

We did it anyway.

President Nixon had recently assumed office, and he was tough on drugs. At the time of Intercept, John Mitchell was the attorney general, Richard Kleindienst was the deputy attorney general, and I was serving as deputy regional director, based in Baltimore. By this date, you might recall, BNDD had been shifted from the Treasury Department to the Justice Department, so I more or less worked directly for Kleindienst (who eventually headed justice as attorney general.) He and I became good friends in the course of our long association.

The idea was simple: We were going to close the entire border and check all traffic coming into our country for drugs.

For twenty-three days, we shut down normal contact and commerce between Mexico and America. We stopped and searched, and it worked. We put a halt to drugs. We also produced another result—very long lines of cars and trucks stretching miles back into Mexico, miles of vehicles waiting to get into our border states.

Throughout the month of September, I traveled up and down the border in a small plane, overseeing the operation. My companion in this journey was a former FBI agent named G. Gordon Liddy, now representing the Treasury Department. He looked after Treasury's interests, while I took care of the same for the Justice Department. It was only a few years later that Liddy would become embroiled in the Watergate scandal, and earn himself first a prison term and then, in the new American tradition, a national talk show.

But that was the future. Now we rode the border, making sure that the president's orders were carried out. And while the program worked, in its harsh fashion, it was a temporary victory. The measure was too severe, too draconian, to last. It also caused so much resentment on the part of the Mexicans that any collaborative effort we might have wanted with our southern neighbors was simply out of the question. To quote a story in *The Baltimore Sun*, "The Mexican press, which does not venture far beyond the bounds of government policy, reacted as if Mr. Nixon and Mr. Mitchell were telling the whole world that all Mexicans were smugglers and defilers of American youth."

So when the operation was lifted after twenty-three days, the drug flow resumed, just like before. Still, it was an interesting exercise, demonstrating that we could stop the drugs, even on this long, thoroughly porous border. Of course, we also stopped tourism and trade. So the issue was what cost were we willing to bear, economically and politically, to achieve our goals.

Just four months after Operation Intercept opened and closed in a cacophony of political posturing and media hysteria, I was appointed the regional director in Mexico City. I was thirty-eight years old, and the youngest regional director in the bureau's history. I didn't get ahead by playing poker with the bosses. I got ahead by working day and night.

Turkey had been the center of the drug war in the early sixties, when I was stationed there, and Latin America was rapidly emerging as the nexus for the worldwide drug conspiracy in the seventies, just as I arrived. With my appointment to this new post, I now held the distinction of being the only U.S. narcotics enforcement agent to serve in the two hottest places in the world for drugs, Turkey and Latin America. In fact, I didn't simply serve in both regions, I was the boss of both shops. Nobody else, before or since, can make that statement.

Nor can anyone else's family, for it was time for Ava to pack up the house and kids and move again. Since Turkey, we had had an addition to the group, our daughter. You might recall that our son was almost two years old when we moved to Turkey. Eight years later, our baby girl was the two-year-old in the family.

Now, in January 1970, we were on our way to Mexico City. Professionally, I was leaping directly into the frying pan, for not only was all of Latin America our next battleground, but Mexico commanded the highest profile of all the region's countries.

It was a daunting task, but I had some specific objectives in mind, and some ideas to achieve those goals. And the place to start was with resurrecting and reinventing Operation Intercept.

That might sound like a relatively straightforward job, restarting a program that has already been up and running. However, anyone who's ever worked for the government knows that nothing could be more difficult. The usual vicious bureaucratic in-fighting over credit and control is magnified a thousandfold when the object or program or agency at stake has a history.

No matter. I had a somewhat different plan in mind, and was determined to see it through. It took a lot of talking and more than a few late-night drinks, to convince the attorney general, the deputy attorney general, and several other of the highest officials of the American government, that Operation Intercept had to be reborn as Operation Cooperation.

Eventually, they came around to my way of thinking. Kleindienst used to travel quite often to Mexico, and we'd talk for hours, planning new strategies, and reviewing the progress of programs already under way. His support, and the support of the president, showed me just how invaluable real leadership is in any fight. Our ambassador in Mexico was not contemptuously obstructionist or aggressively troublesome. Nevertheless, in line with State Department priorities, he was also not overly interested in stirring up diplomatic problems with talk about dynamic drug enforcement.

However, once it became clear that the president of the United States had made the drug war a priority, regularly dispatching the number-two man at Justice and other officials to Mexico City to meet with me, then the ambassador and his staff fell in step with the program. The same applied to the CIA, which had a strong presence in the region and never hesitated to assert its self-appointed authority over any issue. Without the president behind me, I would have wasted a ludicrous amount of time waging turf battles with the spy agency. With the president's backing, the CIA, the ambassador, not to mention customs, the FBI, and the rest, had to acknowledge my primacy in the drug war.

In short, when the dust settled, nobody was willing to mess with my agents or with me. And that meant I could do my job without having to constantly look over my shoulder.

Here's an example: A Panamanian air traffic controller was being paid off to help drug transport planes sneak through to the U.S. I wanted to get him, but I had no authority as long as he stayed out of the Canal Zone, which was American territory and on Panamanian soil. The man had one weakness, however—he loved softball. He loved playing softball, and he especially loved playing in a game that was regularly held in the Canal Zone at the military base with American soldiers. And that's how we nabbed him, luring him onto the base with the promise of softball. We got him and locked him up, and shipped him back to the United States by private jet to stand trial for international drug trafficking.

I received a fair measure of political heat for my efforts. The American ambassador wasn't too happy, and neither was the Panamanian government. The air traffic controller was close to the Panamanian leader, General Manuel Noriega, and other Panamanian leaders. Awkward situation, from a diplomatic viewpoint—good police work, from a law enforcement standpoint. The bottom line was, I had Washington behind me, and nobody got too seriously in the way, and the job was accomplished.

Chalk one up for good police work.

Back to Operation Intercept, and my plan for its successor. Operation Cooperation was implemented and immediately successful. American agents, money, and technology helped Mexican police track down marijuana fields, heroin shipments, drug laboratories. Virtually every week brought a new achievement, another victory.

Senator Charles Percy of Illinois had been "deeply disturbed" by Operation Intercept. The success of Operation Cooperation had made just as powerful an impact. In fact, he felt moved to insert a newspaper article into the Congressional Record, which listed some of our accomplishments:

"In Tijuana, officials of both countries ran down a dope ring that had been supplying heroin, cocaine and marijuana for the past fifteen years. In San Antonio, the former head of the Mexican secret service and his accomplices were picked up with marijuana valued by police at forty-four million. Close to three thousand pounds of marijuana was taken, and eighteen persons were picked up in a raid on a ranch in the state of Michoacan. Three barge loads, about eight thousand pounds, were seized on the California coast after their trip from Mexico—all this and more, in May alone."

The drug trade was changing. The violence was accelerating. The Mafia used to control the drug traffic. They were always tough but had their boundaries. They wouldn't kill police or reporters or family members. But in the U.S., the mob was under serious assault by law enforcement, and overseas, we had broken the Turkish Connection and damaged the European link with the drug trade. All this had happened just as the narcotics markets and profits exploded. Such a market vacuum violates basic economic imperatives and so cannot exist for long. Thus, as the Mafia's control weakened, others rushed to fill the breach.

Entrepreneurs throughout Latin America were among the first to take advantage of this opportunity. The drugs that had been coming through Canada and New York were now moving through South America and Panama. I fought in Mexico and throughout

Central America, and then expanded the fight south. I opened an office in Buenos Aires, because the routing for drugs used to come through Argentina and Paraguay, then into Panama, and north to Miami. When Miami got hot, the drugs started coming in across Mexico in increasing quantities. French heroin, called white powder for its purity, was often routed to Chicago and New York. Mexican heroin, or brown heroin, was easy to find throughout the southwestern states.

The Mafia's relatively restrained rules about murder were summarily tossed out by the Latin drug rings. The Colombian drug dealers in particular rapidly established well-deserved reputations as killers who would torture and murder not only their rivals and enemies, but also their parents and wives and children and friends.

The Mexicans were no slouches when it came to violence. The war between the dealers and police could be ugly and bloody. Mexico resembled Turkey in several respects—the terrain was rough, the cops were underpaid, the people were poor, the government sometimes ineffective and corrupt, the drugs abundant, and ever more so, the danger real.

Not every bust made the papers.

I was running an investigation into a fairly sizable drug ring. We had progressed to the point where I had two undercover American agents and three Mexican federal police officers ready to make a large marijuana buy. They were carrying a nice bundle of cash, driving deep into the mountains, approximately one hundred miles outside of Acapulco.

Unfortunately, my agents deviated from my instructions not to veer far from the main road. My information and my experience told me that trouble was brewing. The local law enforcers, who more closely resembled a gang of security guards for hire than a legally authorized and directed police unit, could not be trusted.

No matter. When the agents did exactly what they were told not to do, and were lured off the road, the ambush was sprung. The deal went bad, the shooting started. Way up in the mountains, far from supervisory oversight or intervention, the local police were no good. They were compromised and corrupted, and they were out to kill my men and steal the cash.

Two of the Mexican *federales* were critically wounded. The American agents returned fire and killed five of the attackers.

Somehow, the agents and *federales* escaped. But that was not the end. We couldn't leave it at that. No way. Not the Mexican government, and not this American official.

Not long after, I accompanied a contingent from the Mexican army. We headed into the mountains. It didn't take long for us to find the village police who had attacked the agents. A ferocious gun battle erupted. Several of the locals were killed, and many were captured. The Mexicans dealt summarily with the murderous cops.

I know I constantly refer to the fight against drugs as a "battle" and a "war." After reviewing some of these stories, perhaps you have a better understanding of why.

The problem of corruption is a matter of money, mortality, and morality. It destroys lives and souls. It tears apart families and governments.

And with so much money floating through the drug world, so much easy, available, untraceable money, it is pernicious and pervasive.

For most honest people, confronted with evidence of corruption on the part of a colleague or business associate, the impulse is to turn him in, or simply turn away. This impulse, this repulsion is not only entirely normal, it is healthy.

However, it is also a luxury.

As an agent or administrator in the field, that luxury is not an option. The job has to get done. The locals have to be consulted and considered. The politicos and generals and cops have to be wooed and won over.

They're either with you or against you. If they're against you, you're dead. If they're with you—well, that can mean many things. But at least you're not dead.

I had to deal with General Noriega. I had to go down into the bunker that served as his headquarters and let him know what we were doing, more or less, and consult with him on strategy and resources and schedules. I had to work with him.

I knew Noriega's reputation. I knew the stories about payoffs. There was always talk that he was a crook, along with many other members of the National Guard and the government.

The Panamanian government wasn't that dissimilar from other governments with which I dealt. And that was the name of the game—dealing. You either dealt with the powers-that-be or you didn't, and then you might as well not be there. And we had to be there, whether I was with the Bureau of Narcotics or the Bureau of Narcotics and Dangerous Drugs or the Drug Enforcement Administration, because it was in the fundamental interests of the United States. I wouldn't claim that the Panamanians or the Mexicans or the Colombians or anybody else were always straight with us, were always gung ho to pursue any bad guy, and make every case. But the locals were the only game in town, and we were there to play. And play we did.

The American government cannot reform every corrupt or inept government and society around the world. Of course, considering that our own government is hardly infallible, it would be presumptuous to think that we could. Regardless, we have to protect our borders and our people to the best of our ability, even if that means sometimes dealing with those who do not come close to matching ordinary standards of decency and honesty.

Now understand, there are limits to such tolerance. Some governments are beyond the pale of contact of any kind.

In any war, most of the ordinary rules of society, the common standards of decency, are thrown out the window. Nonetheless, boundaries are set, and some rules and principles maintained—the precepts laid down by the Geneva Convention, for example.

In our drug war, the boundaries we must establish and abide by are those of our own values. So we must act whenever we can, whenever we have a chance of achieving success, whenever we can thwart the flow of drugs into our nation, whenever we can accomplish our goals without compromising our basic values.

Sometimes it wasn't foreign corruption but our own cowardice that interfered with our efforts.

Paraguay provided an example of cowardice. It all went back to Turkey and the French Connection, and the massive, international drug/criminal/subversive organization that arose out of that conspiracy. (I include subversive, because many of the people involved in drugs in South America were also involved in insurgent groups and activities.)

As the moviegoers among the readers will recall, at the end of the film, *The French Connection*, the mastermind behind the organization got away clean, disappearing into thin air. (While I am not inclined to call upon a Hollywood movie for factual verification, and the facts in that otherwise fine movie are more than a little skewed, the general idea about there being a mastermind who got away is true.) I spent more than a decade, one way or another, on and off, fighting this conspiracy.

Now the final chapter was about to be written. I had tracked down Armand Ricord, the mastermind behind the French Connection, the top heroin trafficker on the planet, in Paraguay. Unlike some of the Colombia kingpins, who adopted wildly extravagant and public lifestyles, Ricord maintained a low profile, living simply, quietly, not attracting attention. He went about his day and his business, doing without his own mountaintop compound or private zoo or army of bodyguards. He was smart, and he had his connections in the Paraguayan government and throughout South America, all neatly and regularly paid off, allowing him to run the biggest smuggling ring in the country and operate throughout the world.

Ricord had picked an interesting place to nest. Paraguay was a dictatorship controlled by General Alfredo Stroessner, a nasty man who kept his landlocked nation poor, and had a penchant for sheltering Nazis escaping from Germany at the end of World War II. Stroessner seized power in 1954, and would stay in office for forty-five bleak years until his ouster in 1989, when civilian government was restored. But until then, Paraguay was a strange and isolated place.

Regardless, it was a place, so the State Department had an ambassador and an embassy on the ground in the capital city of Asuncion, and that ambassador's first priority was protecting his bit of turf. Having U.S. drug agents messing around in his little patch was definitely not on his program.

As per protocol, I informed the ambassador of my investigation, and the ambassador told me that I couldn't work operationally with the local police.

Of course I can, I replied.

So now we were in the middle of a bureaucratic jurisdictional dispute, intragovernment variety. When faced with such a problem, the only solution is to go to the top as quickly as possible. I called Dick Kleindienst.

The U.S. deputy attorney general immediately grasped the situation and went to work. In short order, the ambassador got the word—cooperate.

I didn't have such ambitious plans for the ambassador and me. I just wanted him to stay out of the way. After that, the rest was easy.

It had to be fast and covert. A private 707 jet was flown from the United States to Paraguay in the middle of the night. Armand Ricord was captured and hustled aboard the jetliner, which flew directly to Dallas, allowing us to forego extradition problems between the two nations.

Ricord stood trial and was convicted. After a decade, my personal battle with the organization known the world over as the French Connection, a battle I had waged from the bottom to the very top of the organization's vicious, murderous tentacles, beginning in the mountains of Turkey and ending in an airport outside Asuncion, Paraguay, was finally over.

In 1973, I was named section chief, Office of Intelligence, for the Drug Enforcement Administration (DEA), the latest bureaucratic incarnation of federal drug law enforcement. I was once again based in Washington, D.C. It was certainly not as exciting as going undercover in Chicago or Beirut, but it was a job that was essential to the agency.

After my Washington stint, I was transferred to Boston and eventually to Phoenix. As the DEA moved me from office to office, city to city, I faced the same outrages. A few brief tales from the Boston days:

Item: I discovered that two former federal narcotics agents were selling drugs and government secrets to drug traffickers, including the routes of U.S. military air patrols along the Mexican border. Most treacherously, the feds supplied the names and identities of informants to the dealers, instantly placing the lives of these confidential sources in grave danger. When one of the ex-agents was arrested in Washington, he was carrying a printout from a DEA computer listing informant names and other invaluable information on it. The men charged between five hundred and two thousand dollars per name, sometimes providing a photo as well. Not very much money for a person's life.

Item: Seven people were rounded up in Holyoke, Massachusetts, and another three in Chicago in the course of breaking a million-dollar drug ring. Eleven pounds of heroin was grabbed, with a dealer-to-dealer value of one hundred fifty thousand dollars and a street value of more than one million dollars.

Item: A second-year offensive tackle for the New England Patriots was arrested for selling cocaine on two occasions to an undercover agent. His capture was a small though highly publicized piece of smashing a major international cocaine ring. His conviction ended his career.

Item: Three people were nabbed in a luxury apartment complex, along with a half-pound of cocaine and an ounce of heroin. As a bonus, approximately one hundred thousand dollars in stolen gems was also recovered.

In 1978, I came to Phoenix, Arizona. As Latin American cartels took charge of much of the international drug business, the always porous border between Mexico and the United States became busier and more dangerous as the key transshipment point. And while we tend to think of Latin America in terms of the cocaine trade, the cartels were increasingly interested in diversifying, in pushing any product that had a market. (In fact, with the upsurge in heroin use, heroin labs were starting to be discovered in Latin America.)

When I came to Arizona, as head of the DEA for the region, the drug consumer could find available any narcotic that suited his taste or purpose. Lysergic acid diethylamide—LSD—was experiencing a dramatic surge in popularity. Heroin, marijuana, amphetamines were in abundance, soon followed by crack, angel dust, crystal meth, and anything else that could be grown, mixed, manufactured, ingested, inhaled, injected, bought and sold.

Above all others, cocaine reigned as number one, and it still holds the most prominent place in the drug universe. Cocaine emerged in the seventies as the most lucrative business in the United States, bigger than cars, computers, or clothes. At times, it seemed as if everybody wanted in, everybody, of course, who was willing to step over the line and try for that easy money—laws, risks, and consequences be damned.

Item: Three men were arrested, and one million dollars in drugs was confiscated in Mesa. The largest component of the haul was eight hundred thousand Valium tablets.

Item: A twenty-five-member federal and state task force raided a ranch house in the desert outside Camp Verde. The ranch contained a sophisticated drug laboratory, as well as numerous weapons, guard dogs, and communications equipment. Two men were arrested.

Item: A long-time supervisor for the Phoenix Country Club, who oversaw functions at the prestigious club, was arrested and charged with acting as a major importer of drugs from Mexico. Club members were quoted as being "completely shocked" by the arrest.

Item: Three men were taken into custody at a private residence located on the grounds of the exclusive McCormick Ranch in Scottsdale. A laboratory was discovered inside, with the capacity to manufacture four pounds of methamphetamine every forty-eight hours. One pound of the drug had an illicit value of one hundred thousand dollars.

Item: A Phoenix hair stylist was held on a five million dollar bond, and charged with possession of cocaine with intent to distribute it. The arrest was part of a DEA investigation into a cocaine ring with ties in California, Iowa, Missouri, and Florida.

Item: A man was arrested in a Phoenix hotel room with five pounds of cocaine worth five hundred thousand dollars on the street. Nothing unusual there, nothing that didn't happen far too frequently.

What rendered this arrest deserving of note was that the man was the former head of the Phoenix office of the Arizona Criminal Intelligence System Agency, an official state bureau that acted as a clearinghouse for information on drugs and drug dealers in Arizona. He had worked for the agency for almost six years, and had been dismissed a month before his arrest for unspecified "administrative reasons."

Item: Fifty-three people, including two Phoenix firemen, were indicted by a federal grand jury. All were suspects in a major cocaine ring based in Phoenix and stretching across seven states. More than one hundred DEA agents and local police units moved out at predawn in Phoenix, as part of a coordinated effort to catch drug traffickers in Arizona, California, Florida, Hawaii, Iowa, Kansas, and Missouri. Apart from the firefighters, occupations of the traffickers ranged from clerk to stockbroker, janitor to lawyer.

Not long after the raid, one of the kingpins of the ring was also charged with conspiring to murder witnesses in the case after he approached fellow inmates in the Maricopa County jail, seeking to recruit hit men. His offer for the elimination of potential witnesses was four thousand dollars per murder.

Item: In 1979, I initiated an investigation that eventually led to the largest heroin case ever made in Arizona, and the second largest ever made in the United States. An Iranian national living in our country on a resident alien's visa, and claiming to be an unemployed musician, was arrested with approximately twelve pounds of heroin. This was not brown heroin from Mexico or even the white variety from Turkey and France. No, this was heroin from the "Golden Crescent" of Afghanistan, Pakistan, and Iran, processed in

Iranian laboratories, marking its first appearance in Arizona. This heroin was so pure that its street value was at least twenty million dollars.

But this is far from the end of it. The drugs had been transported from Iran to Kuwait, and then flown by suitcase to Phoenix. Dubbed "the Kuwaiti Connection" by the media, this was not a case of an individual acting alone; this was a major conspiracy, with links to many gangs and perhaps even governments. Remember, this was going on at the same time the regime of Ayatollah Khomeini was holding Americans hostage in our embassy in Tehran. The political dimensions could not be ignored.

Of the twelve original defendants, including the ringleader and his wife, nine were Iranian. Clearly, they were associated with a Middle Eastern gang that might very well have been connected to the anti-American government in Tehran. Khomeini's fundamentalist Islamic state was short of cash, having effectively cut itself off from most of the rest of the world. The drug trade was a fast way to make a lot of money, and strike a blow against its supposed enemies in the bargain.

The defendant was let out on bail, and arrested a few months later with another suitcase with $1.75 million in heroin stashed inside. Four more confederates were arrested, two of whom were Iranian.

The real questions were how much heroin had slipped into the country before they were discovered—how many others were part of the ring throughout the country who remained uncovered—precisely what rank the defendants occupied in the ring's hierarchy—how deeply involved the Iranian government was in the smuggling operation.

I have made the point more than once that drugs must be fought at every level. Now you can see the other side of that reality, i.e., how the drug cartels conspire with governments (as well as banks, airlines, and anyone or anything else), to achieve their objectives. Sometimes partners in these illicit ventures have different goals in mind, which may or may not overlap. In this instance, the traffickers might have been only interested in making as much money as they could, while the ayatollah might have been interested in both making money, and inflicting harm on the United States.

When the stakes are this high, the methods employed by the bad guys can be nothing less than brutal and cruel. While I would never advocate our government and law enforcement agencies adopting those attitudes and techniques, we must recognize the enemy for who and what they are, and respond accordingly.

So those are a few of my tales, a handful of my stories from the front lines. They're not all pretty or neat or comforting, but that is the reality on the streets, in our schools, in our homes. This is the war I have been waging for my entire adult life. This is the war that many American law enforcement professionals have been waging their entire careers. And this is the war that many Americans have been victimized by for their entire lives.

I have spent this chapter recounting some of my victories on both American and foreign soil, victories that have brought me personal and professional satisfaction, victories that have made a difference in our endless conflict.

I am not embarrassed to tell you that I am proud of what I have accomplished. I am a professional. I have always worked hard, I have always done the best job I can. I haven't waved the flag every time I've caught someone.

But I have always been aware of what is at stake. I have seen the devastation, I have seen the stunning cost. I understand why we can never give up this fight.

All this talk about victories might seem hollow. After all, I have already stated that the drug war is a failure. We are fighting a battle we are not winning.

Nonetheless, the victories I have recounted prove that we *can* win. We *can* make a difference. If we can stop them here, in Phoenix, and then there, in Chicago or Washington or Boston, and then we can add to that progress real success in Latin America and Southeast Asia and the Middle East, then we have achieved a great deal. Our problem has always been a lack of consistency in our drug policy implementation. Our problem has always been the many agencies of the government not working in unison. Our problem has always been our inability to use one triumph to build another and then another and another.

If we did all that, for once and for the long haul, the major goals of the drug war could be attained. And that would be more than an achievement. That would change our nation, that would better our nation, in more ways than we can imagine.

And so we have no choice but to continue the fight, continue to fight all the way, with all we can give.

CHAPTER FOURTEEN

Winning the Drug War

The preceding chapter provided you with something of a quick tour of the history of the drug war, through my special perspective. Now that you've seen the past, let's talk about the future.

The first question that must be asked is whether we have the national political will to take on drugs the way I think we need to take on drugs.

That is not an easy question to answer, because it raises so many other questions? How far are we willing to go? Does the government really want to get tough with other nations? Are the bureaucrats really willing to reorganize law enforcement to render the entire structure more efficient? Will the politicians really take the politics out of the law enforcement effort? On and on.

So let us begin.

I must start with a brief statement against legalizing drugs, because that is the foundation for all our efforts. We cannot win a war we do not all believe it is right to fight. The nation will not unite to pull out all the stops to battle a scourge until it has agreed on the virulence of that scourge. So I start with my view on the danger of drugs.

A posse member watches over a prisoner cleanup crew

We've all heard the same stories, such as how narcotics were legalized in certain European cities, and how those cities did not benefit in any manner from encouraging casual users and addicts to flock to their centers. We've all heard the same arguments, pro and con, such as the monetary benefits that would accrue to the government if we legalized drugs and taxed their sale on one hand, and on the other, how much revenue the nation would lose from soaring health costs and declining production on the job.

While all that is interesting, my rationale is simpler, grounded in historical experience. I'll explain through the use of an example—the example of pornography.

Pornography used to be illegal in the United States. Given its widespread availability, that might be hard for some readers to imagine. However, those of us a bit older surely remember a time when eight-millimeter stag movies (often supposedly shipped in from Denmark or Sweden or some other land of allegedly lascivious behavior), were the hottest tickets around.

Pornography's illegal status resulted in one very concrete fact— an awful lot of Americans wouldn't buy the movies. They wouldn't buy them, even if they could find them. Simple and absolute, no contest, no question.

Now that porn is legal, now that the statutory prohibitions have vanished, so have all moral and ethical prohibitions. Now that all that has been swept away, pornography is seemingly everywhere, in book and video stores, in movie theaters, and on television, at corner newsstands, and sundry shops—everywhere. The customers are no longer just the usual suspects, college boys and dirty old men. Now, everyone is included—fathers and mothers, sons and daughters, friends, family, co-workers.

Pornography is everywhere, because the law has given it an implicit stamp of approval. How you personally feel about that, or whether you are wondering about other questions that must be considered, such as First Amendment rights, put all that aside for purposes of this discussion. This example is about cause and effect, and so I ask: Did pornography suddenly become all right just because stores sell it, and the state collects its slice of tax money?

Not necessarily. At the very least, a lot of people who study these matters assert that pornography desensitizes the viewer to an entire spectrum of human emotions. At the very worst, a lot of people maintain that pornography causes violence against women. I've never heard anybody say pornography does anything good for anybody other than the guy making money off it.

But none of that matters now, because it is legal, and people are flocking to get it. They're not concerned about pornography's possible negative effects, because if the state permits them to do it, they will. They're going to watch it, even if scientists could knock on their doors, sit down in their living rooms, and prove that pornography is harmful to their mental health—they'll watch because it is legal.

Obviously, the same query applies to items of harm to our physical health, such as with tobacco. If tobacco was discovered yesterday and cigarettes invented today, and all the health risks known from the start, would we legalize them? I doubt it. (The same question can be asked of alcohol, though the answer, given the physiological ability of most people to use alcohol in safe measure, is not as certain.)

As far as tobacco and alcohol are concerned, the cat has been out of the bag for a long time. At this point, the same might be true of pornography. I don't know. However, I do know that the legal prohibition against drugs keeps literally millions of Americans from using them.

For that reason alone, drugs cannot be legalized. Nor should any drugs be decriminalized. Does it make any sense that it's illegal to sell it but not to own it? Of course not. We have to be consistent. We have to be logical. If we are ever going to seriously impede the flow and use of drugs, we have to stop them across the board, stop them cold.

Now that you know where I stand, let's discuss some of my recommendations and remedies.

Let's begin with politics. Most of us think of law enforcement as a nonpolitical endeavor, but the reality is that politics plays a crucial role in how we attack crime—*if* we attack crime—both here and abroad.

First of all, we have to undertake a thorough reorganization of the federal law enforcement machine.

In the manner of bureaucracies everywhere, federal law enforcement has become overgrown and inefficient. The United States government has no fewer than forty agencies involved in drugs. That means forty major agencies competing for a piece of that huge taxpayer money pie. You can walk into any agency and find that they have their own little group, contending to get its piece of the billions spent on drugs. Even Housing and Urban Development (HUD), has its own force.

Every agency wants some of the money, and, consequently, they all wind up spending way too much of their time and energy fighting other agencies for funding and turf and power. We can only guess at how much of the money earmarked for fighting the drug war is being wasted, expended, and lost in these bureaucratic sideshows.

We need one top law enforcement agency on drugs, and that is and must continue to be the Drug Enforcement Administration. The chief drug agency used to be under the Treasury Department's jurisdiction. Then a bureaucratic juggling act placed the DEA in the Justice Department, where it resides beside the FBI. That means that both the DEA and the FBI work for the same bureaucracy, with both agencies possessing concurrent jurisdiction. Stated in more direct terms, you have two agencies doing the same thing, working for the same boss. Does that make sense? Who else operates in such an expensively inefficient manner? Could any private business survive for long duplicating and confusing the labors of its employees? Only a bureaucracy, which isn't accountable through the normal mechanisms of profit and loss, or answerable to shareholders who hold financial stakes in its operations, can maintain without bothering to justify such an illogical and wasteful state of affairs.

For years, the much larger FBI has been trying to take over the jurisdiction of the DEA, trying to absorb the DEA. I'm totally opposed to that. Drugs is such an important crime, we surely need one agency dedicated to drugs and nothing else.

In addition, it is probably not wise to invest too much power in one agency. Merging the FBI and the DEA—as well as Alcohol, Tobacco and Firearms—(ATF), which is currently under discussion—will create a huge federal police force. That is a prospect that few people would welcome.

One of the chief rationalizations supporters of this merger mania inevitably cite is the overlapping nature of the drug trade. For example, consider a hypothetical Russian gang, based in Moscow, that is selling weapons to Iraq and funneling some of those profits into a massive drug smuggling operation with a Syrian connection. The FBI, with an office in Moscow and initial interest and jurisdiction in dealing with that Russian gang, might claim that its agents need to control the investigation. The DEA, naturally, believes it should manage the drug smuggling end of the affair. Thus, the critics observe, wouldn't it be more efficient to simply join the agencies together, and let the FBI run the whole show?

Absolutely not. By controlling everything, the details, and the myriad of cases that can come out of an international investigation, can get lost in the process. Experts in weapons and drugs collide, whether they're situated in the same office or across the street from one another. Having separate agencies does not mean that they cannot work together, that they cannot coordinate their investigations.

Obviously, with the FBI operating an office in Moscow and the DEA shut out, a problem does present itself. However, the solution is to fix the problem rather than create a new one. Open a DEA office in Moscow.

Let the DEA, with its single-minded focus on drugs, handle drugs. Let the FBI handle the weapons angle. Let them cooperate and coordinate when prudent.

This is hardly a radical idea. The Secret Service is in charge of all matters involving counterfeit money. If the FBI or ATF or anybody else stumbles across a case involving counterfeiting, they turn it over to the Secret Service, no questions asked, no doubt about it.

No one interferes with its jurisdiction or expertise. Why should it be any different for the DEA?

I can give you one reason. There's only so much money, power, and glory in the counterfeiting game. Drugs, on the other hand, are quite a different subject. That's one very strong reason.

Congress has had more than several hearings on the proposal to combine the agencies, prompted by the FBI, and the DEA still exists only because Congress has rejected the Bureau's appeals and instead has insisted on maintaining DEA's independence.

This is not to say that changes are not constantly afoot. I have three different badges from my days as a fed, because every new president steps into office determined to reorganize the war on drugs. The implementation of their proposals, when they have been implemented, has invariably resulted in adding more layers of bureaucracy, which in turn has done nothing but hamper, or even block the real work.

And the bureaucracies just keep getting bigger, and the bigger any organization gets, the fewer people you have doing the job. Instead, you have chiefs and deputy chiefs and assistant chiefs. You have people earning tremendous salaries, enjoying generous perks and playing the role of corporate-type administrators. In this business, that doesn't cut it.

In police work, activity breeds activity. You cannot uncover and accumulate intelligence sitting in an office in a white shirt and tie, working on a two-year-old conspiracy case. While you're on the phone, leaning back in your leather chair, the dealers are busy selling dope on the streets.

Before I get ahead of myself and begin discussing law enforcement methods, here's a short and self-evident counterproposal. Instead of subsuming the DEA into the FBI, why not do the obvious, and transfer the couple of hundred or so FBI agents assigned to drug duty into the DEA? Sounds simple enough, doesn't it?

I advise you not to hold your breath waiting for it to happen.

Let's address another fundamental problem. Some years ago, Senator Mike Mansfield, then a very influential member of

Congress, proposed and helped pass a bill that basically stated that law enforcement officers could no longer act operationally overseas. We were officially forbidden from being at the scene, present and accounted for when the deal was going down.

The Mansfield Amendment effectively restricted the role of an American agent to that of adviser or even observer.

Senator Mansfield was prompted by a few incidents between DEA agents posted overseas and drug dealers, causing some diplomatic problems. To claim that the amendment obstructed our drug-fighting efforts would be an understatement. By restricting our ability to initiate, carry through, and complete investigations, Mansfield and his fellow legislators effectively cut off the DEA at the knees. Senator Mansfield set back the American effort to combat drugs by years. In politics, people like to throw around blame recklessly and cruelly. That, as I hope you've gathered by this time, is not my style. In the real world, blame must be assigned when it is appropriate and informative. This is one such instance.

Like it or not, the bottom line on law enforcement is pretty straightforward, and if you didn't know what it is before you read the previous chapter, you know it now: Investigate and act, seize the drugs, put the handcuffs on the bad guys, case closed. It can get down and dirty, but there is no other way.

The DEA currently has more than four hundred agents (about 10 percent of all DEA agents), working in most U.S. embassies. They essentially function in a liaison capacity, consulting and advising as their foreign counterparts conduct (or attempt to conduct, or pretend to attempt to conduct) the war.

So now the DEA can't do its job anymore, not in the manner it needs to get done.

It is not my intention to bad-mouth any law enforcement agency, especially the one I called home for so many years. Nonetheless, I must say that when you compare how much we accomplished in the old days—when I was working in Turkey, and the entire U.S. Bureau of Narcotics totaled not many more than two hundred extremely active agents, backed by a minuscule six-million-dollar budget—with how the battle is progressing today, you can agree that something is wrong.

Another fundamental problem goes all the way to the top.

Every American president's top priorities are national security and the economy. No one can question just how profoundly the international drug traffic endangers both. Drugs flow into our nation, and drug money flows out, to Mexico, Central and South America, to the Far and Near East. The economy is hurt in many ways, including the decreased productivity of workers. The devastation to our citizens, our families, and our communities must be seen as a threat to our national security.

So what can the president do? I'll explain, courtesy of yet another example. As you already know, we broke up the French Connection, in operation for at least thirty-five years, in the late sixties and early seventies. This occurred during President Nixon's tenure, when all this country had to fight the drug war was the undermanned, underfunded Bureau of Narcotics. While that was a tremendous victory, it would have languished in isolation, a separate triumph in a raging tidal wave of Turkish opium cresting our shores, but for the efforts of Richard Nixon.

That's the reality. Obviously, it's not my natural inclination to diminish the scope of my work as a drug fighter, but this discussion is not merely about me, it is about the health and future of my country. And, we have to acknowledge that this war, same as every war, must be fought at every level, from the front lines, where I usually operated, to the White House.

So, the truth is, the war in Turkey was won because we hit them high and low: we struck hard at the suppliers and dealers, and then the president struck even harder by convincing the Turkish leaders to dry up opium by outlawing legal cultivation. Nixon announced, quite simply, to the Turks, "You will do it or you will receive no more foreign aid."

And that was it for the Turkish connection. Say what you will about Nixon, he was a tremendous drug fighter. He loved it. We used to go to the White House and regale him with war stories about drugs, stories about our undercover operations, and all the rest.

Nixon didn't stop with Turkey. He personally applied pressure to other countries and their presidents and prime ministers and generals as well. His leadership in this war gave us the opening to crack down on the Marseilles laboratories and the Corsican Mafia that comprised many of the components of the French Connection.

After Nixon acted, the rest was relatively easy. We cracked down on the Mafia in New York City. And we basically wiped out that French Connection, which was *the* drug connection. Other opium and heroin sources have sprung up, such as several in Asia's Golden Triangle, which are powerful and dangerous, but that is not the point. The point is, why after so many years did we wipe out this tremendous, international criminal organization? One reason stands out above all others: Because the president of the United States declared that it would happen, and he set the forces in motion to make it happen.

The president is not the only individual in a leadership position who is vital to the success or failure of the war on drugs. Who do you think is the most influential person in Washington, after the chief executive, in this fight? I bet you don't know.

Well, I'll tell you.

The second most important person in the government is the secretary of state. He represents the foreign policy of the United States, dealing directly with foreign leaders and the global media, spelling out our beliefs, detailing our agenda, negotiating our treaties and policies. Just as important, the secretary of state controls all our ambassadors posted overseas, who in turn relate on a daily basis to the presidents and prime ministers and generals and sheiks, who in turn control all the governments' agencies.

Now let me ask you another question: Have you ever heard a secretary of state go public and proclaim that we will fight this drug problem, no matter what? No! One after another, I've listened to them talk about not rocking the boat, not having any international incidents, blah, blah, blah. But I've never heard a secretary of state announce we are going to get those foreign governments to go down the line with us and take care of this problem, or we will cut off all foreign aid. Period, end of discussion.

In fact, George Shultz, secretary of state under Ronald Reagan, has actually talked about legalizing marijuana. After seeing all that he must have seen while in office—amazing!

Talking about cabinet officers, I met with Henry Kissinger when he was National Security Adviser during his visit to Mexico in 1970. During a meeting lasting several hours, the primary topic was Colombia and the prospect of substituting crops, as we did in Turkey. But when Kissinger became secretary of state, he forgot all about it, same as every foreign affairs chief before him. All the heroin and cocaine and most of the marijuana comes in from foreign countries. So again—why isn't every secretary of state laying down the law to our many foreign friends?

Think about it. Think about that wasted power and authority. Think about the many wasted opportunities. Think about what this nation could accomplish if our government resolved to take another course, resolved to use its skills and power to full advantage.

More than soldiers or money, it would require character and backbone.

Maybe that's too much to expect from a politician. But, you know, everybody seems to run for sheriff each November. What I mean is, every politician wants to be viewed as the toughest on crime. Now that the election's over and the politicos are safely ensconced in office, let's see what they're going to do about crime.

Now I recognize that the economies of some countries have grown dependent on the drug trade. I also recognize that many officials in those countries are corrupt. But don't you think we have corruption in these United States? Don't you think some of our local economies have grown dependent on drugs? Consider Florida, where the 1980s witnessed the peak of the inflow of cocaine into the state from South America, and it was said that one of every ten dollars deposited in the local banks came from drug profits. Should we have abandoned the Sunshine State to the cartels? Of course not. Instead, we fought back, and cut back the influence and power of the drug trade.

That's what every community and every country must do. It might be a tough sell, and we might have to get tough, using aid programs, military programs, and other sensitive programs.

I don't want all this talk of toughness to give you the wrong idea. I am hardly suggesting we throw out the Constitution and do away with the Bill of Rights, as some knee-jerk commentators automatically assume. In fact, I'll give you one example to prove my all-American, freedom-loving heart is in the right place.

I've always opposed handing the Pentagon a role in the drug war, including the offshore reconnaissance duties they've been performing, despite the enthusiasm of several presidents and much of the media. I'm worried about giving the military that small opening into civilian responsibilities. Once that breach has been scaled, where does it stop? Before we know it, they'll be patrolling the borders, and what's next after that? The military in hot pursuit across the borders, and then we go down that slippery slope, and we suddenly have troops in foreign streets.

We've set a very dangerous precedent, and it isn't necessary. Why doesn't the government give those resources and responsibilities to the legitimate agencies? Beef up the Coast Guard, beef up Customs, beef up the U.S. Border Patrol.

Now is the time for a few words about methods, and an example will start us off.

President Salvador Allende of Chile was a Marxist leader when Marxists were America's Public Enemy Number One. American politicians and government officials rained down their contempt, fury, and threats upon the Chilean president.

Consequently, it will come as no surprise to hear that relations between the U.S. and Chile were chilly at best. Even our ambassador couldn't get in to see Allende.

At the time, I was the regional director of the DEA for Mexico, Central and South America. Politics aside, I had a job to do, and if

I was going to do it well, I had to find a way to deal with the Chilean authorities.

And I did.

As director, my responsibilities didn't let me get out in the field as often as I liked. I had agents who did most of the legwork, the investigating, the fighting. I was an administrator and a diplomatic officer. My role, more or less, was to meet with the heads of the countries and the national police and convince them to cooperate with us. In this politically delicate situation, cooperating meant that they allowed us to help them, help them as they carried the load in attacking drugs.

So my main mission was to generate interest among these high officials in the drug war, and get them to do the job. However, as was standard among Latin nations, the Chileans had neither the money nor the expertise to conduct the war as it needed to be fought. Thus, I had to deal not only with geopolitical questions but also with inadequate force ability. Not a happy set of circumstances.

Allende's cousin was the chief of the national police, and I knew he was the key to a successful relationship between my office and his nation. I walked onto the scene on a positive note, because I had already established pretty good relations with cops in countries throughout the region. I was a known commodity, and, I am proud to state, was widely considered a straight shooter, in words and deeds. In the context of those years, that basically meant that the Chilean police chief knew I really was DEA, hunting drugs, and not CIA, hunting something else.

That was the beginning. Then, even though I had other responsibilities, I frequently ventured into the field. It was just like in Turkey: I'd go undercover up in the boondocks one day, escorted by some local law enforcement officers, shoot it out with the bad guys, seize the drugs, and then the next day I'd meet the chief of the national police and the generals of the army. And soon enough, the police chief and the army generals would hear about the gun battles and arrests from their subordinates, because that kind of news always travels fast. They would hear about who could be trusted in the heat of the action, who stood fast when the bullets flew, and who didn't.

Signed pacts or handshake deals or old school ties might be great, but nothing binds men together like danger. Nothing proves that one man can trust another like the sound of gunfire.

So between all that and more than a few rounds of drinks, the president's cousin learned to trust me. And so Allende trusted me, at least enough to receive me and listen to what I had to say.

This is not to suggest that I supported Allende or his regime. It wasn't my duty to get involved in geopolitics. Those judgments and decisions did not fall within my jurisdiction.

I was simply fighting drugs, as always, whether in Chicago, Turkey, or Santiago, Chile. That was my mission. I made certain that Allende, his cousin, and everybody else in officialdom understood that. And they could respect that mission and support it.

So that was one method, an on-the-scene method, so to speak, of fighting drugs.

Let's examine another issue that could fall into the method's category:

Law enforcement has fallen into a trap, perhaps an almost inevitable trap, and it's as simple as this: Whatever the federal government does, the state and local authorities follow in lockstep. When Nixon got tough on drugs, he urged the feds to conduct major raids, knocking down doors and grabbing the drugs. And we did, and so everybody else did, too. The locals organized themselves in similar fashion and went charging into the streets following the feds. On the other hand, sometimes it works the other way around, with the feds pushing the locals to step into line with their lead. Either way, the result is the same, and that doesn't always make sense, because the feds and the locals must have different priorities. Each must concentrate on its mission, on its expertise. The feds must aim for the cartels, the international dealers, the larger picture. The locals have to stop the drugs at the street level, making it too hard and unrewarding to stand on that corner and wait for the customers to pick up their junk.

That doesn't mean that the feds and the locals shouldn't work together whenever useful. Many cases involve concurrent jurisdiction. A drug shipment originating overseas might land in my county. Thus, both my department and the feds would have an interest in the case. Obviously, my narcotics detectives would be most knowledgeable about the fate of that drug shipment once it hit the Maricopa County streets, while the federal agents would be the experts on the other end of that pipeline. Working together could make both their jobs easier.

In essence, the working relationship between the feds and the locals shouldn't be much different than the way I described how the rest of the government should regard the DEA—give each agency its jurisdiction and its due, and work with the agency, not around it or over it or against it.

Another methodology problem: Invariably, the government reacts to the drug of the day. A couple of years ago it was crack cocaine. Drop everything else and go after crack. Just before that it was cocaine. Now, particularly in our region, it's methamphetamine. I predict that in two or three years, heroin will be the top drug. And each time another drug gets top billing in the press and with law enforcement, all ongoing efforts are put on hold as cops and money are redirected to go after whatever's the latest, most exciting, most awful, most popular drug.

Instead, we have to be consistent, we have to target all drugs, not on a day-to-day basis, but all the time. Our fickle enforcement policies have meant that we've ended up with a situation where any local TV station can go out and film drug transactions, hour after hour, day after day. If news crews can do it, why can't the police find and grab the bad guys? Of course the cops can, if they are ordered to do so. Law enforcement has to put manpower on the streets, acquire intelligence, make arrests, and keep up a constant presence instead of hit-and-run tactics.

One more time: We have to get back to the streets. When I was with the old Bureau of Narcotics, we used to work nickel-bag cases. But we did it with discrimination, always with a reason. Does this guy get it from that guy, who gets it from that guy, up and up? Let's start from the bottom and try to work up. The result is a two-pronged assault: The police are taking guys off the streets while they're also accumulating intelligence.

Here's still another point about methods, and it's related to what we just discussed. Every cop has his informers, the snitches who supply a great deal of the information on which the police rely to make their cases. So when the word comes down from the top to hit methamphetamine laboratories, each cop asks his best informant whether he knows anything about meth labs. And the informant will probably answer, "Oh, yeah, I can do that for you," because meth labs are popping up all over the place.

In other words, it's the easy case. However, does anybody ask that same informer, "Hey, while you're at it, what do you know about heroin coming in from Mexico?" No, the cop usually zeroes in on the topic at hand and forgets all about the other drugs. Law enforcement has to use all its resources, even its snitch resources, to the fullest.

If a kid is selling drugs, put him away. If a kid is using drugs, the courts have to use common sense. Don't ruin a kid's life if he can be saved. The degree of the crime must be considered. My philosophy is to go after the dope peddlers. Cut it off at the source.

Through it all, while we are juggling the many components of our drug problem, it is important to keep things in perspective.

And another thing: Sometimes we overemphasize some of the problems we face, and throw up our hands in frustration, and neither attempt nor accomplish anything. Similarly, sometimes we oversimplify the problems, and think that the quick and easy solution is the best, a path that again leads to failure.

In all my years overseas, I never had a case ruined because of corruption, whether we're talking about Turkey or Argentina or Mexico. Maybe, because I was on the scene, pressing hard, maybe the corrupt authorities had no choice but to follow through with the case. Certainly local corruption made my job more difficult, though absolutely not impossible. When corruption was an issue and an obstacle, I found a way around it, and found honest people who wanted to do their jobs and clean up their own backyards.

I never ignored corruption, and on more than one occasion, presented evidence of the same to the local higher authorities. Sometimes they acted on my information, and sometimes they didn't. In any event, I got the job done. In any event, it's always better to have an American agent on the scene so that agent can push, prod, or assist the locals, whatever is necessary, as well as report back to Washington so our leaders can do the same at their level, persuading or perhaps bulldozing the foreign government into line.

So never give up, even if our foreign counterparts are thoroughly compromised and corrupted. There are always good people who want to help. There are always cases to be made. There are always victories to be won.

As for oversimplifying the problem: Our government sometimes acts as if the dilemma rests solely on the shoulders of one person or even one cartel. "If we could only get rid of him," so the feeling goes, "we can clean up this mess." It didn't work when we eliminated Diem in Vietnam in the early sixties, and it didn't work when we invaded Panama and captured Noriega in the eighties. Vietnam only got worse, and I don't know if anything has changed for the better in Panama. Problems as enormous as the international drug industry are neither the result nor under the control of one man. Rather, they are a systemic societal problem, ranging from the socioeconomic conditions of the farmers in the countryside to the processors and dealers in the cities, to the stability and maturity of the political process, on and on. And that's just on one side of the equation, because we have not yet calculated the socioeconomic and political conditions on the receiving end, on the drug-using end.

Hey, everybody likes to go after the big guys. I've certainly done more than my share of major head-hunting. Nonetheless, I've also contributed many more than my share of nickel-bag busts. Both count.

Example: For years, we focused on the specter of the Medellin Cartel in Colombia. Finally, the Medellin Cartel started to break up, partially because of our work, and partially because of competition, and also management difficulties. So when the Medellin Cartel crumbled, at least in part, we congratulated ourselves. Unfortunately, the cocaine kept flowing into the U.S., and that was because the Medellin Cartel was replaced by the Cali Cartel, a smoother, more businesslike group. Now the power is shifting again, to other players and brokers. So targeting individuals and groups and cartels is all well and good and smart, until our concentration blinds us to the larger questions. Consider the French Connection again. We stopped it through a wide effort, which included: (a) fighting growers and dealers in the mountains of Turkey, (b) gaining the assistance of the Turkish government, (c) stopping the laboratories in Corsica and Marseilles, (d) gaining the assistance of the French, Italian, and other governments, (e) breaking the pipeline in Canada and New York, and (f) coordinating the efforts of local and federal agencies in the U.S.

Through the course of a long and difficult process, you can be sure that we encountered corruption. You can also be sure that we uncovered some bad guys who qualified as Mr. Bigs. Yet the corruption did not deter us, and the big shots did not distract us from achieving an overall triumph.

Drugs are the enemy. The bad guys are captured by their power, same as the addicts and users are enslaved by them.

Drugs have taken up a great amount of space in this book about crime and punishment, as they must. After all, if 70 percent of all crime begins with drugs, in one form or another, shouldn't we concentrate on eliminating them?

That goes for the jails as well. Along with other jails and prisons, I instituted the first random drug-testing program in any jail system in the country. We cannot allow the problem to follow the drug abuser into the system. While we have him under our control, we must see to it that he is stopped from getting and using narcotics. That's also why I started a drug treatment program. Drug treatment programs on the outside are so overcrowded that they need all the help they can get.

The bottom line is that if we can get them straight and sober, maybe at least a few of them will change their lives around and not commit more crimes, and get themselves tossed back into jail. Maybe, maybe not—either way, it's definitely worth the effort.

The methods and measures that are available to us are many, but our choices are not, for there is but one real choice: We must fight, and we must win the war against drugs, or, more precisely, the war against people who use and sell drugs. I am convinced that this war can be won. Anything this country has set its collective mind to accomplish, it has accomplished. This battle is, first and foremost, a matter of educating the public to the real threat, as well as the horrific cost of doing nothing. Once the American people comprehend what awaits us if we keep heading in the present sorrowful direction, then the rest is just a matter of courage and will.

America has never lacked for either.

PART IV

Final Thoughts, Future Considerations

CHAPTER FIFTEEN

The People and the Press

A t the end of October 1995, I was invited to attend the Phoenix 500, the eighth annual running of the NASCAR Winston Cup Series, held at the Phoenix International Raceway. The race always fills the stands, attracting more than one hundred thousand fans to the track from across the country and around the world. The Nashville Network televises the event to an audience estimated in 1995 at forty million.

Before the race started, Ava and I were brought down to the track. We sat down in the back of a convertible, or really *on* the back of a convertible, and they drove us around as we waved to the crowd. The convertible stopped in front of the main grandstand, and we got out.

Buddy Jobe, who owns the raceway, was there to greet us. To thank him for his invitation to watch the race, I presented him with a pair of pink "Go Joe" boxer shorts. (In case you haven't heard about the pink boxers, wait, because you will in a moment.)

Pink shorts are the answer in more ways than one

Buddy Jobe thanked me most profusely and then introduced me to the crowd with the kind of broad enthusiasm that comes naturally to many Southwesterners.

"Thank you, Sheriff Joe," Buddy said to me, and then addressed the massive crowd.

"This is the guy who spent a night down at the jail all alone with one thousand inmates," he announced, "who had no reason to be there other than to say, 'Hey, I'm here, I'm a man, and I'll show what a real man can do!' And he did it."

The crowd cheered. Buddy had a little more to add. "And I'll tell you what—this is a real man. I'll tell you what—thank you, Sheriff. We appreciate you, and you're a credit to your profession."

The crowd applauded and yelled, Buddy and I shook hands, and the race got under way.

Why, you might be wondering, am I bothering to relate this story? Was it simply an opportunity to let somebody say something nice about me? A little pat on the back from a leading local personage?

Actually, no. I have a point.

And it starts with underwear.

By this time, you might have heard something about the pink boxer shorts. Then again, you might not have, so let me explain. We were issuing boxer shorts—white boxer shorts—to the prisoners in our jails. Then we discovered that inmates were stealing the shorts. Some did it to sell them, while others gave them to their family or friends. They managed to sneak them out while working outside the jail or smuggled them out courtesy of their visitors. You might have trouble believing that anyone would want to wear communal underwear pinched from the pen, but that's why they're criminals and you're not.

Don't think this larceny was small potatoes. Lost boxers cost the taxpayers *forty-eight thousand bucks a year.*

Clearly, something had to be done—exactly what that something was required a little pondering.

Then it hit me. Oh, yes.

And that's where the pink shorts enter.

It occurred to me that all these tough guys (at least they think of themselves as tough, though most of them are just punks), wouldn't be caught dead wearing pink. They would no longer want the shorts, and neither would any of their family, friends, or customers. Even if they might consider stealing them, the pink would be easier to spot, harder to smuggle.

So the dye went in the washing machines, and out came the shorts—totally pink.

And then the funniest thing happened: The boxers were a hit. I'm talking about a *huge* hit. The local media picked up the story and ran with it, and then the ripples started spreading. People heard about the program in Colorado, in California, in New York. CBS interviewed me on its morning show to talk about the shorts. Court TV did a piece on this unexpected fashion trend. The BBC called for a quote. The BBC on boxers—amazing! Now I wasn't surprised when the tents intrigued the press, or when the mall patrol or the chain gang or cutting off inmates' coffee captured the media's attention, but this—even *I* didn't anticipate this.

But that didn't mean I wasn't prepared to take reasonable advantage of this phenomenon.

The interest in the shorts was so great that it created its own market. Thus, it was only smart to satisfy that market by producing pink boxer shorts for sale, proceeds to benefit the aforementioned Sheriff's Posse Foundation. If you will recall, the foundation seeks to raise money to reimburse posse members for some of their expenses, which, as I have previously outlined, can be considerable.

In no time, the shorts were ready to go on sale. We made a few improvements for the retail market, adding a gold sheriff's star to one side and my signature beneath it. Chief Hendershott's fifteen-year-old son, also named David, suggested that the words "Go Joe" should be inscribed on the shorts, and they were, on the other leg of the boxers.

The foundation didn't have a lot of money to lay out up front on production, and we didn't know what to expect, so just 3,000 were ordered. The posse itself took the lead, and a group of volunteers set up and manned a few tables in Wal-Marts and other business establishments. And then the posse members waited.

But they sure didn't wait long because one, two, three, the boxers were sold out. So we ordered a few more—20,000 more to be precise. And the posse got out the tables and started selling those. And, by God, sell they did.

So when more than one hundred thousand people assembled at the Phoenix International Raceway, the posse recognized a prime location when it saw one, and lugged ten tables and a van full of boxers to the track.

I decided to take a look after my lap around the asphalt oval and headed to the area around the grandstands. There were rows of booths selling all sorts of goods, from food to souvenirs. Some were doing well, some were not doing so well.

Our table was doing just fine. A man bought a pair, and asked me to autograph them for his son. A woman purchased two pairs and had me sign her shorts. A line soon formed, and I spent the next three-and-half hours autographing boxers. By the end of the day, between the Phoenix International Raceway and the malls and other locations around town, the posse had sold thousands of pink boxer shorts.

Even more astonishing was the variety of people who bought the underwear. Most of them were from Arizona, of course, and they universally urged me to keep doing what I was doing:

"We're behind you, Sheriff! Put more of those bums on the chain gangs! I like seeing them out there working!"

"You're the best thing that ever happened to Phoenix."

"Sheriff Joe! We support you! Go get 'em!"

"Good for you for cutting out coffee. If it were up to me, I'd have the prisoners on bread and water."

That was pretty much expected, par for the course. But the enthusiasm did not only hail from Arizona natives. Five officers from the Los Angeles Police Department bought shorts and asked how they could apply to transfer to the Maricopa County Sheriff's Office. I gave them a phone number to call, along with a very brief primer on my budgetary conflict with the Board of Supervisors, and wished them well. A woman from Michigan, a couple from Colorado, a whole bunch from Texas, a man from New York—all had heard something about what we were doing in Maricopa County, and were buying shorts in order to show their appreciation or support—or maybe they just liked pink cotton boxers.

But it didn't stop at our shores. Two gentlemen from England made their way to the head of the line. They had seen me on the BBC. They each went home with a pair of shorts.

We're ordering many, many more pink boxers.

Amazing!

What I'm attempting to demonstrate by this rather unusual circumstance, this side issue, you might say, is the power of the press. All those boxer buyers had heard about the shorts courtesy of the televised or print media. But this doesn't mean that the media is seeking to promote me—not by a long shot. I would never claim that the press and I are entangled in a mutual admiration club. The media has not necessarily embraced all my measures and programs, though the media has gladly covered and reported on virtually everything we've proposed and implemented.

In fact, I'm sure it won't come as a shock to hear that the media is awfully eager to broadcast bad news, whether that news is destructive, hurtful, sensational, immaterial, or inappropriate. In other words, the media is never shy about publishing or televising any information that could be considered harmful to society (or to individuals, for that matter).

Why would the media be willing to behave in such a manner? Because bad news sells. Because scandal sells. Because gossip sells. Because exploitation sells.

But gross, cynical commercialism is not the media's only impetus. There is something else at work, something just as vital and as compelling as the profit motive. The media prides itself on its fundamental belief that it has a special role to play in society. And the media is absolutely correct: It *does* have a special role to play, a precious role that is instrumental in safeguarding our rights by providing us a check on the powerful people and institutions that have so much influence over us. If a well-informed citizenry is essential to the vitality and success of a democracy, then the media is the instrument that provides that underlying information and knowledge.

However...

The media also acts on occasion as if it is not only an important segment of our society but a separate, better, more privileged, more righteous segment. The media has declared itself the new high priest of American civilization. As such, it no longer need concern itself with its own flaws or conflicts, but has raised itself above ordinary questions of honesty and decency. The media is busy ensuring that *everyone else* adheres to its standards of right and wrong. The media has seized for itself the mantle of ultimate arbiter of morality and ethics, and it finds most of us seriously wanting.

Now don't get me wrong. I'm not climbing up on a soapbox to urge that we impose restrictions on the media, or that the public boycott the press. I certainly don't believe in such ideas, and my actions prove it. I'll talk to any reporter who walks through my door and asks a question. That's been my policy since I was elected, and I don't see any reason to change, no matter what the media chooses to print or broadcast. I believe in the First Amendment. I believe in the people's right to know exactly what their elected officials are doing. I believe in full disclosure.

A reporter can give me his best shot today, and phone my office tomorrow, knowing I'll take the call. You spend half your life contending with murderers and drug dealers and criminals of all varieties, the kind of people who'll skin you alive if there's five bucks in it. You don't get too frazzled by some journalist trying to get his byline on the front page of the morning edition by quoting "unnamed, confidential sources" "speculating" on "alleged" mistakes, misdeeds. Whatever, they are headlines on Monday and forgotten by Tuesday.

Believe it or not, I even have some journalistic heritage in my blood. My mother's father published an Italian-language newspaper back in Springfield, Massachusetts, for many years.

The bottom line: The media is a business; sadly, no different from most other businesses, willing to do whatever it takes to make a profit. Movie producers like sick, twisted stories about violence and sex, because the audience buys the tickets. Shoe manufacturers shift their factories from the United States to Third World countries, because that's where they can exploit slave labor and save a handful of dollars. And journalists like negative stories and controversy, because that's what sells their products, their newspapers, magazines, and television shows, best of all. The media is more than willing to drag down anyone and knock any new idea, safe in its ivory tower, for the sake of ratings and sales.

That's the simple reality of the situation. Get used to it, deal with it, because that's the way it's going to be for a long, long time.

The truth is, I really don't care what the media says, and not because I'm made of stone. No, I have one good, rational reason for my relaxed attitude, and that's because I know I am not alone. I'm far from the first to realize what's going on. I'm far from the first to remark on the elitism and contempt and cynicism and condescension. This whole situation is hardly a secret concealed from the American people. And that leads to a fascinating situation as far as my specific situation is concerned. The way the public feels about journalists and their entire profession, when they say something good about me, that's fine, and when they say something bad, that's even better, because however they say it, the message gets through. Once again: Regardless of how the media positions my words or actions, *the message gets through to the people.*

I'm not saying that this is how it works for everybody. A lot of innocent people have been hurt by the media, often through casual or reckless or malicious misrepresentations. The Maricopa County Sheriff's Office has been misrepresented often enough, no doubt about that, and so have I. But partly because the department has earned a deep reservoir of goodwill with the public, partly because I have been in the press so often, the truth gets through regardless of how it is presented, partly because the public understands the reality on the streets better than the media elite, and partly because of the clear, unblinking comprehension the public has of the press, the misrepresentations haven't harmed our crime prevention and crime-fighting efforts.

As a matter of fact, I recently encountered a prime example of misrepresentation. A reporter for *George*, the new political/entertainment magazine (or maybe that's entertainment/political magazine), which received an inordinate and thoroughly undeserved amount of press attention prior to its appearance, phoned my office for months, saying he wanted an interview. Somehow, however, month after month, the reporter never made it to Arizona, and never spoke to me. Then one day, lo and behold, an article popped up in *George* on jails in the country, in which the following statement appeared: "Some 5,900 men live year-round in the city of tents... Arpaio's jail is mostly for inmates who have been convicted of no crime." Putting aside the singularly poor sentence construction (isn't the writer saying that the inmates have actually been convicted and the charge was "no crime," a misdemeanor probably somewhere between jaywalking and robbery?), even the most casual reader of this book knows that the tents are restricted to those convicted and sentenced, and that the compound holds thousands fewer than what *George* claimed.

But that wasn't the end of the misrepresentations. George quoted Lisa Allen, the public information officer for the Sheriff's Office, as saying, "...these inmates are disgusting. They're just animals."

Lisa Allen did not say that. It's not in her character or personality. But let's put that aside and deal strictly with practical matters. After fifteen years as a television reporter in Phoenix, Tucson, and Denver, not to mention stints in the marketing and public relations fields, Lisa would not be so stupid or careless to say such things to a reporter. Any way you look at it, the facts don't add up. The quote is either insulting, malicious, or moronic—take your pick.

Lisa wasted no time in informing *George* of its mistakes. As of this writing, I don't know what *George* intends to do about it, if anything. Not that the two-line retraction ever gets anywhere near the attention of the bold-type accusation, but it's better—maybe only marginally better—than nothing.

On the other hand, the *National Enquirer* took an entirely different tack. In the singular style of the *Enquirer*, which allows for unusually long headlines, the bold, black letters read: "Modern Wild West sheriff packs prisoners into tents in the scorching desert... & forms a gun-totin' posse to help him clean up the streets."

The *Enquirer's* piece set its "Wild West" tone right from the top and rode it for all its worth:

"Joe Arpaio is America's toughest sheriff—he puts bad guys in tents in the desert instead of spending taxpayers' money on new prisons.

"The modern-day Wyatt Earp has also put together rifle-toting, horseback-riding posses to chase down criminals. And he's ordered druggies and prostitutes to get out of town by sundown!"

The *Enquirer* continued in a similar vein from there, and it was evidently a vein that the rest of the media regarded as rich with opportunity, because the calls and requests came pouring in. That "toughest sheriff in America" line was picked up, sometimes verbatim, sometimes with modification, near and far. The *New York Post* went with the flow, and also referred to me as "the toughest sheriff in America." *The New York Times* and the *Philadelphia Inquirer* adopted what I deemed to be a more strident tack, opting for "the meanest sheriff." Virtually all the media go one way or the other, toughest/meanest, meanest/toughest. Of course, there's always the periodical or television show that prefers the over-the-top approach, such as *The Guardian*, a British newspaper, which headlined me as "...the meanest, cheapest, harshest jailer in America."

Sometimes it seems that much of the media has decided that being tough on criminals means being—well, it's difficult to pinpoint exactly what the media has decided—but it seems that being tough means also being unfair or backward or reactionary.

For example, how many people know that I appointed a woman as my chief deputy, the highest-ranking official after the sheriff in the office, the first female chief deputy in the history of the Sheriff's Office and the only female chief deputy in any law enforcement agency in the state? Jadel Roe worked her way up to reach the top. But that's essentially a nonstory, because, I think, her promotion, her success does not fit the pat story line that so many media outlets are most comfortable presenting.

In similar fashion, the previously mentioned special Girl Scout unit for daughters whose mothers are in jail, is a program that surely belongs somewhere outside the usual theme about me being the "meanest, cheapest, harshest," receives practically no media coverage.

Lisa Allen, our public information officer, found this similarity, or uniformity, among the media, from *The New York Times* to the *National Enquirer*, to be quite a surprise, and not necessarily a pleasant one. Lisa, the former television correspondent, assumed that this uniformity would not, could not possibly exist, that the mainstream media, the respectable organs of the press, were supposed to be better than the tabloids and the rags. But those distinctions seem to be disappearing, judging by what I've been reading.

Lisa took this realization harder than I did. She liked to believe in journalistic integrity. Journalistic integrity: an important concept, a necessary concept, but, alas, perhaps a quaint, outdated concept.

The *National Enquirer*, *The New York Times*, the networks, the magazines, the newspapers—you pay your money, you take your chances. At least that's how I see it.

But enough theory. Let's have an example. I was profiled by the NBC newsmagazine show, *Now*, on July 13, 1994. NBC is a most respected network, one of the big three, with a long and rich history of investigation, commentary, and reportage, all in the best traditions of journalism.

Then NBC came to Phoenix.

In relating what happened next, I'm not going to attempt to prejudice your opinion, the way the press sometimes tries to do. I'm simply going to report what *Now* had to say, word for word, and you can decide for yourself how its report stacked up against that proud history that journalists so enjoy recalling.

Remember, the idea was that *Now* wanted to provide a fair and full accounting of what I was doing as the sheriff of Maricopa County. Nothing complicated or tricky or unusual there.

Tom Brokaw, NBC's star anchor, introduced the piece by calling me "cocky and controversial." (He also mispronounced my name, but we won't get into that.) The story itself was entitled, "Shoot From The Lip."

Okay. I guess we know which way they were going, right from the start.

Fred Francis, the newsmagazine's chief correspondent, did the reporting and provided the narration. For openers, he said I possessed a "1990s knack for self-promotion that would rival Madonna."

I couldn't argue with that.

A minute later, he casually referred to one of our crime-fighting operations as a "stunt," without providing any justification or reason for that insult.

Quickly moving on, Fred went through the jails and noted my nude magazine ban. NBC showed a prisoner complaining that the detention officers confiscated their nude magazines, and also took down photos of naked women clipped out of the periodicals and hung on the walls.

Fred then chimed in with: "I have a constitutional right to read whatever I want in this country."

"You lose some rights when you go to jail, don't you?" I responded.

"Well," Fred said, "you don't lose your constitutional rights to read a magazine."

"A nude magazine?"

"The Supreme Court has said it."

"No," I said, "the Supreme Court has not said it. I am legal."

Then Fred cut away from our direct discussion to a voice-over, and intoned: "In fact, lawyers for the inmates say the top law enforcement officer in Maricopa County is breaking the law. They say the magazine ban is in direct violation of a court order. He gets around it by claiming that nude magazines are a security threat."

While Fred allowed me to state that 16 percent of the inmates are in jail for sex crimes, and that providing them with these magazines would be like giving "a heroin addict heroin," the finished segment let the presumption remain that the courts have ruled that I am breaking the law.

Nothing could be further from the truth. The ban remains in effect to this day, long after that interview, because it is entirely, completely, 100 percent legal. If NBC had proof that the ban broke the law or was a violation of the Constitution, it should have presented such evidence, because nobody else ever has. This is not a First Amendment issue to me. I do not seek to stop anyone *not* incarcerated from reading nude magazines. In fact, I have granted an interview to *Penthouse*, and the inmates can read that interview—once they're out of jail.

Now did not bother to mention that one-third of our detention officers are women. *Now* did not bother to mention the abuse the female officers continually suffered at the hands of the inmates as they walked the halls or entered the cells. *Now* did not bother to mention how some of the prisoners used the magazines to sexually stimulate themselves. Why should detention officers be forced to look at sexually offensive pictures in their workplace? Why should detention officers have to deal with masturbatory incidents?

If women were forcibly exposed to such conditions at IBM or McDonald's or the Pentagon, you can be sure that *Now* would be screaming about sexism and mistreatment and injustice. But NBC had no such worries here, in the Maricopa County jail system. No, *Now* was more concerned about prisoners getting their pornographic fix than about female detention officers, who have about as tough a job as one can find, not being abused. Go figure.

The underlying issue is simple: An individual loses certain rights upon going to jail. The federal government takes away a felon's right to vote when sentenced to prison, and I have taken away the right to drink coffee, smoke cigarettes, and read some magazines while in jail. NBC did the truth and audience a disservice by its glib presentation.

Let's move along. *Now* took on the posse, and its approach was no-holds-barred. Check out this quote from Fred Francis, spoken while the tape showed a QAP graduation class:

"They may look like sworn deputies, but they're just ordinary citizens, packing pistols while chasing hookers and drug smugglers for Sheriff Joe. If this graduation of brown-shirted posse members smacks of fascism, it doesn't bother the sheriff."

Wow! Consider what Fred said. The first sentence wasn't too bad. While of course the posse men and women were "ordinary citizens," hardly an insult to my way of thinking, they had received substantial training. But that's not the real problem. The real, and I mean *really big* problem, awaits in that second sentence. Fred, and thus NBC, actually referred to posse members as "brown-shirted," a direct reference to Nazi Party members, circa 1933 to 1945. This link was reinforced, in case anyone had any doubts, by stating that the posse and the uniform "smacks of fascism."

That is outrageous, demeaning, slanderous. How in good conscience could *Now* compare in any manner whatsoever decent Americans, "ordinary citizens," to use the show's own words, concerned and committed to helping their community, to Hitler and his Nazis? What prompted NBC to construct such a detestable correlation? How is it that apparently only the *intelligentsia* at *Now* could discern this relationship?

Finally, the affront was topped off by the strange assertion that if all this was so, if this neo-Nazi assembly reeked of fascism, "it doesn't bother the sheriff." Well, of course it didn't bother me, because it would never occur to me that anyone could possibly make such a horrific leap! Fred kind of makes it sound like I would welcome totalitarianism!

All this for recruiting citizens to help make their neighborhoods safer, better places to live. Wow again.

Since those questions will not—cannot—be answered, let's keep going through the record.

Not too much later, *Now* got to the inevitable political question. Fred Francis introduced the subject by saying, "Sheriff Joe has such a high profile that people who follow politics in these parts think he's running for something. The statehouse?"

Fred was standing only a few feet away as he interrogated me. "The big rap on you, Sheriff, is that you're sort of a media hog."

These media types are so predictable. They phone and flatter, and do anything they can to come see you, and then accuse you of chasing the publicity. I had my answer ready, and I gave it, fast.

"You know," I said, "you came to me, I didn't go to you."

"True," conceded Fred. "I guess what I'm asking here—are you running for something?"

I had to laugh, and shook my head. "No."

Fred didn't believe me. "You can tell me. Come on. Joe, you can tell me."

His manner was bordering on condescending, but I ignored that and addressed the obvious. "Even if I told you no, you would never believe me."

"That's probably true." Fred had just added insulting to condescending.

"They keep saying, 'You're doing this for political reasons.' I just got elected!"

Fred still didn't believe me. "Joe, I want to hear a Sherman-like statement: 'I don't want to be governor. I'm not ever going to run for governor.' Repeat after me."

I've watched reporters treat dictators and murderers and lawyers with the utmost respect and deference. I wasn't sure why Saddam Hussein rated more courtesy than the sheriff of Maricopa County, but that wasn't the topic at hand, and I was well aware what NBC would do, how the show would manipulate the videotape, if I even looked like I was ducking the question. Not that I wanted to. Not at all.

"I do not want to be the governor," I said clearly. "I want to be the sheriff. The sheriff is the best job in this country."

Incredibly, Fred wasn't satisfied. He was still hard at it. "I will never run for governor," he said, as if reciting a pledge.

"I will never run for governor," I instantly repeated.

Fred was a bit quick on the trigger. "I will—" He caught himself, at a loss for words. Then he acknowledged the undeniable. "You said it."

Fred was getting close to his big finish, and he gave it his all.

"In a country that is frightened and angry about crime," Fred said, "Joe Arpaio, cocky and controversial, is a hero." (So that was where Tom Brokaw got that phrase, "cocky and controversial," for his intro.)

"Though he works in seeming disregard of the Constitution," averred Fred, "his constituents love him. He's scoring big with the voters, and despite his protests, his next shot may be for the state-house."

Despite my following Fred's script, despite my Sherman-like disavowal, Fred chose not to believe me. It was obvious to me that nothing I could say would have convinced him. He didn't believe me because, for some reason, he (or his producer or editor), didn't want to believe me. So *Now* made me out to be nothing less than a liar. The show had no evidence, no rationale, no inside information, but it did not require any. *Now* was NBC News, and NBC News said and did whatever it wanted.

Incidentally, Fred looked disgusted through much of the interview, but that might have been his normal look.

The aim of that relatively in-depth examination was not to pick on NBC (because I could have used examples from a variety of media outlets, domestic and foreign), but to demonstrate that the press is no better or worse than any other aspect of real life in a democracy. The media can be personal and petty, arbitrary and inconsistent, subjective and opinionated. None of that is a crime (if you'll excuse the term); rather, that is human nature, and that is what a television program or a network ultimately is, a collection of human beings giving vent to their hopes, values, and prejudices.

All of that only becomes a crime, or at least a very serious and perhaps dangerous grievance, when the media forgets that its representatives are no more gifted or wise or significant than the rest of us, and that its role is to be a part of the American community, not its judge and jury.

It would be hypocritical of me to only highlight the media reports I haven't liked, because I've procured more than my share of commendatory notices. I've also seen many fair, neutral examinations.

The ubiquitous Rush Limbaugh has been supportive on several occasions, especially when he discussed my cutting out coffee and cigarettes and—well, you know the list. "And he's gotten back to what the original intent of jail is," Rush proclaimed on his TV show. "He says, 'I don't want these people ever wanting to come back to my jail.'"

When Rush offered a perspective on the entire American system of incarceration for his readers in his Limbaugh Letter of February 1995, he generously used my jails to highlight some of his points. Limbaugh was writing about my eliminating coffee from the jail system, and entitled his piece, "Hold The Coffee." Rush wrote:

"When bad guys go to jail, they don't always do hard time. The 'high-security' Sullivan prison in New York, for instance, according to a report in *Reader's Digest*, has outdoor TVs installed—so inmates won't miss their favorite shows while they exercise. At the Massachusetts Correctional Institution, there's an annual 'Lifers' Banquet,' treating convicted murderers and their guests to catered prime-rib dinners. Tennis courts, music lessons, and other five-star amenities are offered at prisons around the country.

"But in Maricopa County, Arizona, Sheriff Joe Arpaio is bucking this trend. So far, he has banned sex magazines, cigarettes, and R- and X-rated TV. Earlier this year he even got rid of hot lunches, replacing them with sandwiches and fruit, saving taxpayers about $1 million a year. Now the sheriff plans to cut out the prisoners' daily cup of coffee, saving the county an additional $94,000 a year. But saving money isn't Sheriff Arpaio's sole motivation. If people want a daily cup of coffee, then they should avoid going to jail, he observes, because 'jail isn't the Ritz Carlton.'" (I know you've heard this before, but I always enjoy reciting the list.) "He says he wants to make jail a place that people don't want to come back to. A revolutionary concept. Jail—the way it oughta be!"

My reason for comparing NBC's report with Rush Limbaugh's is not to pat myself on the back, though that's always fun. (Rush once called me "an American hero," same as Fred did, though with Fred you got the impression he didn't mean it as an endorsement.)

No, the reason for making the comparison is to show that while both NBC's *Now* and Rush Limbaugh took factual situations and bestowed their own interpretations on them, took facts and added opinions, one did so honestly while the other did not. And it shouldn't be difficult to discern which was which.

NBC didn't really care what I had to say, didn't even care what I had pledged in response to its questions. NBC had its theories and its convictions, and those were going to be promoted in the end, with no interference permitted by any annoying facts. That would have been just fine if NBC had informed the audience it was submitting commentary, clean and simple. Instead, *Now* had acted as if the viewers were about to see a neutral, unbiased report, and that simply wasn't the case.

In contrast, Rush Limbaugh has strong ideas, strong opinions, and he makes no bones about it. He is a commentator and an advocate, and presents politics and ideas and events so he can discuss and dissect them. He has his theories and convictions, and anyone who reads his newsletter or books, listens to his radio show, or watches his television program knows what they are. Whether you agree or disagree with Rush, you know what you're getting, and you know where he—and you—stand.

Both neutral reportage and assertive commentary are essential to ensuring a well-informed citizenry, which will be capable of honorably and intelligently safeguarding our republic's health and spirit. But the public cannot be well-informed and well served if reportage and commentary are confused and entangled, and the people are deceived and misled.

Same as here, the foreign media has its honorable members, and then there are the others. The British newspapers especially like big, bold headlines—well, loud and obnoxious—whether they're gabbing about Prince Charles and Princess Di, Hugh Grant and Elizabeth Hurley, or—me. *The Guardian's* profile was headlined, "The Meanest, Cheapest, Harshest Jailer In America." A pull quote from the story read, "Life for prisoners in Maricopa County, Arizona, is nasty, brutish and under canvas," managing to make the tents sound prehistoric.

Television companies from around the world have made the trip to Phoenix to interview me, prepared with varying approaches and conclusions. As I fast-forward through the videotapes that the producers sometimes send me after they finish editing, I'll do my best to give a brief critique of their styles and postures. Accept this mainly for entertainment purposes, because my opinion will be of limited value as the segments were not always in English.

For example, I don't know what they said on German TV, but they said it very dramatically, with a narrator's excited voice, off-center camera angles, and the picture fading from color to some kind of inverted black and white X-ray view, and back again to color. Most sensational of all were the fake gunshots periodically banging away in the background. The gunshots weren't added to show any dangerous situation, because the noise didn't match the action, which was often quite mundane. Rather, I think it was just a general comment on America and our Wild West ways.

Spanish TV sort of resembled one of our local news stations, one located in a very small market. The reporter used a big, square, awkward microphone, which partially blocked his face, or the face of whomever he was interviewing—including mine.

Denmark TV was bizarre. The segment opened with me saying something, followed by some other Arizonans doing the talking. Very nice—Denmark TV broadcasts in English.

However, English was only a part-time indulgence, because when the reporter opened her mouth the words came out in Danish! That's the way the entire story was conducted: Americans did their bits in English, the reporter in Danish, and the audience listened to both. From what I could tell, the station sent me a copy dubbed straight off the air, so what I saw was what the audience saw.

So, I guess the only thing to say is: Either the Danes are very educated or very weird.

Swedish TV's tour of the tents was highlighted by a pair of inmates who rapped their feelings about the facilities for the camera. And now, for your listening pleasure:

My name is Rico and,
I've been thinking about this tent swing.
I'd rather be in the tents,

Than locked up in Riker's,
Pushing with certain other prisoners.
I'd rather be in tents,
I'd rather be kicking back in the tents.
At least, that's what I think they said.

The Swedes seemed to do a good job, but I couldn't be sure because they also went in for that dual-language approach.

The crew from Canadian TV hailed from the French side of the nation, and whatever they said, they did it with snappy pacing and good camera work.

Nevertheless, the top prize for foreign reporters must be split between Britain and Australia.

The television crew from Yorkshire had a singularly British take on its story, as exemplified by its discussion of the Sun City Posse:

"Each year, citizens donate a quarter-million dollars to equip their posse, and almost two hundred people volunteer to make regular patrols..."

A standard shot of sheriff cars vigilantly patrolling the streets of Sun City played over the reporter's calm, cultured voice. Then the reporter smoothly added the kicker:

". . . even though their average age is seventy-four."

The picture shifted to show a couple of elderly women in uniform, and then a handful of definitely older men.

And to give it that piquant twist, the narrator was replaced by the twangy guitar strains of cowboy music—slow, sad cowboy music.

You have to understand, that didn't bother me, because it was true. And it was also true that this sizable police presence helped account for Sun City possessing one of the lowest crime rates in the United States. A Sun City posse man made that assertion, and the report wisely did not attempt to contradict his claim.

Indeed, the correspondent implicitly accepted the posse's effectiveness with his following line: "The sheriff's posse program has led to more arrests and a prison overcrowding problem, which he solved with his usual mix of economy and expediency."

"Economy and expediency"—I liked that.

Australia might have shared my personal gold ribbon with Britain, but its style was way down at the other end of the scale. Where the British were cool and subtle, Australia's version of *60 Minutes* employed an in-your-face approach—literally. Sometimes they pushed the camera so close to the person being interviewed that the subject's features were distorted, the nose splayed from ear to ear, the eyes bulging, the mouth wide and large, like a shark ready to attack—it wasn't a pretty sight.

Regardless, the Aussies were effective and entertaining—quintessentially Australian. They were also very energetic, filming on land, air, and sea.

Check out the correspondent's opener: "America's perennial dilemma with worsening crime has taken a new and, it seems, effective turn. The latest answer to crime is lock up all the baddies, and lock them up for a long time. But nowhere is the line harder than in Maricopa County, Arizona, where they've even re-introduced chain gangs. If you're a bad guy in Sheriff Joe Arpaio's patch, all you can expect is a bad time."

Quick, tough, intelligent, a bit melodramatic, and to the point. The best way to get the gist of the Australians' unique pacing and patter is to take in their overblown and yet perceptive words:

"To Sheriff Joe, the complaints of prisoners are sweet praise. With brutal jails, chain gangs, and vast prison camps, he wants the word out that he is the country's nastiest sheriff."

Quick cutaway to me addressing the prisoners in the tents: "Don't ever say you like the sheriff."

Back to the attractive, blonde Australian correspondent: "Just like the days of the Wild West, the Arizona badlands have a lawman with hang-'em-high ideals and an ego as big as his county."

A little later, the report reviews some of the posse training, and shows how the posse members are doused with chemical spray so they will really appreciate its effect. As the camera revealed, it is not an enjoyable experience. Here's what the correspondent had to say:

"A spray of mace can blind and sting for hours, but Sheriff Joe has deputized his followers with such loyalty, they suffer, if not gladly, then stoically."

After surveying my measures in the jails, taking away privileges and frills, the reporter asked me a beauty of a question:

"Do you have a compassionate bone in your body?"

Yeah, and while we're at it, when did you stop beating your wife? I mean, that's a hell of a thing to say to somebody you've basically just been introduced to. Well, what can you expect; they didn't travel halfway around the world to be subtle.

By the way—I answered in the affirmative.

The Australians were great at encompassing emotions and ideas in one-liners, pulling no punches.

Example: The reporter looked at me and said: "Your critics have described you as a publicity-seeking opportunist."

My answer: "Sure, they're all jealous; they can't get on television. They sure like to hang around me so they can get their faces on television."

And the very last exchange of the piece summed up the Australians' attitude:

Correspondent: "How much tougher and meaner and badder can you get?"

Me: "I don't know. I'm running out of ideas, that's my problem—but I'll think of something."

And that's what the rest of the world has heard about the Maricopa County Sheriff's Office.

I guess the rest of the world doesn't think what it's heard has been too bad, because all those stories haven't stopped the tourists from traveling to Arizona.

Since taking office, I've been profiled or appeared on some 250 news and talk shows, small and large, local and national. Because of all that exposure, I feel safe in saying that I might very well be the best-known local or state public official—and that includes police commissioners, mayors, governors, you name it—in the entire country. Why?

Why is the media from here to there and all points between beating a path to Maricopa County to interview a sheriff? Why is the public responding with such enthusiasm?

Putting the ego-stroking aside, these are legitimate questions, that deserve answers, and the answer is patently obvious. You take a citizenry that feels itself to be under assault, present programs that provide some solutions, and some hope, and present them in a straightforward, unadorned, and honest manner, a distinct change from the speeches offered by the usual dissembling, devious, double-dealing politicians, and presto! You'll quickly gain an audience. No doubt. No question.

Whether helpful or dangerous, amusing or sobering, the media's impact on our perceptions and our lives is pervasive. We must understand how the media works so we can understand its collective power. Then we shall be able to understand why the media acts as it does, and how the media decides and chooses.

Once again, the point is not to understand all this in order to block the media or interfere with its operations. Rather, the aim is both more modest—no course of action is advocated, any knowledge gained is intended entirely for internal consideration—and more aggressive—for an informed electorate will intuitively demand that the press do a better, more complete, more responsible job.

The effect of the media handling of crime and law enforcement cannot be underestimated on the public's sense of security and its confidence in society's ability to win this most crucial war.

Has the media helped in this fight? Before answering that, we have to ask, is it the media's role to help, or is the media's role simply to report whatever happens, good or bad, positive or negative?

First, many, probably most, members of the press will automatically tell anyone willing to listen that their job, their responsibility, is to report the facts, come what may, consequences be damned. That, they will say, is the best way to ensure that the media will not unduly or unfairly impose opinions on the citizenry.

High-minded and democratic as that might sound, it is in fact totally hypocritical. There is no such thing as "the facts." Instead, there are an infinite number of facts for an infinite number of circumstances and conditions and cases. The media, in the form of a television news director or newspaper editor or reporter, selects those circumstances and conditions and cases judged to be most interesting or perhaps most entertaining or perhaps most controversial or perhaps most violent or perhaps most disgusting or perhaps most publicized, and calls those stories news.

But that is not the end of the process, but rather the beginning. Because then the television news director or newspaper editor or reporter must choose which part of each story to highlight: Is it what led up to the event, the event itself, or the aftermath? Which side should dominate the telling of the tale, e.g., the winning or losing side? Whose rendition of the event should be believed, or favored, e.g., the eyewitnesses, the inside sources, the official version? Which pictures are used, which quotes are emphasized, how much prominence does the story deserve?

As you can see, this game goes on forever, because the choices and the options are endless. Putting aside political posturing or wishful thinking, that seems to be the way it has to be. Having said that, I don't mean to excuse the ethical and factual lapses in which the media so easily and frequently indulges. The first and foremost lapse is the overwhelming arrogance—a particularly vocal arrogance—that seems bred into the profession. I guess this cannot be too surprising when an entire class of people, or should I say an entire class of jobs, is accorded power and privilege, authority and respect.

Nonetheless, it is not acceptable, especially because it is so unnecessary, so correctable. Arrogance simply isn't a requirement for asking questions and conducting interviews and investigating leads. I say it again—it's simply not a requirement.

Of course, it becomes almost inevitable when so much of the media evinces contempt for the people and stories it covers.

As far as my business is concerned, I think that much of the news media pays lip service to the idea of supporting the police and presuming law enforcement's good intentions when many reporters (and particularly their masters), really feel a certain contempt, combining mistrust and scorn and some cool disregard for the cops. Not that all media types feel that way, or perhaps not even half, and especially not the reporters who cover the crime beat on a daily basis. But still enough do, enough to put that unsubstantiated doubt into the public consciousness, though you can be sure that none of them would admit to it.

The public doesn't trust politicians? Then go with it, dig up every scrap of garbage, poke into every dark closet, expose every piece of personal gossip and innuendo that's lying about. Get them and get them good, because it's the right thing to do, because it's the noble thing to do, because it sells and makes money and wins prizes.

Celebrities? The public loves them but also loves to hate them, so hit them, but only sideways. That way, the blow glances off and the celeb doesn't clam up, and then go back to business as usual and treat the celebs with the deference they expect, playing the shill.

And the cops? It's a black-and-white deal. Write them up as heroes when they rescue a baby or arrest a serial killer, and chop them into bite-size bits when they are accused of misconduct of any sort by almost any lowlife. And if the situation actually becomes something worth talking about, and the charges are not just the same old politically inspired crap, then the media displays a tendency to go insane with blood lust.

The more I think about it, proportion is the key to journalism. Proportion. An example for your consideration: Phoenix is the seventh largest city in the country, with more than one million inhabitants. If only one murder or rape or other terrible crime was committed every other day, then we'd be talking about a mere 180-odd crimes a year. Nothing to talk about, in the larger scheme. A great victory for crime fighting.

And yet, if the local media were to take those 180-odd crimes and run with them, suck every gory detail out of them for public consumption, the result would be assured and unavoidable. The people would be terrorized, common sense abandoned, forgotten in the screaming headlines and bloody pictures.

That, too, is the power of the press.

Say what you will about the media, the only thing I can guarantee is that the whole communications industry is only going to get bigger and richer and more pervasive and more powerful. Understand the media so you can protect yourself from its excesses and trespasses, and get the most out of its intelligence and reach.

That's what I try to do, and so far it's been working.

CHAPTER SIXTEEN

The Future

I wrote this book so I could speak directly to the people, to each of you, without the media editing or interpreting or spinning my words for me. The topics covered in these pages have been vital to the American future, which hinges, in part, on how we deal with crime and punishment. Despite a certain equilibrium or even progress made in the economy and other areas of American life, every poll shows that Americans feel less confident about the future and less secure about their lives. Many factors account for this profound unease. Surely the violence and lawlessness that afflict much of our society, the disdain for fundamental values, and the disrespect for the rights of our fellow citizens that too many Americans display, contribute to our collective deep confusion and fear.

We know in our hearts, in our guts, that something has gone seriously wrong in our society. We are experiencing horrors that most Americans could never believe were possible in this nation. My God! Not long ago I was standing somewhere south of Phoenix, in the middle of the desert, investigating the sabotage of an Amtrak passenger train by some unknown terrorists. Probably homegrown

Something is seriously wrong in our society

terrorists, most experts agree, willing to murder their fellow Americans for some as yet unknown reasons. Terrorism, here on American soil—inconceivable.

Despite the distressing and frightening nature of terrorism, the vastly more pressing and dangerous problem is not isolated acts of terror, but our widespread communal willingness to separate into suspicious, segregated communities instead of working together as Americans. You mind your business, and I'll mind mine, and the hell with you and everybody else.

That is a recipe for the Balkanization of the United States, the destruction of our country.

Common sense is too easily and too frequently supplanted by demagoguery; trust by paranoia; compassion by indifference; reason by prejudice; faith by fear; fortitude by cowardice.

At one point or another, we have witnessed all of these less desirable traits, or trends, in the realm of crime and criminal justice. Since I began my law enforcement career well over forty years ago, I have witnessed a sea of change in the American attitude toward every aspect of crime. Crime used to be viewed as just that, *crime*, pure and simple—a violation of the law, illegal and absolutely wrong, with sure and swift punishment due. Some time within the last generation, social workers and lawyers and mental health professionals and public policy academics and politicians managed to chip away at this ancient, basic idea, known and respected by all societies through human history.

Instead, these "experts" created a whole new world, populated by "victims of an uncaring society," who "expressed their victimization" by hurting, robbing, and killing other people. According to this thinking, criminals deserved not punishment but understanding, sympathy, and all sorts of expensive government programs. This attitude so permeated the system that it even reached down and infected the cop on the beat, who was transformed into some kind of social worker.

I have offered facts and statistics in the course of this book, and I offer a few more, simply because they are so outrageous and so indicative of where we have gone wrong:

The average time spent incarcerated for robbery in the United States is *three years.*

The average time spent incarcerated for rape in the United States is *five years.*

The average time spent incarcerated for murder in the United States is *eight years.*

And even those scant years need not be too unpleasant. After all, thirty-one states allow television in individual cells as long as the inmates pay for it.

I've discussed some ideas that I know will help fight crime, ideas that have helped fight crime in Maricopa County. Several of these ideas are original, such as the tents, the jail chain gang, and the use of the posse. I'll say it again because it is a notion worth stressing: I'm not a genius, and I didn't need be to conceive and implement my plans and programs. Not at all. What I do possess is a reasonable dose of common sense.

The extraordinary thing is, I'm not doing anything extraordinary. I am using common sense, I am enforcing the law, I am saving the taxpayers' money. None of that is so difficult. None of that requires remarkable insight.

And that's good, because that means that if I can do it in Maricopa County, anyone can do it anywhere.

Other cops know it. The cover story for the November 17, 1995, issue of *Parade Magazine* was dedicated to providing a forum for police officers to discuss how they thought we should fight crime. *Parade* polled 3,600 cops to get to the heart of the matter, and what they said wouldn't surprise any reader of this book. On the cover of the magazine, six cops are pictured and quoted. Judging by the photos, the police officers span a wide spectrum, as was the intent: white, black, and Asian, male and female, uniformed cop, detective, chief. I'm going to recite directly and completely from that cover, because it reveals precisely how clearly law enforcement officers comprehend what must be done.

"It's a combination of education at a young age for children, parents being more involved, having proper role models, fighting the pressures to be cool in school and on the street.

257

"The community needs to get more involved and not rely on just the police to deter crime. People need to make a stand for their community.

"Stricter judges and courts and more jail time for offenders. The police officers do their job just to see the offenders treated leniently by the courts.

"Stop the flow of narcotics into the U.S. It *can* be done!

"Eliminate the ability of judges to suspend, defer and run sentences concurrently. That's like getting four or five crimes for the price of one.

"Become friends with children. Treat our youth as we would want our own children treated."

Common sense. Responsibility. Determination.

It's so obvious.

All right. Very good. Now to the hard part. Namely, what are the odds that we will really fight crime the way it must be fought, and what will happen if we don't?

Criminals and criminal organizations have become more violent, more vicious. I am content to leave it to others to worry about the socioeconomic factors that breed the conditions that supposedly lead to violent gangs and other criminals. (As should be evident from my collection of stories, the role of drugs in raising the level of violence and outright criminality at every level of society cannot be overemphasized.) Whatever the underlying cause of each malefactor's dissatisfaction with society and its laws, my job, and every police officer's job, is to stop all of them dead in their tracks.

The goal of law enforcement is to win the war against crime, a war we started losing years ago, a reality that many people have a vested interest in trying to cover up. Don't misunderstand. Winning the war against crime doesn't mean that lawbreakers will be completely eliminated, that crime will be wiped from every corner of this country forever. Of course not. Even if it were possible to achieve such a pristine state, the cost would be worse than the cure. A free society has to allow its citizens the independence to make mistakes, the autonomy to decide for themselves to transgress, the liberty to act stupidly and even destructively. A free society has to allow its citizens the room to be antisocial. To catch all problems before they arise, to control life so totally that men and women are stopped from offending before they offend, is to win the battle and lose the war.

At the same time, the first duty of every society is to protect itself and its citizens. That's the bottom line. We have to get tough and get smart, from the president down to the cop on the beat. Are we tough enough to do that? Are we smart enough? Are we, as a society, ready to face the truth about crime? Do we have the leaders who are prepared to make the hard choices? Crime will always exist. The question is whether we control it, or whether it controls us. Are we ready for the fight?

Though I hate to say it, it appears that something important and good in this society has crumbled. We frequently don't see the dedication and hard work we ordinarily gave and expected years ago. I think that's one terribly fundamental reason we have so many problems today.

That has to change. We have to demand better from the system and from ourselves.

We've talked a lot about politics in the course of this book, and now I'd like to break it down to a single thought: The power of the people has to be stronger than politics. Stated another way, the power of the people has to *direct* politics.

We cannot simply dislike how the political process, the business of the people, is conducted in this country and thus find an excuse to disdain it. Politics was invented to serve the community. Politicians exist to serve the community.

I'm not embarrassed to say I am a politician. When I decided to run for sheriff, I automatically became a politician. To claim otherwise, to distance myself from my new profession, as more and more elected officials are trying to do, would be a self-righteous, self-serving attempt to fool the public. I was elected by the people to serve the people. That is my job, and I am proud of it.

I have made it clear that I survive in my office because of the support of the people. My victories are the victories of the people over politics as usual.

My time in office proves that we can win. My time in office proves that politics can work. My time in office should prove that it can work anywhere.

In all my years in law enforcement, I can honestly say that I was never really afraid, no matter the situation. It wasn't because I considered myself bullet-proof or invulnerable—I simply got angry when faced with a problem, and my anger superseded my fear.

I think that's how this country has to respond. Put aside our fear, no matter how urgent, and get mad. Get mad at the waste. Get mad at the pain. Get mad at the injustice and inequities and anguish.

Get mad and do something, something good and strong and positive. Money is not the first issue. I have done the job here in Maricopa County, Arizona, without taxpayer money to spare. I never had very much money on hand, whether in Turkey, where I was on my own, surviving by my wits, or in any of my other postings with the BN and BNDD and DEA. I adopted and adapted. I persevered. I received a lot of awards from the government for saving money. I succeeded, because succeeding requires money, but it requires a lot more. It requires willpower. It requires tenacity. It requires boldness. It requires imagination. It requires teamwork. It requires dedication. It requires faith.

Success in the war against crime will require the best from law enforcement.

Success in the war against crime will require the best from government.

Success in the war against crime will require the best from all of us.

Do we dare give any less?

Every year between Thanksgiving and Christmas, the city of Phoenix hosts the Electric Light Parade. One hundred thousand or more people line the streets along a three-mile course down Central Avenue as school marching bands and two hundred floats representing everything from the Arizona Public Service to Santa Claus to UPS kick off the pageant. Since the parade starts at 7 P.M., the bands and floats, and most of the marchers, are lit up in strings and clumps and bursts of different colored lights.

Children and politicians love a parade, and I'm no exception. I rode along with Ava in the back of an old truck decorated with rows of blinking Christmas lights. As we left the staging area and hit the crowds, I heard the cheers and waved back. I waved for three miles. The people were from all walks of life, all races, ethnic groups, ages. I attend a lot of parades and other celebratory functions, and have learned to judge what people think by their response. I heard the shouts I always hear, the approval, the thanks, the urging to run for governor or even president.

In the public arena, nothing means more to me than these moments, not the newspaper articles or the television stories or the politicians' compliments. Nothing means more, because it is on these occasions, when the public has assembled, and its massed numbers grant it a license to shed common inhibitions and give voice to raw emotions, that I know how the people really feel about what I am doing.

I rode down that parade route, greeting the people, acknowledging their cheers and calls. On this occasion, as on many similar occasions, I found myself acutely aware of just how far I had traveled to reach this juncture. In a flash, the years unwound back to Washington and Mexico, back to San Antonio and Turkey, back to Chicago and Las Vegas, all the way back to my youth in Springfield, Massachusetts. In my wildest dreams, I never imagined the remarkable opportunities I would have, the extraordinary people I would meet, the amazing adventures I would survive, the accolades and honors I would receive.

What an exciting journey it has been. What an exciting journey it still is.

All those opportunities and people and adventures gave me the knowledge and experience and skill to understand the position I now hold. I learned how to be a diplomat when diplomacy was required. I learned how to investigate when investigatory skills were necessary. I learned how to be hard when hard got the job done. I learned how to trust my instinct when instinct provided the essential edge. I learned how to lead when leadership was demanded.

I learned all this and more, and have called on every bit of information and expertise and talent I have discovered or developed to accomplish my aims. And this was a confirmation that my efforts have worked, this night of cheers and applause.

The power of the group is an astonishing thing, whether roaring at a football game or a political rally. The effect can be inspiring and uplifting, like Martin Luther King's March On Washington, or it may herald something evil and cruel, like a Nazi rally. The choice is ours. Together we can accomplish anything.

The more I enjoyed the reception at the Electric Light Parade, the more I realized yet again just how profoundly I owed these people, and all the people of Maricopa County, my best efforts. And I realized once again how much I wanted to meet their hopes and expectations.

But the truth is, I cannot do the job alone. The police cannot do the job alone. The federal government, with all its departments and agencies and bureaus and committees, cannot do the job alone.

The choice is ours. It is our collective responsibility to see that we work together and dedicate ourselves and this nation to making the right choice.

It's like I said in the beginning: Win or lose. Right or wrong. Good guys versus bad guys. Sometimes, life *is* that straightforward.

I said at the start that we had a lot to talk about. Well, we've done the talking. Now it's time to go to work. Now it's time to act.

All together.